Influenced by Kojève's interpretation of Hegel as well as his direct political experience of the second world war, Maurice Merleau-Ponty abandoned the religious and philosophical position he had assumed in the 1930s and turned to Marxism. This is the first critical study of the French philosopher's political ideas and the context in which they evolved.

In its origin and its development, Merleau-Ponty's political thought expressed a subtle dialectic between ongoing political events and the apparent truths of Marx's analysis. With the onset of the cold war, the discovery of the Soviet concentration camps, the repression of Eastern Europe, the Algerian crisis, and the founding of the Fifth Republic, Merleau-Ponty began to take a critical look at Marx's ideas of the genesis of humanism in the light of these disturbing political realities. His reconsideration of the basis of Marxism and his conclusion that it had lost contact with history led to a fundamental reorientation of his attitudes. No longer sympathetic to the use of violence to end violence, he criticized Sartre's external justification of communist violence as 'magical' and advocated instead a new liberalism combining parliamentary democracy with an awareness of the social problems of industrial capitalism.

Barry Cooper's study of this important contemporary thinker gives context for an understanding of Merleau-Ponty's politics and, in so doing, brings together the complex of issues and ideas that have shaped modern European political and philosophical thought.

BARRY COOPER

Merleau-Ponty and Marxism: from terror to reform

UNIVERSITY OF TORONTO PRESS
Toronto Buffalo London

© University of Toronto Press 1979
Toronto Buffalo London
Printed in Canada

Library of Congress Cataloging in Publication Data

Cooper, Barry, 1943-
 Merleau-Ponty and Marxism.

 Bibliography: p.
 Includes index.
 1.   Merleau-Ponty, Maurice, 1908-1961 – Political science. I. Title.
 JC261.M47C66   320.5'092'4 [B]   78-16829
 ISBN 0-8020-5435-8

For H and H
gratia illis debetur a filio

Contents

Preface

Jean-Jacques Maurice Merleau-Ponty was born on 14 March 1908 in Rochefort-sur-Mer, a garrison town of about 30,000 near the mouth of the Charente in the cognac area of southwestern France. His youth was comfortable and secure, and he matured in a milieu of doctors and officers, losing his father in the first world war. With his mother, brother, and sister he lived in a close, bourgeois family in Paris, compiling a brilliant record at Lycée Janson and the elite Louis-le-Grand. In 1926 he entered the Ecole normale supérieur and graduated four years later. Following military service and studies in Germany, a year at the Caisse nationale de la Recherche scientifique, the CNRS, and teaching posts at lycées in Beauvais and Chartres, he returned in 1935 to rue d'Ulm as an *agrégé-répétiteur*, where he remained until August 1939. Back in Paris, Merleau-Ponty was able to attend the lectures of Alexandre Kojève at the Ecole pratique des Hautes Etudes. In 1939-40 he was mobilized as a second lieutenant in the Fifth Infantry Regiment and later saw service on the General Staff of the Paris military district. During the war Merleau-Ponty taught in Paris at the Lycée Carnot and later at the Lycée Condorcet. In 1941 he joined a resistance group, *Socialisme et liberté*, which disbanded a year or so later. By 1943 Merleau-Ponty had begun talking with Jean-Paul Sartre about founding a literary, philosophical, and political review, and in October 1945 *Les Temps modernes* was born. Merleau-Ponty received the degree Docteur ès Lettres shortly after the war for work published in his first two books, *La Structure du Comportement* (1942) and the *Phénoménologie de la Perception* (1945). He continued his teaching career at the University of Lyons until 1949 and served for a time on the examining board for entrants to the Ecole normale supérieur. In the fall of 1949 he began teaching at the Sorbonne and three years later was appointed to the chair of philosophy, which a generation earlier had been held by Bergson, at the Collège de France. His appointment was not without controversy: the rightist newspaper *L'Aurore* was particularly scandalized that an 'existentialist' should accede to the pinnacle of French learning. Catholics were scandalized equally because of his atheism and others because of his interest in German philosophy and criticism of the greatest French philosophical tradition. In 1957 he was made a Chevalier in the Legion of Honour (he returned his rosette during the Algerian war). He died suddenly, of a stroke, on 3 May 1961 in his study, a large volume of the Adam and Tannery edition of Descartes open on his desk.

Most simply, his was a remarkable intellectual life. Even those who opposed his election to the Collège de France had to admit their error a few years later. But Merleau-Ponty was not so much a philosopher in the modern sense of the term as in the original sense. Some will say, perhaps, that the Biblical message has superseded the Socratic. Yet even the religious person must bear witness before other men and speak, whatever the meaning experienced in the silence of conscience and prayer. If we recall the twofold description of human nature as given by Aristotle, that man is both a political living thing, a *zoon politikon*, and a living thing able to speak reasonably, a *zoon logon ekhon*, the implication so far as the person of conscience is concerned is that rationality and goodness must also be displayed in coherent discourse. Only by speech, it seems, can false prophets be distinguished from true ones, which means that both must be listened to. To consider such a procedure equivalent to a profanation of the divine word before the human may be to mistake the nature of words that, wherever they may point, are human in origin. In an age that has lost confidence in religion, in tradition, in authority, and has often seemed on the verge of losing its grip upon reason, one thing at least seems clear: if we are to understand what our losses mean it can only come about through speaking of them. In this regard, one's fascination with Merleau-Ponty is not simply with an important philosopher in the modern, professional sense of the term but also with a man who knew how to speak with others, who desired to speak with them and for them. Whatever errors Merleau-Ponty may have made, they can be transcended only by following where he has gone and speaking oneself. But this means one must try to understand those to whom and for whom Merleau-Ponty was speaking before one ventures a consideration of what he said.

Merleau-Ponty had just turned twenty-two when he left the Ecole normale, trained in French nationalism but exposed as well to radical political ideologies that had maintained a strong underground tradition in rue d'Ulm ever since the tenure of Lucien Herr as librarian in the 1880s. Neither his stay at the CNRS, another elite institution with a left-wing tradition, nor Kojève's interpretation of Hegel can be considered anything more than incidental exposures. As he once said: 'One does not become a revolutionary through science, but out of indignation. Science comes afterward to fill in and delimit that open protest.' When a *normalien* he had once protested against the vulgarity of his fellow students' songs; the vulgarity of his fellow citizens had a like impact. Italian, Spanish, and German politics gave substance to the fears of many sensitive Frenchmen. In consequence of the political and the spiritual disorder of the times, fear of the right and disgust with their policies, new groups such as the Comité de Vigilance des intellectuels anti-fascistes, relics from the Dreyfus Affaire such as the Ligue des droits de l'homme, and PCF fronts such as the Association des écrivains et artistes révolutionnaires gained a vast following among the intellectual community. According to Sartre, Merleau-Ponty was never closer to the communists than in 1936, but was repelled by the Moscow Trials. For a time he was associated with Emmanuel Mounier and the 'personalist' group centred on the review *Esprit*. By the time the war began he had moved away from the philosophies in which he was trained and also away from any political activity connected to Christianity.

In the Introduction, I deal with the change undergone by Merleau-Ponty during the 1930s. The balance of the book is a presentation and analysis of Merleau-Ponty's Marxism. Initially Merleau-Ponty was a communist fellow-traveller, sharing the aims of the party, but for his own reasons, not theirs, and refusing to join. Nor did he join any serious alternative, though several friends had become members of various splinter groups. Amid the uncertainties of the immediate post-war period, he refused to anticipate the dogmas of the cold war. This led him to an interpretation of Soviet politics that has been taken ever since as an apology for Stalinism. Merleau-Ponty did not see himself that way. Nevertheless, the generosity of understanding he extended to the Soviet Union was misplaced. The reason lay in his belief and hope that a socialist economy would eventually bring about a regime of mutual recognition, of authentic intersubjectivity, of humanism. This was the lesson he took from Marx and especially from Kojève's interpretation of Hegel. Eventually he was forced under pressure of historical circumstance to change his view of the Soviet Union. The short-cut to humanism through the judicious application of terror resulted not, as Kojève had indicated, in a homogeneous social order but in tyranny. After the Korean war and publicity over the Soviet concentration camps, Marxism could serve only as a critical analytic or diagnostic instrument, useful in bringing to light the evils, stupidities, and contradictions of a capitalist industrial economy and a liberal political regime.

Marx's demystification of class conflict in industrial society provided insight into what was wrong with existing arrangements, but its complete lack of success as the basis for a just political regime showed its limitations. Turning Marx's method of interpretation to Marx's own texts and to the political acts of Marx's followers revealed the adventures of the dialectic during the twentieth century, how it changed from an internal movement of thought and creative political action to abstract rationalization of expediency. Henceforth Marxism was no longer believed to be true on its own terms. There were no bannisters, no recipes, nothing to guide political action but common sense and thought that might rely on Marx but would in no way be subordinate to Marx's formulas. In short, by thinking through Marx's errors as well as his insights, and by seeing where action undertaken on the basis of an integral and ideological Marxism had led, Merleau-Ponty learned the virtue of moderation and the value of a politics of reform.

There has been in recent years a steady if not burgeoning production of studies and celebrations of Merleau-Ponty. Much of this work is very good, and I have made what use of it I could. Most of the writing on his political opinions, however, is less satisfactory because either it seems to ignore the political context within which Merleau-Ponty's arguments were developed or it overlooks the changes of emphasis, and indeed of substance, that his political writings reflected. Sometimes both contexts are ignored, and we are treated to a strange sort of pious fundamentalism. I have tried to avoid this by sketching in the historical background where I thought it important. The inevitable result is that I have had to cite rather more references to contemporary occasional pieces than their intellectual power or scholarly worth would ordinarily warrant.

On the purely technical side, I have consulted translations where available but have undertaken to translate all passages myself in the hope of attaining a degree of consistency that otherwise might be absent.

One of the few unambiguously pleasant aspects of writing a study like this is to acknowledge the help I have received in putting it together. The taxpayers of Canada and of France, acting through their agents in the Canada Council and the Ministère des Affaires étrangères, have provided financial support; Ruby Richardson of Osgoode Hall Law School and Joanne Degabrielle of Secretarial Services were responsible for typing the several versions of the manuscript; Larry Mac-Donald laboured with great energy and remarkable skill to make my often opaque prose more intelligible; three readers made several helpful suggestions (where I refused their advice I am happy to take responsibility; all other mistakes and foolishness are our joint doing); Edward Tiryakian first introduced me to Merleau-Ponty, and John Hallowell persuaded me to abandon the more sterile aspects of political science; all these people and institutions have my thanks. Scholars and friends of Merleau-Ponty have been generous in answering my queries about specific and often trivial points. Here my thanks go to Mme Maurice Merleau-Ponty, Jacques Merleau-Ponty, Leo Strauss, Raymond Aron, Allan Bloom, Gaston Fessard SJ, Georges Blount, Xavier Tillette SJ, Jacques D'Hondt, Mme Jean Hyppolite, Henri Michel, Stanley Rosen, Jean Lacroix, Claude Lefort, John O'Neill, Don Ihde, J.P. Siméon, Daniel Mayer, Michel Rybalka, Louis Genevois, Mme M. Kaan, T.M. Domenach, Pierre Mendès France, Sammy Bawlf at DOW, and Paul Ricoeur. My wife, Ann Kussmaul, has helped in all the important ways and by now knows at least as much of Merleau-Ponty's politics as I know of servants in husbandry in early modern England.

This book has been published with the help of a grant from the Social Science Federation of Canada, using funds provided by the Social Sciences and Humanities Research Council of Canada, and a grant to the University of Toronto Press from the Andrew W. Mellon Foundation.

Toronto
Carpus and Papylus, 1978

MERLEAU-PONTY AND MARXISM:
FROM TERROR TO REFORM

Introduction:
the philosophical basis of
Merleau-Ponty's humanism

This is a study of Maurice Merleau-Ponty's politics. For one reason or another, students of Merleau-Ponty's thought have only superficially examined its political dimension. Most scholars have sought to explain particular aspects of his philosophical work. Some have used his writings as a quarry of raw materials to be extracted and refined for their own constructions. A few have studied Merleau-Ponty's writings sympathetically in order to think along with him and reason through new matters in a style they have learned from him. But this is to be a critical account. It treats his views of public affairs and political theory, how his statements were received by contemporaries, and how his judgments were altered by political events.

It has been said that Merleau-Ponty's star has all but disappeared from the contemporary French intellectual sky.[1] Political scientists have in fact taken the more spectacular brilliance of Jean-Paul Sartre, the more elegant and profound ethics of Albert Camus, or the familiar common sense of Raymond Aron to represent French political speculation in the post-war era. But the neglect of Merleau-Ponty is undeserved. Sartre called Merleau-Ponty his political teacher,[2] and in polemics with Camus and Aron during the later forties and early fifties Merleau-Ponty previewed Sartre's more bitter and personal quarrels with them a few years later. Following his break with Sartre, Merleau-Ponty found himself in agreement with Aron not simply politically but philosophically as well. Merleau-Ponty, in short, was a central figure in French intellectual life after the second world war. And yet, however fascinating a study of the fights, truces, changes of position, retrenchments, and reconciliations of Parisian intellectuals may be, it has also something bizarre about it, something of scholarly gossip. This book examines Merleau-Ponty's relations with his contemporaries, particularly with Sartre, only in so far as they were guideposts to his own development.

With the founding of *Les Temps modernes* after the Liberation, and until the

Korean War, Merleau-Ponty served as its political editor and thus helped define its left-wing views. It was during the immediate post-war period, when the myth of unity in the Resistance still obscured deep political divisions among Frenchmen, that Merleau-Ponty was most favourably disposed towards the Soviet Union and the French Communist Party. From late 1947 on, he gradually moved away from communism and a decade later was calling for a 'new liberalism.' How could a philosopher worthy to succeed Bergson at the Collège de France have given intellectual allegiance (or even neutrality) to Stalin's regime? Are *Humanisme et Terreur* or the political essays in *Sens et Non-sens* or *Signes* to be regarded as independent of Merleau-Ponty's other more philosophical works? To understand his political attitudes and writings, one must go beyond politics. As one distinguished political scientist has observed, the most fundamental political division is not between liberals and conservatives, Marxists and non-Marxists, but between transcendentalists, who are disposed to be religious and philosophical, and immanentists, who are inclined to be ideological and sectarian.[3] Significantly, Merleau-Ponty, like Marx, believed that the criticism of religion lay behind all criticism. Merleau-Ponty's commitment to Marxism grew out of a rejection of Christianity. Behind this shift in perspective lay a rejection of the philosophy in which he had been schooled, a rebellion against the religion of his youth, and a replacement of these two traditions by political commitments derived from a study of Marx and especially of Hegel. These topics will now be surveyed in turn.

THE 1930s

Although Merleau-Ponty's intellectual life during the 1930s was confused,[4] one matter at least was clear: he was unhappy with philosophical dogmatism. Towards the close of a favourable review of Max Scheler's newly translated book, *Ressentiment*, a polemical study of Nietzsche's attack on Christianity in the *Genealogy of Morals*, Merleau-Ponty remarked upon the salutary effects that Scheler's phenomenology would have upon French philosophy. As an example that could well profit by a reading of Scheler, he cited an article by Ramon Fernandez on the state of French philosophy.[5] A true philosopher, according to Fernandez, is denoted neither by his language nor his interests but rather by 'his disposition to believe nothing that is not affirmed by an effective *act* of intelligence, in the most precise sense of the term.' All the 'subterfuge of passion' is to be exposed by this intellectual act; all 'anti-intellectual philosophy is reduced to the intellectual act by which the mind gives itself the right to succumb to a most secret complaisance.' Of course, this 'secret complaisance' was illegitimate, because true philosophy consisted of the acts of the critical intellect. For Fernandez and for neo-Kantian or critical philosophy in general, 'the effective act of intelligence excludes in principle that which embarrasses or astonishes it; to understand is never to seize upon an object of thought as it is, but to constitute a world from chaos.' The consequence is that there is but a single intelligible realm, the realm of the critical, scientific intellect. The universe of experience of art, emotion, sentiment, religion is nothing but 'rough outlines of debased versions of the Universe of science.' At the same time, Fernandez continued, we know from these same philosophers of science that an account of the objects of science could never be coextensive with all that exists. The neo-Kantian reply to this problem was simply to reaffirm its own assumption: anything that cannot be reduced to an object of science must be passed over in silence – in fact we cannot even know that we are silent about it because we have no way to know if it exists. But, Merleau-Ponty countered, 'if objectivity cannot exhaust existence, will it not be the very act of a philosopher to attempt a *recognition*, a description of existence under all its forms? Such would be fairly close to the proposals of M. Wahl or M. Marcel. And it is also the right of a descriptive philosophy that Scheler has made worthwhile.'[6] Philosophy would not have to be confined to the objects of the critical intellect but could describe the life of sentiments and emotions and render the complaisances of M. Fernandez less secret. 'It is certainly true,' Merleau-Ponty concluded, 'that every philosopher knows where he wished to arrive. The whole question is to know if he has truly the right to go there.' If critical analysis did not render an adequate account of religious acts or emotions, Merleau-Ponty's immediate concern, other ways of doing philosophy would have to be tried. 'To give philosophy a definition of intelligence that shuts upon itself, is perhaps to assure it a kind of transparency and protection from the world, but it is also perhaps to renounce knowing what it is.'[7] No clearer statement of the deformation of philosophy into doctrine could be desired.

Merleau-Ponty's criticism of the older generation of philosophers was not simply a matter of conflicting 'points of view.' He charged them with being untrue to philosophy. A particularly poignant consequence was that in 1937 several of the most intelligent philosophy students had failed the *agrégation*. In May 1938 the Société française de philosophie held a meeting to discuss problems arising from philosophy instruction. Among others present were Léon Brunschvicg, C. Bouglé, director of the Ecole Normale Supérieure, D. Roustan, chairman of the *agrégation* jury for 1938, and a number of younger men, including Merleau-Ponty who was then an *agrégé répétiteur* at the Ecole Normale Supérieure.

Georges Friedmann, a few years older than Merleau-Ponty, introduced the theme they were to discuss. A good deal of his talk was an elaboration of technical changes in degree requirements. He concluded by advocating a more rationalist critical science, especially the integration of physiological and psychometric applied psychology with Kantian philosophy.

Later, in *La Structure du Comportement* and the *Phénoménologie de la Perception*, Merleau-Ponty criticized at length such an opinion. Here, however, he began by agreeing that some administrative changes were desirable, but added that the uncertainties of examination 'are found in the situation of philosophy and not only in that of the *agrégation*.' During the twenties, when Merleau-Ponty was a student, 'papers were often a march toward the Kant of the three *Critiques*,' but today students 'take as a departure point what was for us a point of arrival.' They were seeking a philosophical understanding of experiences for which exact science is inappropriate; they were looking for a philosophy of art, which ought not be confused with 'questions of aesthetics.' The question of history, or of other people, which the French tradition had consigned to the province of empirical psychology and sociology, was being taken up for its philosophical significance, and philosophical reflection 'more often is concerned with the total experience of man than with the scientific experience. In this sense, one could say they are looking for philosophical anthropology.'[8] Given such an attitude on the part of philosophy students, the questions asked in the *agrégation* appeared formal, and in any case largely resolved.

In this situation, he continued, two attitudes on the part of philosophy instructors were possible. One could fear for the future of philosophy in a France where anything but critical, scientific reason must needs be irrational. But there was another approach: 'if a philosophy of *existence* makes reason a problem, it is not necessarily, as is existential philosophy, an irrationalism, and if one respects reason it is perhaps more important to know of its fragility than to believe it guaranteed in advance by the nature of things.' Merleau-Ponty provided some specific examples of the kind of reform he had in mind: room must be made in the curriculum for post-Kantian philosophers, Hegel and his posterity: Marx, Nietzsche, 'and even Husserl.' 'If one gives philosophy the meaning of reflection on the total man' other parts of the curriculum, presently included, could be dropped: for example, the very psychology that Friedmann wished to see increased. Ordinarily in lycées, he said, what is given 'under the name of Psychology is a composite education in which theory of knowledge is mixed with generally insufficient notions of scientific psychology. This bloated "psychology" takes the place both of philosophy and concrete psychology without providing either one.'[9] After Merleau-Ponty finished, Pierre Uri continued the discussion for several minutes, and he was followed by A. Bloch.

The first reply of the older men came in a rambling statement by M. Bouglé. He acknowledged there had been some surprises in the number of failures, but then life was full of surprises. Moreover, students had not always thought highly of the curriculum, yet ten or twenty or thirty years later they felt differently; philosophy (i.e., critical, scientific, neo-Kantian rationalism) had done well to preserve liberty, and no small reason was that it was unified in its approach to problems. 'Here, I join my friend and colleague, Merleau-Ponty. I find his remarks profound. Why can these disturbances be more lively today? Because there has been a shift in centres of interest; because the new generation does not share the same point of view as their university teachers ... The things that interest so many of the young are not those that interest us.' Consequently, it was difficult to establish any kind of intellectual harmony between candidates and juries. Now, he continued, Merleau-Ponty has told us a great deal. The young did not wish to be 'demonstrative; they have at the very least suspicion if not horror of $a + b$ demonstrations. Here the jury awaits them as a detour in the road.' But if the student cannot demonstrate his argument and reach a conclusion, the juries are surely correct in refusing to grant a degree. 'Is not the first virtue of a philosophy professor clarity?' The *agrégation* as presently constituted at least has the merit of demanding clarity. 'One proposes a thesis, one argues, one attempts to conclude. Perhaps you will call this exercise a little formal, a little scholastic? Must one also say, Cartesian? In any case, the traditions of *agrégation* in philosophy thus constituted have contributed to the maintenance of those characteristics attributed to the French spirit, and on this point I believe the jury is right.' When a jury fails a candidate it is only because of his inability in certain philosophical or pedagogical areas – a fear of demonstrating what is advanced as a thesis or an inability to argue methodically, 'and it is in that where the *agrégation* contributes to the form of thought characteristic of our country and which I judge worthy of maintenance.'[10] Criticism of neo-Kantianism had become, by some serpentine route, criticism of the French spirit if not France itself.

Bouglé called for an end to this intellectual disarray through a re-establishment of scientific discipline in matters pertaining to thought. The next speaker, D. Parodi, agreed with Bouglé, and M. Roustan took the floor. He had been instructed, he said, by the opinions which the younger men had voiced, although he agreed with very few of them. What he had learned was that they had forgotten the needs of secondary education and the role of the *agrégation* with respect to it, namely the production of lycée teachers. 'M. Merleau-Ponty has told us that he was surprised to have had to wait until last year to become familiar with Hegel, which means, if I am not mistaken, that he is criticizing the *agrégation* for not having had to introduce him to Hegel earlier.' This is understandable enough, but there is another problem. 'It is not a matter of questioning the importance of Hegel, or Schelling, or Fichte, or even Husserl and Heidegger. But is it proper to direct a candidate who ignores Kant towards Hegel or some such other of these philosophers? Is it not proper to study Kant before Hegel, Leibniz before Kant, and Descartes before Leibniz?' There will always be gaps in instruction, but one's education does not end with the *agrégation* and one can learn Hegel, Marx, Nietzsche, Husserl by oneself. True, the young are of the opinion that 'philosophers as classical as Descartes or Kant have made some inexcusable errors. What would happen if we replaced Descartes by Nietzsche, and Kant by Husserl in our programs?'[11] Roustan had finally come to the heart of the matter. It was not so much a question of wrapping oneself in the Tricolore and guarding the French spirit while it travelled from Descartes to Kant as it was of maintaining doctrine. Roustan did not give us a glimpse of what would happen if Kant were replaced by Husserl, and we are left merely with intimations of unspoken and presumably unspeakable horrors. Merleau-Ponty had warned a few years earlier that a philosophy that defined itself by a self-enclosed rationality would succeed only in protecting itself from reality at the cost of knowing what it is.

GABRIEL MARCEL

Merleau-Ponty's rejection of dogmatism did not at first imply a rejection of Christianity, as can be seen in his review of Gabriel Marcel's *Etre et Avoir* in 1936.[12] During the twenties and thirties Marcel had been especially critical of idealism and empiricism, which, he said, were indistinguishable insofar as they both denied the reality of incarnation.[13] In addition, he criticized the prevailing Thomistic formulas that dominated theological discourse. In his review Merleau-Ponty noted both these aspects of Marcel's criticism as well as the positive response that Marcel developed to replace the positions he argued against.

The aspect of Marcel's philosophy that bears on the origin of Merleau-Ponty's early political thought is his criticism of Kantianism. As with Descartes' *cogito*, which is made into the criterion of existence or the guardian of the 'threshold of the valid,' the 'one' of Kantian thought is nobody's, belongs to no existing flesh and blood person. Kantians ignore the existence of the person, Marcel said, in order to open the door to progress through science. This science or 'objective thought,' he said, was constituted by an act whereby we detach ourselves from our awareness of existence in order to construct a second reality along objective, scientific lines. Accordingly, he wrote of a 'functionalization' of reality, an act of the mind that imaginatively converts all matters of human concern into 'problems.'[14] A 'problem' is something that the scientific imagination can grapple with; it is encountered as a roadblock or barrier and may be manipulated and surmounted by a specific technique. Indeed, technique defined the problem.

The same issue was indicated by the notion of characterization. We 'characterize' something when we enumerate its properties one beside another and consider them to be independent, autonomous, and external. When, for example, we characterize a river as hydro power it is converted from being a river into a problem for engineers to overcome by building a dam. Moreover, engineers can perfect, or at least improve, their ability to solve these kinds of problems, increasing thereby what we call our 'power' over nature. The pragmatic effects of 'science' so understood give the idealist philosophy that underlies it such widespread appeal. But the effects of 'science' and 'progress' are ambiguous: 'You cannot read a newspaper article on the occasion of some catastrophe without ascertaining that it is treated as a kind of revenge by the beast we believed we had tamed.'[15] For Marcel, the desire to construct the world according to one's own view of it, to hold that the single citadel of order is man and the world a chaos of 'raw material,' and, most important, to characterize man as a technical potential, is both a gigantic act of *hubris* and the source of despair when the concerns of existence, which objective, scientific thought so carefully excluded from the mind, reappear as vague, haunting anxieties that, precisely because they were excluded, are incapable of being recognized.[16] It seems hardly necessary to add that an objective materialist view has even more trouble with the despair that expresses its own bankruptcy.

These views were a prelude to what, in Merleau-Ponty's opinion, was Marcel's most important insight, his understanding of the body and existence. According to Merleau-Ponty, Marcel approached the question phenomenologically. For example, the awareness expressed in the statement 'I am my body' brings to light the reflective awareness of myself as a 'participation in the world.' The reflective knowledge is indubitably linked to the awareness of the existence of oneself as body; that is, there are no independent criteria by which 'I' can judge whether 'my body' is existing in a world that is also existing. The reflective act of judgment presupposes an already existing judge, and in any case my first experience is not of judging whether I exist (which, strictly speaking, makes no sense) but is of existence itself. The 'presence' of existence of which we are reflectively aware when speaking of a 'presence' is, Marcel wrote, 'neither that of something nor of someone, and perhaps can be expressed, at least indirectly, by the words "absolute presence." '[17] One cannot even say that the universe is present to me, since that would already imply a duality, which is what Marcel and Merleau-Ponty both sought to avoid.

Nor can one characterize existence, because it is not an object that manifests characteristics. Rather one must use the image, familiar to Plato and Aristotle, of a participation that transcends the realm of problems and solutions, what Marcel called 'metaproblematic.' The metaproblematic defies rigorous description, Marcel believed, because it is anterior to discursive thought. What we call reflection is, as it were, a second reflection, a reflection on a primordial articulation of experience. This secondary reflection is a communication by symbols to another who, understanding its meaning, is able to reconstitute an equivalent personal experience and give it his own expression. The activities surrounding this secondary reflection may be indicated by the metaphor of drama and described by the term 'mystery.'

A mystery, unlike a problem, is not confronted as an object; rather, it absorbs the subject. To Marcel, mystery 'is something where I find myself committed, the essence of which, consequently, is not to be entirely before me. It is as if in this zone the distinction of *in me* from *before me* lost its signification.'[18] Both the modes of commitment, such as love, suffering, or faith, and the existence that is committed are 'mysterious.' But we must not understand our existence as something separate and distinct from our commitment, for it is of the essence of love or suffering to constitute the existence of the person, or rather to constitute the person. The counterproof is easier to grasp: it makes no sense to speak of 'me' involving 'my existence' in love or suffering as if in fact I could decide not to experience this love or suffering while maintaining a 'state' of 'being-in-love' or 'being-in-suffering.' The modes of existence likewise are not problems but mysteries; reflection upon existence, which is what Marcel understood metaphysical activity to consist of and which Merleau-Ponty called phenomenology, is reflection upon the theme of mystery.

A phenomenological, or in Marcel's sense a metaphysical, consideration of bodily existence or corporeity at the very least overcomes the difficulties that a scientific or problematic approach raises. Corporeity, the so-called problem of body and soul, is a mystery. Formulas that presuppose a scientific attitude, such as 'I have a body' or 'I sense my body,' will therefore always be inadequate because the logical elements of the problematic expressions are in fact derived from the mystery they attempt in vain to express. The most misleading 'problem' of all is that of evil. To look upon evil as a problem not only gives the progressive an opportunity to advocate the Promethean task of overcoming it but also obscures the real question. Evil is not a 'breakdown in goodness' or a 'flaw' in the world. First of all, it is suffered. That which is not suffered is no longer simply evil. To suffer, Marcel wrote, 'is to be wronged in what one has, in so far as what one has becomes constitutive of what one is.'[19] Those who speak of the problem of evil cannot know of what they speak. Consideration of the mystery of evil and suffering and the obvious relationship between suffering and corporeity suggests that, while all evil is suffered, not all suffering is evil. The example of the martyr makes this clear.

Martyrdom also means that we must revise, or at least deepen, our understanding of the statement 'I am my body' because the act of sacrifice signifies that 'I' can make 'myself' disposable in some measure for the sake of others.[20] One can, for example, bear witness against evil – which of course if not at all the same as 'comprehending' evil as a 'problem.' Considered this way, the meaning of corporeity is transformed. In Merleau-Ponty's words:

With *Etre et avoir* the philosophy of M. Marcel has been amplified, so to speak:

it tends to become a comprehension of life, of the ensemble of situations lived by man, each with its own ambience. More and more, the centre of perspective is shifted from the body and comes closer to the soul. For if my body is more than an object that I can possess, we can no longer say that it is myself. It is 'the frontier of what I am and of what I have,' at the limit of being and having. The central fact of metaphysics is doubtless no longer, as we recently said, the presence and separation of my body: rather in the new work of M. Marcel, it is the presence and absence of my life, the adherence of my life to myself and at the same time my power of sacrificing it, my refusal to confound myself with it.[21]

Gabriel Marcel's arguments show clearly what was implied by Merleau-Ponty's endorsement: that no gap or conflict existed between religious and philosophical experience.

Merleau-Ponty went on to compare Marcel's philosophy of existence with established Christian philosophy. We are ill prepared, Merleau-Ponty said, to consider existence philosophically. 'It is astonishing to see how prudent or timorous philosophers have been when it is a question of forging new terms for the very aspects of existence to which they hold most.'[22] The analysis of the existence of the Christian soul using Aristotleian terminology is a case in point, for it is essential in Christianity that the soul have the potential for damnation or salvation, a notion quite foreign to Aristotle's concept of the soul as the 'form of the body.' In Christianized Aristotelianism, whatever maintains its form is ipso facto saved; but in Christianity, Marcel argued, the soul cannot be saved unless it can be lost, and there can be no place for salvation except in a universe that admits of real injuries, which means there can be no hope of salvation unless there is equally the possibility of despair or damnation. Thus it is on philosophical grounds and not on the basis of vague and irrational religious feelings that one must acknowledge that sacrifice and despair, martyrdom and suicide, spring from the same ground. For Marcel, the possibility of suicide was a central datum for metaphysics. Thomism ignored it. 'By facing despair, metaphysics must take up its position. The ontological problem is inseparable from the problem of despair – but they are not problems.'[23]

Thomists erred to treat ontology and despair as problems; these are mysteries that philosophy has every right to investigate. By the same token, philosophy can hardly be excluded from considering other mysteries, including the mystery that Thomists, among others, call revelation. But the mystery of revelation is not an interruption of a world that would otherwise be full of problems and solutions. 'Whatever a revelation may be,' Marcel wrote, 'it is nevertheless only thinkable insofar as it is addressed to a *committed* being, in the sense that I have tried to define, that is, participating in a non-problematizable reality that sustains it as subject.'[24] Indeed, for a sufficiently aggressive 'scientist,' revelation can also become a problem. Usually, making the mystery of revelation into a problem is the first step of an argument against divine being. But, on the other side, the so-called proofs for the existence of God are equally indicted, for they were simply theistic responses to an alleged problem. Or, as Merleau-Ponty wrote, 'we must also habituate ourselves to consider the "proof" as a mode of secondary thought.'[25] Proof is a term that properly belongs to the solution of problems. With respect to God, proofs are essentially counterproofs in that the 'attributes' of God can be denied only by falling into contradiction, that is, the theology to which we are led by philosophy is a *theologia negativa*. The positive, experiential ground for which philosophical theology is the counterproof is a mystery.

Phenomenologically, love is the appropriate term to describe the experience of that mystery which is poorly indicated by the phrase 'the relationship between God and man.' Love is a co-presence that in itself cannot properly be characterized by one of the terms, since the entire commitment of a possible co-existor is what constitutes co-presence. For example, when we are present with a beloved we do not, at the same time, co-exist in such a way as to characterize them, even as beloved. When we take the necessary distance to accomplish the characterization we cease to be present to them. Similarly, we do not co-exist with God but are present to Him in worship. Our ideas of God, accordingly, are nothing but the abstract, intellectualized expression of a co-presence that, at best, may be symbolized in ritual and liturgy. When one takes part in, and is committed to, these actions, said Marcel, one experiences 'an order where the subject finds himself put in the presence of something over which all grasp is precisely denied. If the word transcendence has a signification, it surely is this: it exactly designates this kind of absolute, impassable interval which is hollowed out between the soul and being where being refuses us a hold. Nothing is more characteristic than the very gesture of the believer who joins his hands in prayer and attests by this same gesture that there is nothing to do, nothing to change, but simply that he is about to give himself.'[26] The real 'proof' of God, Merleau-Ponty agreed, was in the experience of which the gesture of prayer is but a token and the discursive thoughts of formal proof a mere intellectual confirmation of that which is known with a certitude greater than any verification.[27]

Faith in God, love of another, indeed all commitment, presupposes the possibility of betrayal. Fidelity to one's commitment is not a matter of pride in keeping one's word because it is one's own. Nor is it a matter of duty to certain principles, but the active recognition of a performance, a real presence that can be maintained by commitment or forgotten and obliterated. Again, in Marcel's view this has nothing to do with irrational religious sentiments but only the theoretical analysis of experience.

Perhaps the core of Marcel's philosophy is contained in the following statement: 'A phrase came to my lips as I was looking at a dog lying in front of a shop: "There is one thing which is called living, there is another called existing: I have chosen to exist." '[28] We have a choice, and nothing obliges us to choose 'existence' over 'life.' Moreover, nothing obliges philosophers to choose existence over life. As Merleau-Ponty remarked, 'the objection that comes to mind when confronted with such a philosophy is that it lacks any kind of *obligatory* force ... An option is there, and it could not be otherwise.'[29] But, he continued, one cannot help but wonder if reflection could not control this option more closely. 'The author knows better than anyone how the place made here for philosophy properly understood is a narrow one. And after that, if the "I have seen" is a final argument, does not this philosophy authorize all kinds of pseudo-intuition as well? How will we distinguish authentic intuition from illusion?'[30] But, he said, let us look more carefully at this objection: is it not an attempt to create a problem where mystery abides? Is there in fact no solution to the danger of the false prophet? And if not, is this not simply another example of our perennial temptation to degrade mystery into a finite series of problems? Yet, Merleau-Ponty continued, we *do* distinguish between true lyric and madness, 'and when it happens that the words of an infant or a madman express the sounds of true poetry, our surprise and the sort of shock that we feel warns us that there we have two absolutely different registers. Thus we are invited to clarify that immediate distinction of what is below reason from what is above it.'[31] For example, Merleau-Ponty wrote, do not the very existences of which we have knowledge display 'a certain structure, do they not present to us certain partial aspects, sensible as such, aspects of which each one is an invitation to go further?' But, he said, M. Marcel knows this; he maintained the possibility of dialectic and even spoke of a 'hyperphenomenology.' Finally, Merleau-Ponty concluded, we should recall that we are dealing with an unfinished philosophy, and nothing could be more unfair than to oppose scientific 'refutations' to Marcel's suggestions or to construe Merleau-Ponty's comments as unfavourable.

These early writings of Merleau-Ponty, though not on political topics, were nevertheless important in the formation of his political opinions. Not that they showed him to be pious; rather Scheler and Marcel were important to him philosophically. Their arguments concerning the nature and amplitude of human experience convinced him rationally. The distinction between believing in a creed, system, or dogma – whether Christian or Marxist or liberal – and giving a discursive account of common human experience could not, he felt, be overemphasized. Whether that description were called philosophy or theology is a secondary matter; what counts is that the argument express the real contours of lived experience in such a way that the reader or hearer is able to recognize its truth. Systems and dogmas are derivative. This, or something like it, was Merleau-Ponty's philosophical or interpretative position before the war.

KOJÈVE

It is insufficient, however, to point to Merleau-Ponty's distaste for dogma if one seeks to understand his rejection of Christianity, let alone his commitment to Marxism. Nor is it enough to say, as he did himself, that he was drawn to the left by the teachings of Christianity, for he also knew that the City of God was not the Earthly City. Anyone as familiar with the philosophy of Scheler and Marcel as Merleau-Ponty was not going to be persuaded simply by abstract argument on theological or philosophical topics. Whence, then, his new commitment?

The most obvious factor, which we will consider in detail in the next chapter, was the second world war. He began it as an irenic second lieutenant and ended it in the Resistance, gun in hand, patrolling a *quartier* of Paris in search of Germans. Yet the sheer experience of war does not determine one's response to it, and it was certainly not responsible for Merleau-Ponty's 'loss of faith.'[32] On the contrary, he had already formed new commitments before the war began. The moment of disillusion with Christianity and with the meditative phenomenology of Scheler and Marcel was one with the moment of restoration of a new commitment: the agent was Hegel.

For four years before the war Merleau-Ponty had listened to the exposition by Alexandre Kojève of Hegel's *Phenomenology of Spirit*, and it was on the basis of Kojève's teaching him how to read Hegel and Marx that he was able to understand, or rather, 'unmask,' Christianity.[33] The substance of his Hegelian argument on religion may be summarized as follows: 'perhaps ultimately the religion of God-made-man ends up, by an inevitable dialectic, in an anthropology and not a theology.'[34] In Kojève's more explicit words: 'For Hegel, the real object of religious thought is Man himself: every *theology* is necessarily an anthropology.'[35] Or, as Hegel himself said, religion (including Christianity) is consciousness of absolute being in the form of representation, *Vorstellung*, not in the form of the concept, *Begriff*, that is, argument. Accordingly, the task of conceptual thought is to dissolve the form of representational thought and expose as un-hidden truth, the *a-letheia*, beneath.

We need not consider the details of Kojève's argument here nor raise the more difficult question of the soundness of his interpretation.[36] Three aspects, however, are important. The first, which every commentator on his book has mentioned, is the absolute centrality of what Hegel called the pure concept of recognition, namely the dialectic of master and slave, which began with a primordial and pure struggle for prestige. From the moment of this anthropogenic fight, the animal homo sapiens ceased to dwell in a state of nature and became a historical, temporal, active, and negating being. Henceforth a human being was a dynamic being-in-the-world not a static being-of-nature.

A second and equally significant point is that Hegel's *Phenomenology of Spirit*, which according to Kojève contained the introduction to the final, definitive, and complete philosophical teaching, was concerned with the historical details of the pure concept of recognition as they emerged in empirical history. In other words, Hegel wrote his book in a kind of code, which Kojève deciphered. The real contents of Hegel's *Phenomenology* dealt with the whole of 'history,' where that term was taken to mean the fights of historical masters and the labours of historical slaves. That is, 'history' was concerned with the technological and political transformations of humanity. The data ordered by Hegel's book stretched back as far as the empirical knowledge of his day would allow, to Egypt, and ended with the contemporary events of the French Revolution and the Napoleonic Empire. To be more precise, it ended with Hegel who comprehended, justified, understood, or 'forgave' the Spirit whose appearance as 'history' he had accounted for. That is, the *Phenomenology* was an account of the whole of history, which, being accounted for, was over. Henceforth, nothing genuinely new would occur, and actual events would simply bring into empirical existence the principles established by the French Revolution and the Napoleonic Empire.

The third significant aspect of Kojève's interpretation was his elaboration of the details that the Revolution and Empire established in principle. Formally, it was the final, perfected, and unchangeable political order, which accordingly brought to an end the dialectical changes outlined in the pure concept of recognition and actually undertaken historically. This political order Kojève called the universal and homogeneous state.

The Biblical story of the fall of mankind told how human beings lost their innocence; in Hegel's version human beings lost their nature. The whole of history is a redemptive drama laboriously played out by the slave living in terror of the master. By transforming the external world of nature the slave came to recognize it as his own work and ceased to fear it. Since fear of nature, including the fear of death at the heart of the slave's 'nature,' is the motive for belief in God, when nature is no longer feared men become atheists. In addition, during the course of history the slave had before him the ideal of freedom, which he saw incarnate in the master. But it was simply an ideal, an abstract ideal, a nothingness. Thus, when the slave attempted to actualize the ideal directly the result was the actualization of nothingness, death. Historically this took place during the terror directed by Robespierre. Terror, as Hegel said in a famous passage, is abstract freedom made actual. And, Kojève added, it makes mankind finally disposed to admit of a state where they will be truly, not abstractly, free.

The citizen of the Napoleonic state, having purged the final remnants of his slavish 'nature' in the Terror and thereby completed the last act in the self-education of humanity, completely understood himself. 'He lives in accord with himself. Thus he is completely satisfied (*befriedigt*), and he is so by the *mutual recognition of all*.' The Napoleonic state realized the secular world-immanent ideal of the Revolution, *Liberté, Egalité, Fraternité*; 'the synthetic man is realized in it, the veritable *Bürger*, the true citizen, the synthesis of master and slave: the soldier who labours and the labourer who makes war.'[37] Because it is universal, I am recognized by *all* men, who are my equals; because it is homogeneous it is *I* who am recognized and not my family, my wealth, my social class, or my nation. Concretely, only the Leader of this state is really satisfied, but all citizens are satisfied *in posse*, for each citizen can become Leader, each can actualize his desire for recognition 'on condition of accepting the risk of death (element of mastery) that implies competition (= political struggle; this risk guarantees the "seriousness" of the candidates as well) in this State, and on condition also of having previously taken part in the constructive activity of the Society, in the collective labour that maintains the State in its reality (element of servitude, of service, that guarantees the "competence" of the candidates as well).'[38] The universal and homogeneous state, then, is a synthesis of power and wisdom.

MERLEAU-PONTY'S ANTHROPOLOGY

Merleau-Ponty did not subscribe to the entire Kojèvian thesis, and yet his two most famous early works, the *Phénoménologie de la Perception* and *Humanisme et Terreur*, float in a Hegelian ether.[39] The latter work is an analysis of violence and recognition within the context of power 'perfected' in the USSR by the 'wisdom' of Marxism. A Hegelian echo is found in the very title of the *Phénoménologie*. More particularly, it contained a Hegelian understanding of human being. Philosophers have acclaimed the book a classic of the twentieth century, and since a political scientist ought to show some deference before a fine philosophical text a brief apology is required. First, although political science has no warrant to doubt the judgment of philosophy, two things should be made clear. As Merleau-Ponty himself pointed out,[40] one reads a classic text as an interrogative invitation, so that, whatever the questions philosophers have asked of the book and however profound the replies they received, one is justified in reading it in a particular way if one can show it to be consistent with other, chiefly political, pieces of the same period. In other words, there can be no intention of making an attempt (in any case futile) at giving a balanced summary of what took an original mind over five hundred pages to say. Since my purpose is simply to document the genesis and nature of Merleau-Ponty's philosophical assumptions insofar as they bear upon his politics, I must be strictly selective. I focus upon a single aspect of Merleau-Ponty's anthropology, his notion of historical contingency, for this appropriation from Kojève enabled him to conceive of humanism as the goal and purpose of political, that is, historical, action without embracing the apparent finality of the Hegelian System. As all who have read the *Phénoménologie* know, innumerable other questions may be asked of the book, and other readers can find other things; but that is simply to confirm it as a classic.

The world, Merleau-Ponty and Kojève agreed, implied man. Man is a world-immanent temporal being, the source of unrest and negativity in the world, a being whose presence and activities are the ground for the contingency of existence, of being, and of truth, a being whose 'purpose' is the achievement of freedom, authentic intersubjectivity, the recognition of man by man, all of which are rigorously equivalent terms. 'Existence,' Merleau-Ponty said, 'is indeterminate in itself by reason of its fundamental structure insofar as it is the very operation by which what has no meaning takes on a meaning.' Existence 'takes up a de facto situation. We will call this movement by which existence takes up for its own purposes and transforms a de facto situation, transcendence. Exactly because it *is* transcendence, existence never definitively goes beyond anything, for then the tension that defines it would disappear.'[41] Existence as an operation or movement is 'transcendence' only in the sense that men can transcend one situation by going forward into another; this temporal movement constitutes what Albert Camus called horizontal transcendence, a transcendence within the world. The structure of this transcendence is conditioned and even determined by time: 'if we rediscover time beneath the subject, and if we relate to the paradox of time those of the body, the world, the thing, and the other, we will understand that there is nothing to discover beyond.'[42] For Merleau-Ponty, there is *nothing* to discover beyond an exploration of the philosophical understanding of time. The fullest and most comprehensive understanding of man results anthropologically from an understanding of human temporality, politically from an understanding of his historical situation.

The power of making promises and covenants, of committing oneself to a project and so disposing of the future as if it were present, has traditionally been understood as providing stability and reliability in an otherwise unpredictable world. For Merleau-Ponty, however, this aspect of temporality was primarily reflected in the contingency of knowledge and the historicity of the world.

He introduced the problem by wondering whether one can knowingly be committed to an illusion.[43] False love, for example, is more than self-deception and less than knowledge. It does not appear as false and is not known to be false until after disillusionment. Yet I could be under the illusion of love only because I was in a situation that I could not control but that, at the same time, I was not entirely unaware of. Thus while awaiting my beloved, I am both bored and thinking it foolish to have arrived at our meeting place so early. I am aware of my ambivalence but unwilling to do anything about it. In principle I can be illusioned and disillusioned because I commit myself to a situation and this commitment hinders the effectiveness of my knowledge. In the actual and living tension between an intellectual knowledge of one's situation and the concrete existential commitment to it, the greater weight of priority must be accorded the latter. My true love is assured, therefore, only by my constant commitment, and it can be proved false only by my taking up another commitment. This much, at least, Merleau-Ponty retained from Marcel.

The example chosen was intended by Merleau-Ponty to be of more general significance than a description of the dynamics of personal fidelity and betrayal. It was an illustration of the structure of human being as such. 'It is true,' he said, 'neither that my existence possesses itself nor that it is estranged from itself, because it is an act or a deed, and an act, by definition, is the violent passage from what I have to what I intend, from what I am to what I have the intention of being. I can effect the *cogito* and have the assurance of genuinely wishing, loving, or believing upon condition that first of all I effectively do wish or love or believe and that I accomplish my own existence ... There is no way to attain "sincerity" except by forestalling these scrupulous doubts and throwing oneself, eyes closed, into "doing." '[44] Human being, in short, is the continual act whereby I commit myself to a future that is ontologically distinct from my past, an act of continual negation of what is given *qua* given. This does not mean that each act reverses prior commitments but only that if prior commitments are confirmed it is not by necessity.

The structure of existential commitment must therefore extend to the realm of intellectual knowledge as well. The core of our knowledge of truth, according to Merleau-Ponty, is found in the experience of establishing and resuming concrete relations with ourselves and with others. In short, he said, the experience 'of *participation in the world*, of 'being-in-truth' (*l'être-à-la-vérité*) is not distinct from being-in-the-world.'[45] It is only by actually being launched and committed to a specific set of thoughts that I can discover other evident truths, so there can be no question, according to Merleau-Ponty, of confining oneself to phenomena while retaining the possibility of acceding to a real being beyond appearance. Rather, we must understand being as what appears: 'I think, and such and such a thought appears true to me; I know well that it is not unconditionally true and that the total explication would be an infinite task; but that does not deny that at the moment when I think, I think something, and that every other truth, in the name of which I would devalue this one, if for me it can be called truth, must accord with the "true" thought of which I have the experience.' Error and doubt, he said, do not cut us off from truth, because we remain surrounded by the world, which allows us to resolve particular mistakes. But the 'mistakes' of the world should not be seen as flaws in an otherwise perfect whole, nor a threat to rationality, nor a problem to be solved: that would make them out to be merely ontic contingencies. 'Ontological contingency, that of the world itself, being radical is, on the contrary, what founds once and for all our idea of truth. The world is the real for which the necessary and the possible are the only provinces.'[46]

For Merleau-Ponty, knowledge must be personal if it is to exist at all; dogma, which claims to be necessary but is ultimately a contingent formula, is derived from pre-dogmatic experience; and the world implies man. In addition, however, Merleau-Ponty insisted, with Kojève and Hegel, that the very being of man is an act of negation. Thus, the world to which he imparts negativity is what it is because it is what it has come to be. It could have been different; it will be different tomorrow. Change is not simply *événementielle* but evidence of the ontological contingency of the world qua world.

This raises a question of the utmost importance for Merleau-Ponty's political thought: in a contingent world how can one be committed? If the world as such is contingent, if all our commitments might be revoked, all our promises broken, where shall we look for criteria to judge our individual and collective actions? If the sheer fact of commitment is ontologically prior to the objects worthy of our commitments, must we not conclude that it is we, by our actual commitments, who confer a provisional and contingent value upon whatever objects we favour? But if it is the act of commitment that confers value, then it is a matter of relative indifference to what we are committed. And this, to follow Nietzsche, is nihilism.

On the other hand if we produce a short list of criteria of true and false or good and bad and loudly proclaim their validity independent of our own commitments is this not transparently dogmatic? If someone should produce a second list we are reduced to the first alternative, of imputing validity because we are committed. Merleau-Ponty sought a way beyond this dilemma by discovering in the immanent logic of our actual individual and historical commitments a configuration that expresses and eventually achieves a non-arbitrary meaning. We shall look first to his account of meaning in individual commitment and then to history, which is the story of our collective commitments.

Commitment is always conditioned by a particular situation, a specific, given conformation of things. Because the world is contingent, I can take up my present and alter the significance of my past as I choose my future. Thus, what is given cannot determine my choice, and a particular choice cannot restrict my freedom. Indeed, without commitment there can be no freedom. But this only sharpens the issue: to what is one committed? What should one choose? Here is Merleau-Ponty's reply:

Freedom is entangled in the contradictions of commitment and does not realize that it would not be freedom without the roots that it thrusts into the world. Shall I make this promise? Shall I risk my life for so little? Shall I give up my freedom in order to save freedom? There is no theoretical reply to these questions. But there are these *things* that irrefutably present themselves, there is this loved one before you, there are these men who exist enslaved around you and *your* freedom cannot be willed without leaving its singularity behind and without willing freedom for *all*. Whether it is a question of things or of historical situations, philosophy has no other function than to teach us to see them clearly again, and it is true to say that it is realized by destroying itself as separate philosophy. But here it is necessary to fall silent, for only the hero lives his relation to men and to the world right to the end, and it is not meant that another should speak in his name. 'Your son is caught in the fire, you will save him ... You are willing, if there is an obstacle, to sacrifice yourself to help him. You inhabit your act itself. Your act is you ... You give yourself in exchange ... Your signification shows itself, resplendent. It is your duty, your hate, your love, your faithfulness, your invention ... Man is but a knot of relations; relations alone matter for man.'[47]

This rhetorical flourish, which closed the *Phénoménologie*, is itself something of a knot and may be disentangled in the following way: freedom is a practical question, a question of action, so that the object of one's commitment can never be decided a priori. Freedom cannot be a singular matter for individual consciousness, since my commitment has practical consequences for others; thus truly to commit myself to my own freedom I must tacitly commit myself to the freedom of every other individual. One who actually does that, Merleau-Ponty said, is a hero, and philosophy has no authority to praise or judge heroic behaviour, to speak in behalf of heroism, or preach it. That is why Merleau-Ponty allowed an actual hero, Saint-Exupéry, to have the last word.

Individual commitments, because they engage others, are already collective and historical. The problem is to discover the meaning of our collective and historical commitments, and here Merleau-Ponty followed the same formal procedure he used in his analysis of true and false love and the problem of commitment to an illusion. The great collective illusion was Christiantiy.

Kojève's interpretation of Hegel, we have argued, should be the starting point for any understanding of Merleau-Ponty's religious criticism. It enabled him to demythologize Christianity and so avoid a doctrinaire 'anti-theism,' which he said was a dogmatic reversal of dogmatic theology. Philosophy, he held, was beyond that. 'What the philosopher performs is the movement that increasingly leads back from knowledge to ignorance, from ignorance to knowledge, and a sort of repose in this movement.'[48] Merleau-Ponty saw the experience of repose in the uncertain movement of philosophical life, not the lesser demands of Christian doctrine, as the genuine truth of existence. As Hegel taught, 'there is a perpetual malaise in the condition of being conscious,' man 'defines himself as the locale of unrest (*Unruhe*),' he is a 'sick animal,' and in consequence 'all consciousness is unhappy.' The role of religion in human culture, therefore, is that of a 'cry,' which is unreflective, but which, like the dogmas of the incarnation and original sin, is valuable because it 'reflects the contradictions of man, body and spirit, noble and wretched.'[49] A clear grasp of the significance of religion would make clear the contradictions of human existence and so open them to direction and change.

If we treat religion as the symbolic expression of the social and human drama – in Hegel's language, if we understand religion as *Vorstellung*, representation – we can pierce its opaque symbolism and see it 'returned to its sources and its truth, which are the concrete relations of men with each other and with nature.' Rightly understood as the imaginary effort of man to rejoin other men in another world, the 'Beyond,' we can reject 'this fantasy of communication' and replace it with 'effective communication in this world.' In short, he said, 'religion is more than a hollow appearance; it is a phenomenon founded in interhuman relations. It will only disappear as separated religion by passing into these relations.'[50] Merleau-Ponty was urging not only that his readers change their perspective but also that such a change was demanded by the course of history itself.

Hegel had said as much: 'Reading the early morning newspaper is a kind of morning benediction for the realist.'[51] The newspaper had replaced the Bible, worldly wisdom had supplanted knowledge of God, and God had been murdered because His historical task was done: He 'destroyed the ties of blood and family in order to create the bonds of the spirit.'[52] Now these bonds are to be purged of religiosity and escapism and replaced with effective communication in this world, that is, humanism. Following the Left Hegelians a century earlier, Merleau-Ponty argued that what really was meant by Christians who speak of faith in God was good faith toward other men. 'Is not faith itself,' he asked, 'stripped of its illusions, that very movement by which, joining ourselves to others and joining our present to our past, we act in such a way that everything has a sense, and synthesize, by a precise word, the confused discourse of the world? The saints of Christianity and the heroes of past revolutions have never done anything different. Simply, they tried to believe that their fight was already won in heaven or in History. The men of today do not have this resource. The hero of our contemporaries is not Lucifer; it is not even Prometheus. It is man.'[53]

Man, the contemporary hero, Merleau-Ponty recognized, was Hegel's self-transformed slave 'who preferred life, and who laboured to transform the world in such a manner that in the end there is no more room for the master.'[54] The solitary master depends for immortality on the memory of the slavish storyteller.

The slave makes his own immortality, 'where the deed lives and hurries further on [in history] even if the name of its original creator should be left behind.'[55] Merleau-Ponty glossed Schiller's text: 'For the living there is no other resource – but it is sovereign – than to keep up the conduct of a living man. One dies alone but one lives with others; we are the image they have made of us; there, where they are, are we as well.' We can no longer have faith in a world-transcendent God, he said, but only in the natural movement that throws us towards things and towards others. When man has come of age, his love of life with others replaces the morbid fascination of the master and the pious illusions of religious consciousness.

The achievement of Christianity was to have dissolved the pagan bifurcation between master and slave. The price paid by Christian consciousness was the illusion of faith in a world-transcendent God. But when the criticism of Heaven is followed by the criticism of earth, as Marx instructed, we find beneath those illusions a genuine faith in man. Faith without illusions joins us to others and through them to truth.[56] Man, the synthesis of master and slave, is the contemporary hero, the 'world-historical individual' of our times, because he grasps directly the truth of his own being, which is effective communication in the world, and he knows that earlier religions were simply a cry for authentic intersubjectivity.

Interhuman relations alone matter to man. According to Merleau-Ponty, these are the only kind of relations that men may truly experience. Hence, a commitment to humanism is philosophically justified. Anyone who nevertheless insists on the reality of 'vertical' or ontological transcendence must be disillusioned. The contingency of the world makes all knowledge provisional except consciousness of contingency. From this consciousness emerges a commitment to humanism.

Illusions die hard. Not everyone is a humanist, so that those who are may reasonably anticipate resistance, especially since the humanist's programme of disillusionment involves one's most fundamental experience. Moreover, humanism as commitment is not humanism achieved, only a precondition of it. Like any commitment, a commitment to humanism implies, Merleau-Ponty said, a 'violent passage from what I have to what I intend.'[57] The most important practical implication of an as yet unattained humanism may therefore be terror. Terror, or more generally violence, was for Merleau-Ponty a historical necessity, and humanism its sole justification.

1
The post-war context

I have argued that humanism was the central term in Merleau-Ponty's political vocabulary. It brought together the various interpretations of collective life to which human beings have committed themselves. The intellectual and spiritual change that Merleau-Ponty underwent has been described as cutting himself off from 'vertical' transcendence in the religious or philosophical sense, implying that the act was a mistake. It was motivated by his rejection of religious and philosophical dogma and the existential attractions of Hegel's idea of commitment to humanism or a regime of mutual recognition.

If Merleau-Ponty was right, religious experience is illusion, an ersatz reality sustained in the last analysis by individual and collective neuroses. Merleau-Ponty's arguments were not set forth in a psychiatric idiom, and he claimed that religious commitments were in fact philosophical and historical errors. He thus set about justifying his own commitments by coherent argument. The actual historical commitments of human beings he regarded as a call to humanism and an outline of its eventual triumph, which in itself was desired by all reasonable and realistic people.

In the terminology of Scheler and the Merleau-Ponty of 1935, one may distinguish 'regions of value' and establish intellectually the hierarchy extending, for example, from biological values to sacred ones. While one may, without much difficulty, understand the hierarchy of values described by Scheler, it is entirely another matter to incarnate this knowledge in the commitments of daily life. Nevertheless, if one's commitments ignore completely the experienced hierarchy of values, one's actions will no longer make moral sense. In more positive terms, two presumptions are being made: that the sphere of violence, power, and the rationality that connects means to ends is not independent and autonomous but an integral part of the whole of human existence, and, second, that the whole of human existence also includes a transcendent dimension, sensed in the common human experience of a gap between our values and our ability to live according to them. This experience may be called ontological dependence. When the rationality of moral ends as established by one's knowledge of a hierarchy of values is ignored, the rationality that co-ordinates means and ends is controlled by other commitments that may be called morally irrational or even immoral.

From this perspective the great error in Merleau-Ponty's understanding of human being is found in his opinion that interhuman relations alone matter to man because these alone are experienced realities. Clearly, such relations do matter, but so also does the reality experienced as transcendent to the human sphere as such. For example, from Merleau-Ponty's dogma, 'interhuman *praxis* is the absolute,'[1] one may turn for comparison to the subtle dialectic of authentic self-choosing described by Kierkegaard:

That which I choose I do not posit, for in this case this were not [already] posited, I could not choose it, and yet if I do not posit it by the fact that I chose it, then I did not choose it. It exists, for in case it were not in existence I could not choose it; it does not exist, for it only comes into being by the fact that I choose it, otherwise my choice would be an illusion.

But what is it I choose? Is it this thing or that? No, for I choose absolutely, and the absoluteness of my choice is expressed precisely by the fact that I have not chosen to choose this or that. I choose the absolute. And what is the absolute? It is myself in my eternal validity. Anything else but myself I never can choose as the absolute, for if I choose something else, I choose it as a finite thing and so do not choose it absolutely ... But what, then, is this self of mine? If I were required to define this, my first answer would be: It is the most abstract of all things, and yet at the same time it is the most concrete – it is freedom ... It requires courage for a man to choose himself; for at the very time when it seems that he isolates himself most thoroughly he is most thoroughly absorbed in the root by which he is connected with the whole.[2]

The difference between Merleau-Ponty and Kierkegaard is this: for Merleau-Ponty the only limitations to human commitments are either natural or given limitations or else merely human limitations, that is, the pragmatic consequences of earlier choices. In neither case are these limitations ontologically significant to human beings as such. Rather they should be seen as challenges to action and obstacles to be removed. For Kierkegaard, human being is ontologically limited by its very nature; the 'absolute' of human existence is the free recognition and authentic acceptance of one's own finitude. As Kierkegaard said, an authentic self must exist if it is to be chosen, and yet it cannot exist until it is chosen, the ontological limitation of human existence being expressed by the fact that both statements are indubitably true. Likewise, the 'self' is both abstract and concrete. Kafka tells of the person who wants to find the right road to the true moral law but is unable to do so before the end of his life, precisely when he has no time to choose; then he discovers that he can find the right road only by embarking on it. Here Kafka indicated a prosaic truth close to the Heraclitan as well as the Pauline formulas: the moral law is hard to find unless one has hope (*elpis*); the divine is hard to know unless one has trust or faith (*pistis*).[3]

Merleau-Ponty's political thought thus moved within an unnecessarily restricted field. This 'scotosis,' as Bernard Lonergan has called such an aberration of understanding, did not eclipse the whole of common experience. But certain insights were excluded, and with them the further questions that carry one's perspective to further and more comprehensive levels. But within the field he surveyed, Merleau-Ponty's political thought achieved a remarkable penetration of problems and constitutes the substance of his practical analysis. His political thought contained a number of critical insights the validity of which is unimpaired by the limitations we have suggested. Merleau-Ponty's chief criticism, directed against ideologues whose scotosis was greater than his own, was that either they denied the importance of concrete human relations in favour of pretended necessities and moralizing abstractions or they denied their responsibility for the consequences of their own commitments. Let us examine now his account of the war and the Liberation, which served to confirm in practice his theoretical commitment to humanism learned at the feet of Kojève.

THE MEMORY OF WAR

Because he took so seriously first neo-Kantian rationalism and then Hegelianism, the war and the occupation were an apocalypse for Merleau-Ponty, a revelation of disorder and irrationality on such a scale and with such a significance that, upon reflection, he felt it necessary 'to form a new idea of reason.'[4] As he wrote in the *Phénoménologie de la Perception:* 'the idea of a universe of thought or a universe of values where all thinking lives would confront and conciliate each other is found to be questionable.' Just as nature is not of itself geometrical but only appears that way within a strictly circumscribed context, he observed, neither is human society a community of reasonable minds but only appears that way locally and temporarily. The experience of chaos, he said, both in philosophy and in war, 'invites us to see rationalism in a historical perspective, which, in principle, rationalism seeks to avoid, to seek a philosophy that makes us understand how reason springs forth in a world it did not make, and to prepare the living infrastructure without which reason and freedom are emptied and distorted.'[5] The actual experiences that lay behind these words were set forth in an essay whose importance to him may be judged by the fact that it appeared in the inaugural issue of *Les Temps modernes*.

There are at least two ways, he said in that essay, in which thinking men can abstain from politics or war: the first is to adopt an attitude of desperate irony in order to conceal frustration at being implicated in events that are not to one's liking. Politics is dirty, and one wishes nothing of dirt. One may take revenge through a cynical Machiavellianism and pronounce lofty judgments,[6] but one knows it is a retreat to the Republic of Letters, where aphorisms, art, and the exquisite replace action. Nevertheless, he added, there is an apolitism that is less a retreat than an acquisition of perspective and a commitment that may go beyond what is known or what is reasonable but does not, for that reason alone, go against reason and knowledge. Before the war Merleau-Ponty was ironic, afterwards he was *engagé*; the transition was made during the intervening years when political action was thrust upon him but when he never forgot that we cannot see what we are doing unless we stop and think.

From the vantage point of 1945 it seemed to him odd that France had taken so long to go to war. Because 'we were not guided by facts,' because 'it was even a duty for us to distrust facts,' Munich did not appear to represent German aggression. But folly too is motivated: he lived in a France too happy and too weak to envisage violence, unhappiness, and war in the scheme of life. He had been taught by men who wished to forget war by inculcating optimism and rationalism, but that was simply the philosophy of a scarcely victorious nation, a compensation in the imagination for the memories of 1914. They knew of Nazi concentration camps in the same way they knew Plato and Sophocles. Existence was Edenic. Beyond the placid, formal court of the Ecole Normale Supérieure lay another garden, France, and the anticipated vacations of 1939. Merleau-Ponty had been innocent of the fact that if France was a garden, the rest of the world was not. 'We lived in a certain area of peace, experience, and freedom, formed by a conjunction of exceptional circumstances; we did not know it was a land to be defended; we thought it was the natural lot of men.' Everyone, even those who for one reason or another knew better, refused to be aroused from childhood habits of freedom: 'how could we know that they were difficult acquisitions? How could we have learned to commit our freedom in order to save it? We were consciousnesses naked before the world' and did not know that this was to live in peace, in France, and in a certain state of the world.[7] The only difference between Merleau-Ponty and Germans he knew was that they had let the Nazis thrive and were more immediately implicated in lies; the French had not yet learned of their own complicity. During the phony war and the collapse of the French army,

Merleau-Ponty learned nothing. Donning a uniform was a personal adventure for the young officer, and the Germans could be viewed with compassion as they lay dying.

With the defeat and occupation the strange game where men shot others, who were acknowledged as men, ended. Germans were no longer other men in uniform but masters, and representatives of a Nazi government. Magnanimity may be a virtue of the rich; it may not be difficult to treat generously prisoners who are at your mercy; but he himself was now the prisoner.[8] It is true that one can discover masters and slaves in peacetime society, he said, but 'no slavery is more visible than that of an occupied country.' Those who had never acknowledged that their liberty had been sustained by their tacit bond with others were made aware of it under the German guns. Communists, who before the beginning of Operation Barbarossa saw the war as a struggle between two forms of capitalism, after the Normandy landings spoke of the Liberation like everyone else.[9]

Living out the condition of master and slave put normal times into high relief, and Merleau-Ponty began to wonder at what miracle ever wrested tranquillity and order from chaos and violence. Nazi racism and the subsequent persecution and extermination of Jews shattered the axiom of his youth that declared there are only human beings. If it were true, if there were only human beings, or better, if there were only rational consciousnesses, then existence of the great lie of Nazi anti semitism could not be understood at all. Yet people were being killed and children taken from their mothers, which meant that people could make Nazi lies part of themselves, and that too had to be understood. Moreover, both sides had to be grasped, not only the motives of the antisemite but also that passion which sundered the filiations among men, the blinding force that permitted the Nazis to cause such suffering and devastation under the cover of racial hygiene and seemingly in ignorance of murder. For his own part, there was the discovery that consciousness did not survey its own kingdom. Just as a Jewish man was, for a Nazi, the embodiment of The Jew, so Merleau-Ponty embodied The French: more important than the discovery that roles could be imposed was the discovery that indeed he *was* French, and would stop being French only when he died. People, he learned, could be engulfed from within by hatred and passion and alienated from one another by their own deeds.

For the rational consciousness of his early philosophical training nothing was unintelligible. *La guerre, c'est la guerre.* It was precisely such 'reasonableness' that Merleau-Ponty found so opaque. He could see untutored passions eclipse whatever reason people possessed; he saw people murdered, whatever the reasonableness of their minds, because of their bodies. These things were only mocked by the lofty impartiality of rationalism. 'In this combat,' he wrote, 'we were no longer allowed to remain neutral ... If the arrest and conviction of an informer had depended upon us, we were no longer able to leave this duty to others.'[10] One might try to draw aside to meditate for the duration, to return to the great men who had been studied in school and carve out from a common corruption a small redoubt of virtue. 'For all that, we did not escape from history. Our best thoughts, seen from London, from New York or from Moscow situated us in the world and carried a name: they were the reveries of captives and being so were modified even in their value as thoughts.'[11] There is no way to get beyond history and time; private eternity is but the dream of a madman who thinks he is God.

The concluding part of his essay began with the words: 'In sum, we have learned history, and we are maintaining that it must not be forgotten.' The history he learned was that there could be an effective communication through action.[12] By taking up and living out the role of Hegel's slaves, the meaning of humanism, the recognition of man by man, became the standard by which politics could be measured.

In the Resistance one experienced mutual recognition and authentic intersubjectivity, where one could appear, unencumbered by class, or birth, or religion, simply as an individual among equals. In the Resistance, as René Char said, one could afford to go naked. It was 'that rare phenomenon of an historical action that did not cease to be personal.' Living under German guns and the Vichy regime enabled him to break away from the dilemma of being and doing, a dilemma common to all intellectuals who ponder action. And action resulted in 'that *happiness* through danger that we saw in certain of our friends who normally were so vexed.'[13] It may be objected that Merleau-Ponty confused the brotherhood of the battlefield with a peaceful regime of mutual recognition. That would be an error. Merleau-Ponty knew it was 'all too clear that this equilibrium of personal life and action was directly bound to the conditions of clandestine action and could not survive it ... We have now returned to the era of institutions.'[14] His wartime experience informed the best of Merleau-Ponty's political writing. It amounted to a life-world unmediated by family, class, or nation, a revelation both of the interpersonal depths that lie beneath everyday social relations, which are mediated by institutions, and the goals that institutions are meant to serve but cannot.

The strength he found in these depths exposed as well the frailty of all laws and all institutions. The years from 1939 to 1945 were not revolutionary, he said, but were comparable to revolution because both '*put the uncontested into question*.' The defeat of 1940 was an event in French political life unparalleled by the greatest dangers of 1914-18. For many, including Merleau-Ponty, it was equivalent to revolution because it laid bare the contingent foundations of legality and showed how a new legality was constructed. A person no longer lived within a constituted state but was 'invited to discuss with himself the social pact and to reconstitute a State by his choice.'[15] During an era of stable political and social institutions direct actions are difficult, if not impossible: good intentions, frank words, personal deeds, are mediated, often impersonally. Among Frenchmen during the war the split between what Ricœur has called *socius* and neighbour, between public and private men, disappeared.[16] After the war the caution and calculation that had been reserved for relations with the Germans were found in relations with one's fellow citizens.

The abrogation of personal liberties during the occupation was the price paid for that elusive happiness. Clearly the price was too high. But what of moderation and calculation? What of weighing the meanings that one's words and deeds have for others, even for one's fellow citizens? Then again, caution and circumspection may degenerate into dissembling and propaganda, and in any event are one cost of peace. Merleau-Ponty had no longing for the dangerous happiness of war. He also insisted that although something had been lost something had also been learned, that one cannot escape from history and the consequences of one's subjective certainties. The war, he said, did not teach him to renounce the liberal political values praised by Kantian philosophy. It was still wrong to kill a person because he lived on the other side of the Rhine, to treat another as a means, to hide the truth because it harms one's country. It was still right to wish for freedom, truth, happiness, and honest relations among men. But he learned that these noble and lofty liberal maxims remained nominal and were even worthless without an economic and political infrastructure that allowed them to exist. Even more, he learned that such maxims and the sentiments they expressed also designated interhuman relations. Thus, he concluded, 'it is not a question of renouncing the values of 1939 but of accomplishing them.'[17]

THE LIBERATION RABBLE

The war, the defeat, the occupation, and the Resistance exposed in a public and undoubted way the contingent basis of every constitutional order. No Frenchman could avoid the knowledge that any given regime was sustained by the commitments of its citizens or subjects. Merleau-Ponty's commitments and the life that followed from them were an embodiment of Kojève's lessons: he knew that mutual recognition was possible, and he sought to recapture the experiences of the war under the new conditions of the post-war world. Here Merleau-Ponty encountered what Malaparte called the 'Liberation Rabble,' an amorphous collection of communist, liberal, and free-floating intellectuals.

In the name of the public weal men are called upon to betray and lie and massacre. Such acts may not be vicious, wrote Montaigne, but they are always a misfortune. At the very least one must 'deprive wicked, bloody, and treacherous natures of this pretense to reason.' Merleau-Ponty approved of these words, adding that his opponents wished to ignore them: 'they must have a freedom that keeps a good conscience, and frank speech without its consequences.'[18] Communists, socialists, and liberals had alike forgotten their political responsibilities. They were infantile in the precise sense that, like children, they tried to forget everything offensive: real soldiers knew that glory had often been purchased by means that were less than glorious, while the politicians who honoured them were often compensating for their own impotence. It was so much easier to forget experience, to leave culture alone and solemnly to formulate as venerable verities 'the platitudes that fit our own weariness.' But weary words and a refusal to think had their own consequences: 'exactly because it is out of weakness that they love peace they are all ready for propaganda and war.'[19] What was missing from all political groups, what prepared them for war, was a forgetfulness of the structure of the human condition and the ambiguous meaning of action, which always goes beyond one's purest intentions and can never be guaranteed a meaning: Merleau-Ponty based this political 'ethics of responsibility' on his understanding of Marxism. I shall consider his arguments for Marxism in the next chapter. Here I shall outline the polemical context into which were set his theoretical reflections on, and practical experience of, humanism.

For Merleau-Ponty, political debate, which presumes at least some common ground, was worthwhile only with people whose allegiance was to the left. Not that the right was ignored, but that an element of acrimony entered in such discussions that by and large was absent otherwise. His most lively exchanges were with the self-appointed guardians of Marxist truth, the intellectuals of the French Communist Party.

Communists had little use for philosophy or religion; these things were in no way related to the political struggles of the proletariat. For a communist who, from Marx's teaching, had 'understood' religion to be of no real significance because it was simply false, any attention that philosophy paid to religious phenomena and religious consciousness was a waste of time. 'If one justifies Sartre before G. Marcel,' asked Merleau-Ponty, 'is he not condemned before [a communist such as] Lefebvre?'[20] There is, he went on, a brand of Marxism for which the concerns of philosophy are epiphenomenal because consciousness is part of the world, a mere reflection of objects, or a part of the merely given. Moreover, textual evidence from the Marxist canon, some of Marx's late formulas, Engels's 'dialectics of nature,' Lenin's argument in *Materialism and Empiro-criticism*, and so on support such a view. But it was an inadequate and simple-minded materialism, 'not a dialectical philosophy that necessarily admits of reciprocal relations between different orders of phenomena and the emergence of original relations or structures on the basis of material phenomena.'[21]

A Marxism that sought to escape subjectivity by taking refuge in objectivity was open to all the criticisms developed in *La Structure du Comportement* and the *Phénoménologie de la Perception:* there can be no a priori syntheses either in things or in ideas. This was why attacks upon Marxists who held to materialist doctrine were valid 'less against Marxism itself than against expositions of it that are currently made, or against certain authentically Marxist formulas that schematize the doctrine.'[22] In a more heated mood Merleau-Ponty wrote: 'One would get a strange idea of Marxism and of its relations with philosophy if they were judged by the writings of certain contemporary Marxists.' Of course, 'it is the strict right of each of us to adopt the philosophy of his taste, for example, the scientism and mechanism that have for so long taken the place of thought in radical-socialist milieux. But it is necessary to know and to say that this genre of ideology had nothing in common with Marxism.'[23]

Communist intellectuals have never taken kindly to instruction from outside the Party; their replies were in an equally strong but less elegant language. According to Henri Lefebvre, these existentialists were no more than 'a little group of scouts and snobs whose publicity has been facilitated by the incredible inconsistency of university philosophy (pardon, of the official bourgeois scholasticism), by the emptiness of the dominant mentality, by the moral decomposition of so-called upper classes (badly disguised by an atmosphere of morality and hypocritical bashfulness), and by the inanity of current literary production.'[24] Jean Kanapa wrote: 'The alternative is not new: idealism or materialism. Either the ideology of the crisis of imperialism, decadent philosophy and intellectual reaction, or the only true contemporary form of materialism and of humanism, Marxism.'[25] For G. Gak, existentialism was 'banal subjectivity,' 'the fruit of the capitalist world in decay,' nothing but 'paradoxes and sophisms.' But it was not less dangerous for all that, because in bourgeois society every paradox and every sophism has force when the public opinion of the dominant class is behind it. Hence, it was necessary to struggle against existentialism as against a dangerous spy of the bourgeoisie 'called by it to confuse and weaken the forces of progress and democracy, to stifle their courage and corrupt their consciousness through the poison of pessimism, lack of courage, and lack of perspective.'[26]

The consequences of such talk for any rational discourse were spelled out at a later date by a chastened Lefebvre. In the midst of the publication of his study on the categories of formal logic, the Party line changed: what was needed were weapons, *oeuvres de combat*, that the party militants could use in the field against capitalism. The consequences 'of this imbecilic attitude theorized by paleo-Marxists' meant that 'my work of a philosopher – of a logician – was interrupted and smashed. I have never been able to take it up again.'[27] What the Party objected to, it later seemed to Lefebvre, was that his loyalty was not unconditional.

In the end it was too much even to give reasons for one's loyalty to the Party.

The dialectic of history having been resolved by Party dogma, there was no room for the dialectic of speech. Communists saw existentialism as an index of decadence; Merleau-Ponty saw a similar meaning not simply in communists' misunderstandings of Marx, but in their refusal to discuss the issue at all. The decline, he said, was 'in accord with the pace of our history. Having passed a certain point of tension, ideas cease to proliferate and live; they fall to the level of justifications and pretexts; they are relics and points of honour, and what we pompously call the movement of ideas is reduced to the sum of our nostalgias, our grudges, our timidities, our phobias.'[28]

Turning to the political activities of the Communist Party and the Socialists, Merleau-Ponty found the same substitution of an exchange of anathema for an exchange of ideas. He began by recalling the mad sincerity of nineteenth-century republicans and the immoderate demands for justice by the Dreyfusards; before the war the Surrealists, Alain, Gide, Bernanos, all had been united in their passion to tell the truth, even when it was grotesque and in opposition to the nation or the Party or the Church. Neither the tough-minded André Malraux nor his own communist friend Paul Nizan was 'realistic' enough to swallow the Hitler-Stalin pact. 'Like their intellectuals, the French judged and spoke frankly.' In 1946, all that had changed: 'We have seen, as they say, "where that leads" ... We are all repentant. We will not be caught there again.' The lesson that one should be diplomatic in politics was learned too well, and 'a sanctimonious and insinuating tone reigns nearly everywhere.' Conservatives are calling themselves revolutionary, Communists are part of the Establishment, 'and everyone replies indirectly, so that discussions are dialogues of the deaf.'[29] He had expected duplicity from the conservative right because they refused to acknowledge in public the central importance of the class struggle; but he was surprised to find an equal mendacity on the left.

Merleau-Ponty was disappointed with both Socialists and Communists, and for practically the same reason, their dishonesty. The Socialists were continuing the pre-war ambivalence of the Popular Front, which for the bourgeoisie was presented as a bulwark against revolution, a final attempt at extracting order and justice from capitalism, but which was presented to the workers as the start of socialism. At a time of class antagonism, he said, one is sincere either towards the workers or towards the bourgeoisie. Léon Blum's 'intellectual honesty' and 'objectivity' were praised as virtues, but they were personal, not political, virtues: 'this "objective" manner, this habit of treating the revolution as an already accomplished fact or yet to come, and never as a present for which we are responsible, are duplicities when it is a question not of contemplating the world but of transforming it.'[30] And in any case it was not the workers Blum wished to convince during the thirties but the fascists. Ten years earlier Blum had retouched the Socialist canvas with the conservative tones of the 'national interest,' so it was not entirely without precedent that the contemporary SFIO, the Section Française de l'Internationale Ouvrière, advocated reform on the basis of Marxist theses that contradicted reform. Merleau-Ponty's criticism of the opportunism (or flexible pragmatism) of the Socialists did not mean he wished them to abandon power for principle, but only that they should acknowledge their compromises. The problem was that their Marxist principles had been so long abandoned that the Socialists were unable to recognize what in fact they had done.

Merleau-Ponty seemed at first to be more generous towards the Communist Party, allowing that the communists did not seem inwardly to submit to the very ones they seek to attack. In that, he said, 'they maintain the proletarian style.'[31] How Merleau-Ponty sensed the inner resolution of the communists was unclear from the evidence he presented. They criticized the government but they were part of it; they criticized the electoral laws that set the rules for constituting the next government, but refused to resign. Worst of all, they covered their tracks with a propaganda that still paid service to Marxist themes of an earlier day. 'The function of Marxist ideas is no longer to determine a policy but to comment upon it and provide it with a Marxist *aura*.'[32] Communist Party policy was no more than a style, whatever their lack of inward submission.

Considered together, the two left-wing parties augmented each other's vices. The party with the proletarian style refused to extend a hand to the Socialists: 'after all, worker unity might entail a transformation of the Communist Party itself, and it would be allowable then for the Socialists to introduce their habits of criticism and discussion to it.' The Socialists for their part would have to face up to their own lack even of a proletarian style. Since neither the unity nor an alliance of the left seemed likely, political thought and analysis of events could only be very confused. There were nothing but 'mutilated ideas,' and each person's political position was defined less by a certain number of theses than by his adherence to one of the two present blocs. 'To be communist or to be socialist, *in the order of ideas*, no longer signifies anything determinate. We have come to a state of political nominalism for which French history offers perhaps no other example.'[33] The communists' commitment to an aura of Marxism and the proletarian style was equivalent to the socialists' opportunism in that each set of mutilated ideas justified the adherents' refusal to consider what a genuine union of workers might be. In this way each alone could consider themselves to represent the future of mankind as by a historical right.[34]

Liberals had their own variety of bad faith. Like Merleau-Ponty before the war, they refused to recognize publicly that the world was not a French garden, or indeed that France was not a French garden. Péguy once distinguished between a historical period, when public affairs were little more than administration because authority was legitimate, and an epoch, when tradition and the structure it provides for everyday attitudes had crumbled, so that men must act to found their *constitutio libertatis*. One may prefer periods to epochs, Merleau-Ponty said, but it is foolish to confuse the two; this confusion was the liberals' greatest error. Charles Maurras had been clear-sighted enough to denounce the 'Kantian illusions of democracy,' which said: where the rights of man are guaranteed, no freedom encroaches on any other, and the coexistence of men as autonomous and reasonable subjects is guaranteed; violence is an aberration; the economy, through the mysteries of the unseen hand, assures harmony and justice; the structure of the world conforms to reason. 'We know today that formal equality of rights and formal political liberty mask the relations of force rather than suppress them.'[35] Liberal thinking was less a political position than an abstract moralism because it failed to consider the problems of social structure and looked upon justice as if it were given with humanity itself.

Here Merleau-Ponty again adverted to the teaching of Montaigne. The liberals' insistence upon the importance of good intentions was equivalent to the communists' historical absolute: all acts could be excused provided one's conscience was clear. Indeed, he said, the internal life of a good conscience and a beautiful soul was the most subtle of mystifications because it authorized us to abandon existing men and made us take leave of an effective morality for a dream morality. In practice the norms of sincerity, conscientiousness, and good intentions were but the formal rules of capitalism, bad faith erected into an institution. Moreover, no one, least of all capitalists, paid any attention to these formalities. To tell the truth, to act according to conscience, were but alibis of a false morality; true morality was not occupied with what we think or wish but with what we do; it obliged us 'to take a historical view of ourselves.'[36] If Maurras could be said to have sacrificed the internal realm of conscience to the exterior of power and violence, liberals sacrificed the meaning of these external events, which were not to their taste, in order to guard their conscience in an inviolable purity. The political problem, however, as Hegel said, was to make externally effective the moral truths we know in conscience.

Merleau-Ponty's political thinking was thus conditioned by a field of political and intellectual disorder whose main lines of tension were supplied by liberals, socialists, and communists. In addition, for Merleau-Ponty, Arthur Koestler's noisy testimony symbolized much that was wrong with French political thought.[37] Many of the things Koestler criticized appeared in his heavily autobiographical writings as aspects of his own singular virtue.

In his memoirs Koestler said how his early life had been 'a succession of breathless pursuits of the arrow in the blue: the perfect cause, the ideal Helen, the knowing *shaman*, the infallible leader.' After years of failing to catch the arrow, he continued, 'I began to accept that I was a person of the obsessive type. Blessed or cursed with a surplus of nervous energy, I had to be obsessed with some task if I was not to be obsessed with myself.' Joining the Party, or the Graf Zeppelin expedition to the North Pole, or grinding out books, was therapy.[38] He later remarked that he was indebted to British liberal public opinion for saving him from a Spanish firing squad. 'I have found the human climate of England particularly congenial and soothing,' especially, he said, the 'dignity and grace' with which the British were dissolving the Empire. 'Ultimately, this may be the reason which attracted me to England. I only seem to flourish in a climate of decline, and have always felt best in the season when the trees shed their leaves.'[39]

Images of decline and decay appeared in his writing at various times to characterize the Soviet Union, Spain, Germany, and France, and in other more significant ways he construed public affairs after his own personality. First he denied his internal motivations and pursued the external arrow of revolution, and then, when he recognized that he was a fanatic, he pursued an internal obsession corresponding to a world in decline. In Merleau-Ponty's words: 'One gets the impression of a philosophy in retreat: Koestler withdraws himself from the world, he takes leave of his youth and retains nothing of it.' Rather than save what is valuable in the admittedly inadequate response of youth, Koestler dismissed the problem. For fear of having to forgive, he preferred not to understand. 'Perhaps it is for him a question of health and one would be angry with oneself to interfere with a cure. But he should not present a remedy for his own uncertainties as a solution to the problems of the day ... After all, we do not have to atone for the sins of Koestler's youth.'[40]

Koestler's apparent frankness in confessing that he was an 'obsessive type' was also suspect, for there are two kinds of sincerity: the one does not boast, the other, like Rameau's nephew, enjoys the variety and cunning of its masks and its own extravagant honesty. However sincere Koestler may be, we may still interrogate the apparent necessity he unveils. Must we make a virtue out of misery? Is there anything worthwhile in sitting 'for eight hours at my desk, growing piles over some boring and meritorious piece of research, as an atonement for an unknown original sin?'[41] If Koestler's suffering were sincere he would be quiet; his eloquence testified only to 'a certain ostentatious cult of value, of moral purity, and of the interior man [which] is secretly allied with violence, hate, and fanaticism.'[42] Koestler knew his own self-laceration was obsessive, that he willed his own atonement in order to enjoy confronting a necessity whose discipline was of his own making. 'One likes a man,' Merleau-Ponty said, 'who changes because he matures and understands more today than he did yesterday.' But one who merely reverses himself does not go beyond his former errors; 'he breaks with his past, that is to say, he remains the same.'[43] By refusing to confront the implications of his masquerade, Koestler confirmed, at an individual psychological level, the link between bad faith or hypocrisy and the effective denial of the importance and responsibility in interhuman affairs that Merleau-Ponty found institutionalized in political life.

Whether the equivocation was to be found with Koestler in his 'necessary' obsession with masks, or with the communists in their belief in the historically necessary triumph of their movement, or with the liberals in their clean and beautiful souls, the result was identical, a denial of one's responsibility for commitments made and acted upon. When I am in such a mood, Merleau-Ponty wrote, 'I have the right to withdraw my judgments from the control of others; they receive the character of the sacred; in particular, in the order of the practical, I have a plan of escape at my disposal that transfigures my actions: suffering for which I am the cause is turned into happiness, ruse becomes reason, and I piously make my adversaries perish.'[44]

False piety arising from sacred but violent action was derived, Merleau-Ponty thought, from an intellectual climate whose origins lay as much with the pre-war generation as with his contemporaries' refusal to learn from the defeat, occupation, and resistance. No one seemed to want to acknowledge what innumerable statesmen and political thinkers had observed, that political actors were responsible for the unanticipated consequences of their commitments. When these involved violence, no amount of verbal justification could diminish the suffering of those upon whom the consequences fell. For Merleau-Ponty the only reasonable political commitment was to humanism. But, as was suggested above, action to achieve humanism may involve violence to those whose commitments lay elsewhere. How Merleau-Ponty tried to justify responsibility for violence in the name of humanism is the topic of the following chapter.

2
Recognition and violence

Merleau-Ponty's chief criticism of his contemporaries, as we have seen, was that they were wrong in refusing to acknowledge that intentions and consequences presented a problematic. One might also speak here of a dialectic of intentions and consequences, but in either case the connotation was of an unavoidable practical or pragmatic uncertainty. A problem can be solved, but a problematic must be coped with for better or for worse. To resolve a problematic into its analytically distinct constituent elements is to destroy its characteristic tension between (or among) those elements. Likewise, a dialectic contains its own internal dynamic, for example in the Socratic form of zetetic speech where contradictory opinions are purged but are never resolved into formular dogma. Later and non-Socratic forms of dialectic also retained the factor of contradiction. Thus one may say that any genuine dialectic or genuine problematic expresses a strain towards resolution, not the relief of completion.

For Merleau-Ponty, the problematic of intentions and consequences described in another way the reality of human being-in-the-world. As in the *Phénoménologie*, there could be no final synthesis, no ultimate resting point or definitive 'state,' for it would be equivalent to death and non-existence.[1] This lack of resolution was the defining feature of 'existential' or 'critical' philosophy. Moreover, Merleau-Ponty repeatedly said that both Hegel's and Marx's greatest arguments were in this sense existential.[2] The immediate result of 'existentializing' Marx and Hegel was to allow Merleau-Ponty to speak in his own name and in his own idiom on Marxian and Hegelian themes. This chapter considers his arguments on the problematic of humanism and terror or, more generally, of recognition and violence.

CREATIVE VIOLENCE

The most primitive argument Merleau-Ponty seemed to employ may be called creative violence. The link between creativity and violence is forged with the slightest displacement of nature. There is a difference, however, as Hannah Arendt has tirelessly insisted, between the violence of *animal laborans* and that of *homo faber*: the former atones for his violation of nature through piety, which acknowledges nature his master still, while the latter rejoices in his own strength and justifies his violations by the product he forms. In Hegel's terms it is the difference between the slave who is terrorized into forced labour and the slave who has begun his self-education through making tools to lighten his physical toil and ideologies to lighten his spiritual anguish. We must note too that in the fabrication of both things and ideologies the notion of an ideal or an idea is crucial. In particular, according to Hegel, the realization of the final ideology, Christianity, justified history, under its aspect as slaughter bench, in the same way that cutting down a tree is justified by the table. Now, a table can also be a work of art, that is, a statement or an embodied thought, as well as a use-object; likewise the desire of the slave is mediated by thought and the products of thought, both material and non-material. In the end, for Hegel, the universal and homogeneous state is the final work of art, the embodiment not just of thought but of wisdom, of finality achieved by men who are transient.

Merleau-Ponty's argument did not cleave invariably to this Hegelian or Kojèvian line. Nevertheless, there are statements in his work, contrasting 'a world ready-made and well-made' with an 'unfinished world of revolutionaries,' which may suggest that the ideal of humanism, authentic intersubjectivity, or the recognition of man by man is to be understood as fundamentally akin to the utilitarianism of carpentry.[3] One has an idea, so the argument might run, and the only questions are technical. Nation-building is like boat-building except using human timber, and since everyone knows you cannot make an omelette without breaking eggs our squeamishness at broken heads must be a personal weakness.

Such statements and their violent implications were qualified, however. Merleau-Ponty knew as well as anyone that men were not things and the Hegelian state was a work of art only through a kind of metaphorical indulgence. He knew that both a crude instrumentalism and a more elaborate aesthetic instrumentalism were inadequate for an analysis of politics. Where he spoke of the 'goal' of history, he also denied that Marxism promised a future 'state of affairs' as an end for which the use of certain techniques, such as violence, promised success. 'In reality, there are not ends *and* means; there are only means or ends, however one wishes to put it,' because 'the end and the means can only be distinguished in the conceptions of an intellectual, and not on the terrain of history.'[4] Thus, he said, it was 'absurd' to try to achieve a proletarian goal, that is, a humanist goal, with other than proletarian means.

If anything was incontestable, according to Merleau-Ponty, it was that Hegel's masters never change. The life of a soldier was essentially the same, whether he fought in phalanx, hollow square, or helicopter. All that changed were his weapons, and they were the product of the slave's labour. Consequently he could never learn anything. Even more important, a society of masters, because it implied rule by a few over the many who were slaves, could never be a humanism. In principle the slaves were denied recognition. Only the many, the slaves, could attain the goal of humanism; only the many could be the means to attain it.[5] Thus the goal, so to speak, becomes the means.

On the 'terrain of history' humanism was not even an ideal, but the judgment of an intolerable present. Rather than being the consciousness of an end, it opposed an impossibility, the actual world understood as contradiction and decomposition; rather than the fantastic conception of a paradise on earth, it was the patient analysis of past and present history as class struggle; and finally, it was the creative decision to pass beyond this chaos with the universal class, so as to establish the foundations of human history.[6] From the idea of humanism we are referred back to the experience of war (or class struggle), the judgment of the present as chaotic, and the decision to pass beyond in order to found human history in a lived actuality of mutual recognition.

It is at this point that the theme of violence touched the theme of recognition, constituting the 'theory' of the proletariat. It is difficult to overestimate the significance of the proletariat for Merleau-Ponty's early Marxism; it provided a general orientation to the Marxist dialectic that 'distinguishes it from the dialectic of sophists and sceptics.' The idea of the proletariat distinguished Marxism from every so-called totalitarian ideology, especially from fascism, 'a mimicry of Bolshevism,' because it 'retains everything of Bolshevism except the essential, that is, the theory of the proletariat.'[7] The theory told the story of the genesis and epiphany of mankind, it gave the 'historic names to the mythological combats that [Hegel] described between consciousness in-itself and consciousness for-itself'; it was 'truly the centre of the doctrine, for it is in proletarian existence that the abstract conceptions come to life and life itself becomes self-awareness.' In the name of the proletariat Marx described a situation such that those who lived it, and they alone, had 'the full experience of freedom and universality, which for him defined man.'[8] The forces of capitalist production had created a world market where every man depended upon every other for his life, but only the proletarian, who experienced the world market in terms of alienation, was in a position to transform an ecumenical economic organization into an ecumenical social order of authentic intersubjectivity.

There was an objective premise of the revolution, universal dependence, and a subjective premise, consciousness of this dependence as alienation. Moreover, the two were bound together in a meaningful dialectic, for 'the "objective" situation itself solicits the proletarian to become conscious of his situation; the very exercise of his life motivates his becoming conscious.' Only the proletarian gains 'individuality,' a Kojèvian amalgam of self-consciousness and class-consciousness; only the proletarian *is* the universality that he thinks about; 'only he realizes the self-consciousness of which the philosophers, in their reflections, have traced the outline.' Only the proletariat 'according to the internal logic of its condition, according to its least deliberate mode of existence ... are, and alone are, in a position to realize humanity.' They alone had a mission, 'not providential but historic, and that means that the proletariat, if considered in its role within the given historical constellation, goes toward the recognition of man by man.'[9]

Marxist violence, then, was not simply the 'making' of a revolution, and the 'creation' of proletarian self-consciousness was not a thing to be achieved or a goal to be attained once for all. Indeed, Merleau-Ponty never ceased to criticize communists who thought in such terms. The fundamental reason for his effective rejection of fabrication, of justification by the product, as an appropriate model for the understanding of violence lay in his conception of the historical meaning of the proletariat and the character of historical action. Proletarian self-consciousness was for him a continuous mode of existence, an act of mutual recognition; history, the accumulation of historical acts, must therefore be interpreted as a process.

PROCESS AND VIOLENCE

'There is a revolutionary process for which each moment, therefore, is as indispensable and as valuable as the utopian "final" moment.'[10] The notion of process, however, if applied to history may confuse more than it clarifies.[11] When one thinks of fabrication there is at least the subjective certainty of an ideal for the sake of which fabrication is undertaken. But when the process is as valuable as the achievement, does it matter what we do? More precisely, how can it matter what we do if history is a process and the final 'moment' or 'product' is not held to be its proper justification? And if the 'utopian moment' is emphasized, does not this deny the meaningful autonomy of the process and open the argument to the critical objections already raised by Merleau-Ponty against the fabrication metaphor? If so, any justification of humanist terror must be from outside history.

The process motif was introduced by a quotation from Trotsky: 'every historical process is the prism of just rule when seen by the fortituous. If we may use the language of biology, it could be said that the rational rule of history is achieved by a natural selection of accidental facts. It is upon this basis that conscious human activity, which subordinates the accidental to an artificial selection, is based.' Merleau-Ponty gave a gloss to Trotsky's statement: 'Accidental facts, that is, isolated facts, those which are not required by the total situation eliminate themselves from history by failing to find supports, concordances, and complicities in the historical context, just as monstrous congenital variations, according to Darwin, eliminate themselves by failing to be compatible with the general life of the organism. But this selection only guarantees the destruction of non-viable systems of irrational societies: it does not guarantee the appearance of a new viable form, which presupposes a selection, oriented this time by the idea.'[12] In *Humanisme et Terreur* nearly identical language was used and the implications drawn: 'history only has a meaning if there is something like a logic of history which, while it does not make any adventure impossible, at least, as by a natural selection, eliminates over the long run those that would divert history from contact with the permanent needs of men. Thus, every philosophy of history postulates something like what is called historical materialism, namely the idea that morals, conceptions of law and the world, modes of production and labour are tied together from within the express each other.'[13] Again, in his inaugural lecture at the Collège de France, he said: 'From the course of things themselves we know only that it will sooner or later eliminate irrational historical forms, those which secrete ferments that destroy them. This elimination of the irrational can end in chaos if the forces that destroy these forms do not show themselves capable of constructing new ones from them.'[14] Thus we see that the notion of process held a central position in Merleau-Ponty's political thought from 1945 on.

Darwinian themes are deeply embedded in Marxist thinking. Marx sought to dedicate *Capital* to Darwin; Engels could think of no higher praise in his Highgate eulogy than to call Marx the Darwin of history; his own 'dialectics of nature' made frequent references to Darwin, and even Marx's dialectic of history originated in the natural or biological force of labour-power. In light of the traditional and fundamental separation of nature and history or being and time, Darwin and Marx alike appear to have blended the two categories in their respective conceptions of a developmental process. In this conjunction of nature and history it makes little difference in one sense where the accent is placed, for there is a grave theoretical objection to be made to both Marx and Darwin: when 'laws of evolution,' whether biological or historical, no longer express stable frames within which change occurs, but are themselves expressions of change, theory is swallowed in practice.

One way to seek relief from the ineluctable grind of practice would be to exempt man from the instability of all laws and maintain with Merleau-Ponty that the 'logic of history' was an 'absolute within the relative.'[15] But the comfort of this pragmatic make-believe could not last. These alleged laws of nature and history are no more than a provisional constitution of reality and the result of practice, the wilful or imaginative practice of their inventors. And then, if we must find our way 'at each moment in a general and ever changing situation, like a traveller who progresses into an unstable countryside, which is altered by his own advances, where what was an obstacle can become a passage, what was a right-of-way can become a detour,'[16] there are no signposts at all. Unlike Darwin, for whom human existence was the result of an intelligible evolutionary journey, and unlike Kojève, who claimed to stand at the end of the historical journey, Merleau-Ponty's historical traveller can know neither where he is nor where he is going.

Can nothing, then, be gained from viewing history as process alone, as a 'negative dialectic?' According to Merleau-Ponty's exposition of Trotsky, there may not be a positive or creative meaning to history, but there is a negative one, based on certain (unidentified) 'permanent needs of man.' Clearly, Merleau-Ponty did not wish to introduce the notion of a permanent human nature. What he meant was that although we could not, perhaps, ever say what will happen, we could say what will not. It was Merleau-Ponty's opinion that 'the movement that succeeds at a particular time is not always the most true nor the most valuable,' yet 'if it is to last, it must be.'[17] Merleau-Ponty illustrated this rather vague statement with the example of the rise and fall of fascism: 'if it continued to ignore problems rather than resolve them it would disappear for failing to have joined up again, by a conscious act of will, with the deeper motives from which it was born and for failing to have assumed its proper truth.'[18] The 'deeper motives' were provided by class antagonism; the inadequate palliative, which failed to resolve the motive as a truth, was the 'ephemeral exultation of the nation.' That facism did disappear was sufficient evidence that it 'deserved to disappear.' The conclusion was clear enough: we do not know if actual history is going to consist in a series of 'diversions' from its proper, humanist course. After the fact, the Marxist historian will be able to show that phenomena such as fascism and perhaps 'Americanism or the western bloc' were just so many temporary resistances to the class struggle. But if this were true, might it not make more sense to try and do what one can rather than order all action by reference to the general principles of the class struggle? 'There is no sense in any longer treating the class struggle as an *essential* fact, if we are not sure that effective history remains faithful to its "essence" and that accidents will not constitute its course for a long time or forever.'[19] The issue of a 'negative dialectic' would appear to be the hope that a future historian could show that sacrifice in the name of humanity was not in vain. Schiller at least held out a guarantee.

Kant asked the progressives of his own day: why should an individual, whose only future certainty is his own death, think that the future of mankind has anything to offer him? Similarly, what possible reason could be advanced to convince anyone to throw in one's lot with the proletariat? And Merleau-Ponty was enough of a Kantian to ask 'What does the future of the revolution matter if its present remains under the law of violence.'[20] Perhaps, if indeed there is 'no sense in treating the class struggle as an essential fact' because politics seems not to conform to the 'essence' accorded it by Marxism, then one may be tempted to abandon Marxism, if not for a Kantian politics then at least for a politics not wildly at variance with the apparent common sense of Kant's question of progressives. Whatever else one may think of Kant's political theory, he raised here a genuine existential issue and posed it correctly in terms of individual choice and personal commitment.

NECESSITY AND VIOLENCE

In Merleau-Ponty's first argument, which was probably never seriously entertained, the inadequacy of the fabrication metaphor was explored. In his second one, discussion centred on the notion of process. The historical process was evidently not, in his opinion, endowed with a positive outcome, though the negative dialectic of history operated as a kind of natural selection whose most important and obvious product seemed to be hope. But this conclusion was open to the apparently fatal objections of Kant. Merleau-Ponty was still enough of an Hegelian not to confront directly the issue raised by Kant; his reply was in terms of the necessity of violence.

Merleau-Ponty disputed Kant's objections by questioning the validity of the premises he said they rested upon. 'There would be no sense in preferring a regime that employs violence for humanist ends, since from the point of view of the consciousness that suffers it, violence is absolutely unacceptable, being what negates it; and since, in such a philosophy, there would be no other point of view but self-consciousness, the world and history would be the sum of these points of view.' To ask Kant's question, Merleau-Ponty argued, one must accept these postulates of Kantian individualism. 'But such postulates are exactly what Marxism puts into question by introducing, following Hegel, the perspective of one consciousness upon another.' The world was more than the juxtaposition of points of view and of self-consciousness: 'I am not for him and he is not for me pure existence for-itself. We are, for each other, situated beings, defined by a certain type of relation with men and with the world, by a certain activity, a certain manner of treating others and nature.'[21] Merleau-Ponty recognized the dialectic of doing and suffering as a 'law of human action' whereby the present encroached upon the future as one person intruded upon another. To condemn all violence in order to maintain a beautiful soul was to take one's place outside the realm of justice and injustice. Moreover, such a condemnation of violence was a 'hypocritical damnation' because he who utters it, from the very moment he has begun to live, has already accepted the rules of the game. Among men considered as pure consciousnesses, there would be, in effect, no reason for choosing. But among men considered as the occupants of situations that together comprise a common situation, it is inevitable that one must choose. Accordingly, one might sacrifice those who, according to the logic of their situation, are a menace and prefer those who are a promise of humanity. 'That is what Marxism does when it establishes its politics on an analysis of the proletarian situation.'[22] In other words, argument to justify proletarian violence depended upon the validity of the argument that presented the proletarian situation as universal. That is, Merleau-Ponty was here drawing out explicitly the political implications of his philosophical anthropology.

Thus once again he asserted that our individual commitments are already collective. We situate each other by our personal choices, whatever they may be. There is no transcendent situator of all human beings, which is why Merleau-Ponty wrote of a common situation not a universal one. But even if one eclipses the experience of being situated, and thus limited, as a human being and accept that one can be situated and limited only as a historical being – that is, by other human beings and not by divine being – there is no apparent reason why one ought to prefer a future of 'humanity' to any other future, because concretely our ideals and so our prospective futures may have nothing in common. Merleau-Ponty had therefore to show why 'really' everyone necessarily desires a future of humanism. This argument from necessity constituted, in effect, the sought-for external justification of humanist terror.

It was, moreover, essentially Kojève's position. Kojève's argument took its force from the assumption that all men desire recognition, which for him implied the end of history and the slaughter of those who fail to acknowledge the truth. Kant's query therefore would be answered by violent action and the imposition of the System as the completed Wisdom of history. The System presumed to give a final account of what is, and so to make wholly explicit the criteria for justice and injustice – or rather to explicate necessity, so that the question of justice would no longer be open to scrutiny or debate. But, as we have said, Merleau-Ponty rejected this answer, and in its place suggested the metaphor of the traveller, as we have seen, who passes through an ever-changing countryside, who alters what was there before his passage while he passes through it, and who is altered himself by this same passage. If we are to find a coherent argument which is Merleau-Ponty's own, it must be by working through the implications of contingency.

There was a bleak side to contingency. Historically speaking, it was as if the confidence and pride that the eighteenth century voiced had decayed into melancholy and nausea when the consequences of will and imagination as the ordering forces of society appeared. If one focuses upon process rather than outcome, there is nothing to prevent men from believing that limits are temporary, wilful or even desirable conventions that must disappear as the process unwinds. The process and its alleged conventional order must always stand in contradiction to nature. The mask of convention can be removed to display the natural will or natural desire that keeps the process moving. By nature, one may say, men seek to satisfy their desire for recognition; real justice must be based on this desire. But this means that for the time being justice must be limited to a select group of men, the citizens of the ancient city or, the only contemporary men in a position to realize humanity, the proletariat. Just as beyond the walls of the city the strong do what they can and the weak suffer what they must, so too between the proletariat and the rest violence must prevail. There is no whole, no cosmos, no *homologia*; politics cannot be judged through mimicry of the divine logos, and there can be neither trust, nor friendship, nor peace, because nothing is shared. There is only, in its place, a common suffering entailed by the dynamics of alienation, which may indeed cure melancholy and nausea, perhaps only by obliterating the power of reason to give such moods a name.

This bleakness was anticipated by Merleau-Ponty. Marxists, he said, 'have often compared revolutionary violence to the intervention of a doctor at a birth. That is to say, the new society already exists, and violence is justified not by remote ends but by the vital necessities of a new humanism already outlined.'[23] Two implications followed. First, the metaphor of childbirth must be taken seriously: if a new world may be waiting to be born from capitalism, it is always possible that the mother may die and the child be stillborn. Second, since 'new worlds' are constantly being 'born,' all historical change must contain an element of violence. Merleau-Ponty saw in these two implications further justification for the principle of contingency and openness towards the future: 'Historical terror culminates in the revolution, and history is terror because there is a contingency,' but at the same time 'a contingent future, once it has come into the present, appears real and even necessary.'[24] To be sure, he said, this is a 'harsh notion,' but it makes politics serious. Merleau-Ponty's argument moved easily between historical contingency and vital necessity, between a contingent commitment to humanism and the necessity of such a commitment once our consciousness has been disabused of its illusions of transcendence. If humanism were a genuine option we would still be faced with Kant's question, unanswered on its own terms: why choose humanism? But if not, Merleau-Ponty's politics must be justified not as an option with which one may quarrel, but as a revelation of necessity. Yet this would appear to place the whole matter in the realm of practice. One may, as a practical matter, perhaps defy necessity for a time, but there seems no point in arguing against it.

I have emphasized Merleau-Ponty's reliance on, and his independence from, the Hegelian or Kojèvian System. In the absence of the System, the direction and meaning of history must come from the actions of men. According to Merleau-Ponty, violence was the condition for action, including the counterfeit action of doing nothing. 'Either one wishes to do something, but this is on the condition of using violence,' or one respects formal liberty, and one renounces violence. But this meant renouncing socialism and the classless society, that is to say, consolidating the reign of the 'Quaker hypocrite.' The innocence of good intentions was as fraudulent as the innocence of pure consciousness: 'For us, there are only situated consciousnesses, which are themselves blended with the situation they assume and which may not complain that they are identified with it, or that the incorruptible innocence of their innermost heart has been neglected.' Just as in history, so in individual actions that constitute history, there was no room for alibis: 'we are what we do to others, we renounce the right to be respected as beautiful souls. To respect one who does not respect others is, in the end, to despise them; to abstain from violence against the violent is to make oneself their accomplice. We have no choice between purity and violence but between different kinds of violence. Violence is our lot insofar as we are incarnate.'[25] Here, then, we may see the discipline of necessity; we are conditioned by the necessity of violence for our politics in exactly the same way that we are conditioned by the necessity of our eyes for our sight.

Within this necessity, however, questions, or rather one question, can arise. 'What counts, and therefore what must be discussed, is not violence but its meaning (*sens*) or its future.' The question therefore is not to know if violence is accepted or refused, but whether the violence that is practised is 'progressive' and tends to suppress itself or whether it tends to perpetuate itself. The first problem, however, was to recognize the necessity of violence and to combat 'Quaker hypocrisy.' Just as naming a Freudian complex may be the first step on the road to mental health, so naming violence may be the first step in ending it. But nothing could be guaranteed: 'A nominally liberal regime can be oppressive in reality. A regime that recognizes its violence *might* conceal more true humanity.'[26] This argument, or rather this hope, could be undermined by the consideration that the practice of 'progressive' violence, the acknowledgment of detours and deceptions for what they were, may just as easily turn into habit and an endless perpetuation of violence whose justification is truly hypocritical. In any case, the communists' argument that Marxist violence was preferable because its aims were incontestable would seem to be no argument at all.[27] It was just another kind of beautiful soul.

The dialectic of the necessity and contingency of violence may be resolved into its two constituent elements. As contingency, violence may some day be ended, but we can have no knowledge of that day before it dawns. Nevertheless it was the day to which all human beings (all whose consciousnesses had been purged of transcendence) were necessarily committed. At the same time, as necessity (prior to that day), violence was justified not on its own terms but by the context of a violent world. Of course, to resolve the dialectic in this way is to turn it into an abstraction and destroy its poignancy. The whole problem, so far as Merleau-Ponty was concerned, was that the new day had not (yet) dawned and we can meanwhile only hope for it while being compelled to employ violence against those whose hopes are different.

As Merleau-Ponty indicated, to take violence seriously was already to transcend the historical plane where it appeared and to judge it on the basis of an ethics whose ground clearly cannot be itself violent. Since history was the context of violence, that ground could not itself be historical. If one's act was a genuine judgment and not a reductive prejudice, it would imply a higher not a lower vision. Here, then, one must question Merleau-Ponty's charge that all non-violence was 'Quaker hypocrisy.' In the first place, it would be hard to see why hope, as Merleau-Ponty had outlined it, was any less equivocal than the preachings of the most sanctimonious advocate of non-violence. In the second place, the genuinely non-violent person does not simply wish for a non-violent world, he commits himself to it, even to the point of suffering rather than inflicting violence. Unlike Merleau-Ponty, therefore, one may distinguish between the theorist, whose understanding of public affairs tells him that both violence and love are equally historical, and the political actor, who is faced not with questions of understanding but with practical choice. The choice of the political person who may have to rely on violence can be met on equal terms by the non-violent person whose refusal of violence is an affirmation of truths beyond history. The dialectic (and ambiguity) of non-violence is therefore not less severe than the claims of self-suppressing violence. But it is different, and this difference is genuine, which means that non-violence cannot be reduced to hypocrisy.

'Violence is everywhere,' he wrote, 'but no one could look it in the face.' To understand terror can only be 'a literary matter,' and whoever professed to understand it simply gave voice to the prejudice of the universal spectator. His pretense was sustained by forgetting that 'the past and the remote have been or are still being lived by men who lived or yet live their unique lives' but could be broken by 'the cries of a single man condemned to death.'[28] The non-violent person would never deny that the universal spectator is a prejudice,[29] which did not mean there could be no genuine non-violent action. It meant that one must distinguish mere cowardice from non-violence. The coward shies from historical violence, his soft and perhaps beautiful soul slipping away from what is hard and ugly into a realm of exquisite self-indulgence. If non-violence is more virtuous than violence, it must be more just. And justice entails a concern with the ugly as well as the beautiful souls. The non-violent person, then, if not simply soft, must pass by way of the 'harsh notions' of history to something beyond them. If progressive violence, the violence self-consciously employed to put an end to violence, is born from historical desperation and not simply from ideological intoxication or the lust to conquer, we must recall that there is yet a desperation deeper than historical violence. But here we pass once again beyond Merleau-Ponty's horizon; the desperation deeper than that which results from the inflictions of humans can be indicated only by the mythical expression, the wrath of God. No man may face the wrath of God (or Zeus), but faith in this mythical truth may give the non-violent man the courage and love to face historical violence.[30]

Merleau-Ponty made his readers uneasy because he pointed to the threads of violence that decorate the social fabric. The liberal historian who praised the great cardinal Richelieu forgot how he appeared to Urbain Grandier, to say nothing of the North American Indians slaughtered through the implementation of his policies. The liberal saw himself as a consumer of violence but never a producer or, if a producer, one who was excused by the beauty of his soul. Against the bad faith of Koestler and the fanaticism of communist intellectuals Merleau-Ponty insisted upon frankness and responsibility. The deeds of the Communist Party were to be judged, not applauded, but on terms that made sense to Marxists. Here was a 'theory of the proletariat' that was truly secularized; there was nothing of 'historical' significance in proletarian violence beyond the contingencies of human injustice. That is, proletarian and colonial violence were not by definition senseless, irrational, and so on. The great insight of Merleau-Ponty's reflections on violence was in reminding his readers that the meaning and direction of violence appeared in its consequences and that it was itself not the result of a phantom evil spirit hovering over an otherwise happy and peaceful kingdom.

On the other hand one must acknowledge the limitations of Merleau-Ponty's argument. He interpreted away as an expression of abstract individualism Kant's quite legitimate question: why should someone whose only future certainty is his own death be committed to a future of humanism? Because we are not 'pure' self-consciousnesses, our actual contingent commitments involve the impinging of one body upon another. The motion and hence the conflict of incarnate consciousnesses constituted, according to Merleau-Ponty, the violent core of our historical being. And since he held that human being was essentially historical, this meant that the only legitimate political questions must deal with whether violence is 'progressive' or not. For this reason, non-violence had to be reduced to hypocrisy, much as experiences of transcendence were reduced to illusions. This same mixture of insight and neglect can be found in Merleau-Ponty's comments on Machiavelli, a theorist whose fame in no small measure derived from his teaching on the nature and usefulness of violence.

COMMENTARY ON MACHIAVELLI

In his *Discourses* Machiavelli wrote the following account of violence:

Wherefore the prudent founder [*ordinatore*] of a republic, whose intent is to govern not for his own good but for the common good, not for his own successors, but for the common fatherland, should endeavour to have sole authority: nor will a talented and sagacious man reproach him for taking any extraordinary action, which is of aid for founding a regime or constituting a republic. It is well said that while the deed accuses, the effect justifies; and when it is good as was that of Romulus, it always will justify, because he who is violent in order to wreck, not he who is violent in order to repair, is blameworthy.[31]

The usual interpretation, that Machiavelli was saying that the end justifies the means, is misleading because it is abstract. Machiavelli had a particular end in mind, the founding of republican Rome. The doctrine that the end justifies the means would have been too Machiavellian even for Machiavelli. As Merleau-Ponty said, 'it is the pious ruse of those who direct their eyes and ours toward the heaven of principles in order to turn them from what they are doing.'[32] Rather than pass moral judgments, Machiavelli's detractors should suggest an alternative to violence for the founding of a regime. The famous *Exhortation* at the close of *The Prince*, despite its apocalyptic motifs, was a call to repeat the great deed of Romulus.

In *Humanisme et Terreur* Merleau-Ponty said that 'Machiavelli is worth more than Kant.' He meant that 'in the actions of all men, and especially of princes, where there is no tribunal to which one appeals, one must look to the consequences.'[33] Merleau-Ponty admired Machiavelli because the Florentine described well 'that knot of collective life where pure morality can be cruel and where pure politics demands something like a morality.' Once having recognized the realities of struggle, Machiavelli discovered its sense, that the prince must know when to act like a beast and when like a man; in other words he must be able to distinguish the two. If the prince employed violence, he should make plain his reasons, so that violence would be episodic and authority never absolute.

But how could Machiavelli's teaching have benefited humanism? First, Merleau-Ponty said, because it introduced us to the proper milieu of politics and allowed us to measure the task if we wish to introduce truth to it. And second because it 'indicated the conditions of a politics that would not be unjust: it would be what satisfies the people.'[34] Citizens are quick to forget the ferocity of origins when there is consultation between the prince and his subjects. 'Then the individual grows through the very gifts he makes to power and there is an exchange between them ... If Machiavelli was a republican it was because he found a principle of communion ... By the mastery of his relations with others, power clears away the obstacles between man and man and puts some transparency into our relations, as if men could not be close without keeping a kind of distance.'[35] The exchange of opinion, which constitutes what Hannah Arendt has named the 'space of appearance,' establishes political communion. At the same time it guards against the rise of a dictator whose speech moulds a single public opinion after his own and so prevents further exchange. Here Merleau-Ponty's discussion followed Machiavelli's, and his exegesis was exemplary. His critical remarks were less satisfactory.

Merleau-Ponty began by quoting Machiavelli's advice that, because most men judge on the basis of appearance, if a prince cannot be pious, temperate, and just, he should at least appear so, and commented: 'What he wished to say is that, even if genuine, the qualities of the leader are always prey to legend, because they are not *touched* but *seen*, because they are not known in the movement of the life that bears them, but are set in historical attitudes. Thus it is necessary that the prince have a feeling for these echoes, which his words and acts arouse.' Machiavelli's insisting that in public affairs men should learn how not to be good, which clearly was not a counsel to be evil, was predicated also upon the seemliness of the public realm for the appearance of goodness, 'for the public judgment according to appearances, which converts the goodness of the prince into weakness, is perhaps not so false. What is a goodness incapable of toughness? What is a goodness that wishes itself to be goodness? A meek manner of ignoring others and finally of despising them.'[36] But Merleau-Ponty's understanding of the relation of goodness to seeming and being was not that of Machiavelli.

Machiavelli's praise of *virtù* was the response of a political man to the *fortuna* of the world, which is ordered by sight, not touch. He objected not merely to the corruption of the Renaissance papacy but also to the influence of genuine spirituality, visible in the mendicant orders, in political affairs.[37] Thus, his insistence on the importance of 'looking to the consequences' in considering the acts of political men did not imply that intentions did not matter but that men were not touched by them. The intentions of men, which never appeared in the light of the public realm, mattered only to God, but God is invisible. Men, however, are not, and when they speak with the imputed authority of God they need to be reminded of what they presume lest the whole of the public realm disappear and be replaced by invisible spectres conjured by prophets. In other words Machiavelli's teaching on being and seeming had nothing to do with hypocrisy. Human beings are what they truly are before God, but in the human world *virtù* is only appearance. Thus the goodness or badness of a person, which lies behind appearance in the darkness of the heart, are literally unfit to be seen.

For Machiavelli, God was the guarantor of truth and being. For Merleau-Ponty,

God was an illusion. God's presence or absence, however, makes a difference for the relation between being and seeming. In the *Twilight of Idols* Nietzche told the 'history of an oversight,' 'how the "true world" in the end became a fable.' 'We have abolished the true world,' he said, 'What world then remains? the apparent one perhaps? ... Oh no! with the true world we have abolished the apparent one as well.'[38] Nietzche's vision of instability was expressed already in Merleau-Ponty's image of the traveller. Once again the name of Marx was invoked to restore order and reveal the hidden meaning of a true world. The contours of this true world emerged in a new context in Merleau-Ponty's criticism of Machiavelli.

Machiavelli, said Merleau-Ponty, should be praised for his frankness, but not for his fatalism. 'History is a struggle, and if republics did not struggle they would disappear. At least let us see that the means remain bloody, merciless, and sordid.' But seeing was not enough. Machiavelli was not wrong to insist on the problem of power, but he erred to content himself with merely evoking a power that would not be unjust without searching for its definition. What discouraged Merleau-Ponty was his belief that men were immutable and that regimes succeeded each other in cycles. 'There were always two sorts of men, those who lived history and those who made it.'[39] For Merleau-Ponty, therefore, Machiavelli's error was in believing that the dialectic of master and slave had no issue. It was an understandable error, Merleau-Ponty said, because of the times he endured. 'What could he reasonably wish for if not an Italian nation and soldiers to make it?' In this confused and ignorant Europe, 'where were the universal people who could make themselves accomplices of an Italian city-state?' No such universal people were present; the time, as Hegel might have said, was not ripe. Thus Machiavelli's fatalism was excused by his historical situation, and he was more to be praised for having grasped, within the strictures of Italian nationalism, the problem whereby 'the people of all countries would recognize, act together, and join up with each other.' For, Merleau-Ponty said, 'there is no serious humanism but the one that looks for the effective recognition of man by man across the world; thus it could not precede the moment when humanity gives itself its means of communication and communion.' The means did not exist in Machiavelli's day, but 'they exist today, and the problem of a real humanism posed by Machiavelli was taken up again by Marx a century ago.'[40] Merleau-Ponty did not say what the required means were, but as he made an immediate reference to the 'vital movement of the most exploited, most oppressed, most powerless men,' the essential difference of modernity would seem to be the existence of a world market and a world proletariat.

Merleau-Ponty concluded his 'Note on Machiavelli' by exploring the fortunes of humanism in the wake of Marx's analyses. On the basis of the condition of the proletariat, namely alienation and powerlessness, Marx 'sought to establish a revolutionary power, that is, one capable of suppressing exploitation and oppression. But it was apparent that the whole problem was to constitute a power from the powerless.' The dilemma was either to follow slavishly the fluctuation of mass sentiment and mere subjectivity, or else to delegate the interests of the proletariat to the Party and so institute a new ruling class. The solution could only be found in an absolutely new relationship between power and those subject to it. There was a need for political forms capable of controlling power without annulling it, and for leaders capable of explaining to the subjects the reasons for a policy, and if necessary of obtaining freely the sacrifices that power ordinarily imposed.[41] But, Merleau-Ponty went on, such new forms of government, the soviets, were crushed following the Kronstadt uprising when the leaders of the Party saw them as a threat, as indeed they were. 'One sees reappear within the revolution the struggles it was going to surpass.' And, as if to prove Machiavelli right, while the revolutionary government resorted to the classic deceptions of power, the opposition found sympathizers among the enemies of the revolution. 'We can conclude that one hundred years after Marx, the problem of a real humanism remains intact and thus can show some indulgence towards Machiavelli, who could only glimpse it.'[42]

The grave defect of this as of other historicist readings of Machiavelli was that it failed to take the teachings of *The Prince* and the *Discourses* seriously on their own terms. However we judge Machiavelli's political teachings, it is inadequate to say, with Merleau-Ponty, that he was a kind of proto-Marxist humanist, if for no other reason than that Machiavelli and Marx did not conceive of human being, time, and history in anything like the same terms. If, as Merleau-Ponty admitted, the problem of humanism remained intact, one may wonder whether in this respect at least Machiavelli, unadorned with the Marxist heritage, was not correct in maintaining that politics is always a realm of power, corruption, struggle, and deceit, from whose discipline upon occasion there emerges a man of *virtù* and greatness. To take Machiavelli seriously with respect to violence, however, entailed a rejection of the goal of humanism and mutual recognition. This Merleau-Ponty was not prepared to do. 'History,' he said, 'despite its detours, its cruelties, and its ironies, already carries within itself, with the proletarian situation, an efficacious logic that solicits the contingency of circumstances and the freedom of individuals and directs them towards reason.' The reason that emerges from the process of history was defined by Marxism and is that 'history has a meaning, in other words that it is intelligible and that it is directed, that it goes towards the power of the proletariat ... a "universal class" [able] to overcome social and national antagonisms and the conflict of man with man ... Proletarian power and the growth of the world proletariat is the norm of history.'[43] In other words Machiavelli's political teaching was effectively refuted by Marx's doctrine of proletarian universality. But this 'refutation' begs the question, because what is in dispute between Marx and Machiavelli is precisely the possibility of a 'norm of history.' If Machiavelli believed that political history was a story of war and bravery, diplomacy and treachery, and that men in some fundamental or basic way did not change, one can scarcely admit as criticism Marx's opinion that such sordid doings were confined to pre-history. One need not be a Machiavellian to wonder just what the power of the proletariat was supposed to mean, especially when, as Merleau-Ponty admitted, the only so-called proletarian revolution he knew seemed to confirm Machiavelli's opinion, not Marx's. The power of the proletariat, in short, did not refer to a factual, empirical reality; not now, and not in Marx's day. At best, it symbolized the hope for mutual recognition, which brings us again to the question raised earlier: why ought one to hope for humanism?

THE POLITICS OF HOPE AND RESIGNATION

Hope is not a firm basis upon which to develop a political position. Yet, if the relationship between recognition and violence was problematic, hope was the appropriate dialectical mood, never reaching the certainty of success or despair. One who was hopeful could anticipate a regime of mutual recognition but not count on it. Humanism could become in effect a paradigm by which existing regimes could be judged, at the same time as a goal for political action. In this way the irresponsible certainties of communist intellectuals would be avoided, along with the cynicism of modern Machiavellians. And yet hope was a fragile and exposed mood, too easily shattered by conflicting interpretations. Merleau-Ponty tried to overcome, or at least obscure with rhetorical bluster, the obvious embarrassment of having to rely on such fragile and vulnerable assumption. 'Why accord a reprieve to this philosophy?' he asked of Marxism. 'It has not succeeded in establishing itself in the facts; it was a utopia.' Thus, we may as well forget about it. But no. A final point would rescue Marx's teaching from oblivion: 'The decline of proletarian humanism is not a crucial experience that annuls the whole of Marxism,' because, he said, it remains a valuable, indeed unsurpassable, criticism. 'Even if it were incapable of giving form to world history, it remains strong enough to discredit other solutions.'[44] Such an appeal could only hope to persuade the converted to reaffirm their faith.

To make plain the fervour of his own commitments Merleau-Ponty employed a familiar rhetorical strategy. First, he restated his faith: Marxism was the 'philosophy of history,' the sole valuable expression of a 'logic of coexistence.' Second, he set forth the apocalyptic alternatives: 'to renounce [Marxism] is to cross out historical Reason, after which there is nothing more but dreams or adventures.' And third, he secured his faith against the trifling objections of fact and argument: 'Perhaps no proletariat will come to exercise the historical function that Marxism accorded to it. Perhaps the universal class will never be revealed, but *it is clear that no other class would replace the proletariat in this function.* Outside Marxism there is only the power of the few and the resignation of the others.'[45] Merleau-Ponty's passionate hopes were also tempered with resignation: 'Eh bien, continuons' said the inhabitants of hell in Sartre's *Huis clos.* So with Merleau-Ponty: he wrote his polemical works because there were yet those who failed to understand that the way towards 'humanism' had been indicated by Marx. This polemical context may prevent the boredom of resignation from growing acute, but one's mood would still be informed by the tacit suspicion that, if there was nothing outside Marxism, there was not much inside either. Like Pandora's jar, only hope was left inside.

One may summarize Merleau-Ponty's teaching on violence, as follows: because human being is temporal (in both senses of the term) there can be no meaningful discussion of transcendence. History, therefore, is a world-immanent process. Because the ultimate desire of human being is the desire for recognition, humanism is the norm of history, because the actual process of history is contingent, because human being is incarnate, and because process implies innovation, the mode of passage from one moment of the process to the next, from one historical situation to another, is violent. The dialectic of recognition and violence thus resolves itself into a single theoretical question by which the meaning and direction of history must be judged: is this violence progressive? That is, does it lead to humanism? Several implications followed. First of all, non-violence is hypocrisy or, more charitably, simple-mindedness or faith in illusions. Likewise, persuasion and discussion that calls into question the premise of the 'norm of history,' namely proletarian power, is undercut. In the example of Kant's straightforward and common sense objection to progress this was done by introducing the abstract individualism of his epistemology; in the example of Machiavelli, evidence that supported his opinion was ignored and his alleged shortsightedness was explained by the historical period in which he lived. Specifically, Machiavelli's inadequacy was attributed to the absence of a world-wide economic order, established by nineteenth-century capitalism. Machiavelli was praised for seeing the true problem through a glass darkly; but not until Marx could it be seen in its full amplitude and in full light.

Merleau-Ponty presented his opinion in the form of an argument or an exegesis, and I have attempted to show where that argument failed, where his interpretation was misguided. It is clear, however, that his intentions were not merely theoretical. His discipline of necessity was intended to be practical: it pointed to but a single resolution of the problematic of recognition and violence, the eventual and, under pain of falling into chaos, inevitable establishment of a regime of humanist, mutual recognition, proletarian power. But these equivalent terms did not refer to any worldly and empirical reality. They were symbols that took their meaning within the 'second reality' of an intellectual's imagination. For this reason Merleau-Ponty transposed the whole discussion into a mood of hope. All one's theoretical objections, all one's contrary empirical evidence, may be met and dismissed by the appeal to hope. In this context, appeal to hope is an appeal to abandon our common sense experience of everyday reality as well as our experience of divine reality and take our bearings within the imagination, where humanist, progressive violence provides the only means to achieve proletarian power or mutual recognition.

The ambiguities discussed in this chapter resulted from that shift in the discussion to the level of the imaginative. In more prosaic terms, he moved from Marx's 'theoretical' reflections on politics and economics to the 'practical' realm of a meaning to history. If the 'theoretical' rhetoric of his discussion were successful, we would, in practice, change our attitude and all our former objections, both 'theoretical' and 'practical' would melt away because we would know what to hope. On its own terms this position is impervious to criticism. But for that very reason it leads us, so far as critical argument is concerned, to a dead end. All one can do is submit his words to analysis. If the result is less satisfying philosophically or politically than one would like, and if the analysis is sound, one must conclude that Merleau-Ponty's political thought was severely flawed. However, one cannot live always in the imagination, and Merleau-Ponty was also a man of great common sense. Some of these ambiguities and inadequacies were cleared up or at least modified when he came to consider the thoroughly practical, common sense, though not, perhaps, everyday question of the actual historical fate of Bukharin.

3
Historical responsibility and the Soviet Union

CONTEXT AND MOTIVES

Over half of *Humanisme et Terreur*, published in 1947, was devoted to an interpretation of the Moscow Trials; Merleau-Ponty disputed Arthur Koestler's interpretation in his famous novel *Darkness at Noon*, as well as the current liberal interpretation and Trotsky's view. The evidence used in his argument was primarily from the *Report of Court Proceedings* of the March 1938 trial of Bukharin, Rykov, Yagoda, and eighteen lesser known men. It was the only full-length analysis of political events that Merleau-Ponty ever undertook; *Les Aventures de la Dialectique*, his only other book devoted entirely to a political theme, was presented in the hope that it would 'illuminate experience, not on the terrain of politics but on that of political philosophy.'[1]

Merleau-Ponty's motives for reviving a topic that had puzzled men a decade earlier, in what must have seemed another age, were complex. According to David Caute, the Moscow Trials 'did not materially alter the balance of opinion on the French intellectual extreme-Left.'[2] True, the fanatically committed Stalinist intellectuals believed Vishinsky's story of treason, but these did not include Sartre, Merleau-Ponty, or even Nizan.[3] Simone de Beauvoir captured the mood: 'We had never imagined the USSR as a paradise, but we had never before seriously questioned the Socialist enterprise. It was disconcerting to be driven to do so at the time when policy of the Western democracies had so disgusted us. Was there no corner of the world left where we could pin our hopes?'[4] Sartre reported that the Trials profoundly influenced Merleau-Ponty: 'From the few conversations that we had later, I had the feeling that before 1939 he was closer to Marxism than he ever was later. What made him draw back from it? The Trials, I imagine; for, in speaking of them at such length ten years later in *Humanisme et Terreur*, he must have been dismayed by them [at the time]. After that, the Nazi-Soviet pact hardly bothered him.'[5] In light of Merleau-Ponty's association with Mounier and the Christian temper of his articles in *La Vie intellectuelle*, Sartre's views must be qualified. There is no doubt, however, that the memory of the Trials had an impact.

More recently, the trials of Laval, Pétain, and their collaborators had put the notion of a 'political trial' into a new perspective and raised again some of the issues debated in the wake of the Moscow Trials. It was in the context provided by post-war purges in France that the success of *Darkness at Noon* must be understood. Koestler's own view of the purges of collaborators was that they were undertaken mainly by the Communist Party, which 'used these chaotic weeks, just as they had done in Spain, for a systematic settling of accounts with their opponents under the pretext that they had been collaborators.' He accounted for the successful sales of his book as follows: 'In this oppressive atmosphere, the novel on the Russian Purges, though dealing with events that lay ten years back, assumed a symbolic actuality, an allusive relevance which had a deeper psychological impact than a topical book could have achieved. It happened to be the first ethical indictment of Stalinism published in post-war France; and as it talked the authentic language of the Party, and had a Bolshevik of the Old Guard for its hero, it could not be easily dismissed as "reactionary" and "bourgeois." '[6] Koestler's attitude towards both the French purges and the Russian ones seemed to be a common one. ' "There! that is what they want to set up in France," said an anti-communist upon setting down *Darkness at Noon*.'[7] These opening words of Merleau-Ponty's book evoked the immediate polemical context. He intended to dispute Koestler's 'ethical indictment' no less than his 'authentic language.'

There was another motive for Merleau-Ponty's writing. It was perhaps the most elusive, but it may have been the most important. In January 1946 Merleau-Ponty published an article, 'Pour la Verité.' It was the third article he had published in *Les Temps modernes*; the first had dealt with his understanding of the war, the second, 'La Querelle de l'Existentialisme,' was a defence of Sartre's *L'Etre et le Néant* against Catholic and Marxist attacks and an attempt to integrate existentialist themes into Catholic and Marxist traditions. The third article took the offensive. It discussed the baseness of contemporary political talk, the question of the Soviet Union and its relation to Marx's teaching, and the task of men such as himself. In the twelve months following the publication of this article came the bulk of his reflections on Hegel and Marx and Soviet politics. It was therefore a pivotal and programmatic statement.

Marxism, Merleau-Ponty said once again, never excluded the possibility of setback. There was no necessary content to the negative dialectic; empirical events may not conform to 'true history.' 'Now, are we not, according to all appearance, at this point?' The Russian Revolution, which should neither have happened when it did nor where it did according to Marxist teaching prior to Lenin's *State and Revolution*, was not followed by European revolutions, as the Bolsheviks had hoped and expected. 'The tactics of "Popular Fronts" have modified the [national] proletariats and the recruitment and theoretical stance of communist parties too profoundly for one to be able to await the off-chance of a renewal of an open class struggle, or even to propose words of a revolutionary order to militants who *would not feel* them.'[8] No longer, he said, could politics be understood in terms of the two clearly defined antagonists, bourgeoisie and proletariat: 'the history of our times, we see, consists in composites.'

The obvious conclusion suggested itself: was not scepticism or relativism a healthy attitude? Have events not proven that no perspective was better than any other? But no one, according to Merleau-Ponty, could be a consistent sceptic, least of all when it came to drawing practical conclusions, which meant that, in the end, everyone was obliged to settle on one perspective, to develop something like a philosophy of history, and to treat some events as important and others as trivial. Neither scepticism nor 'a Marxist proletarian politics along classical lines' remained possible. 'Our only recourse is in a reading of the present as complete and as faithful as possible, which does not prejudice its meaning, which even acknowledges chaos and non-meaning (*non-sens*) when they are to be found there, but which does not refuse to discern a direction and an idea when they are manifest.'[9] In the concrete context of post-war politics this meant acknowledging one's ignorance of the Soviet Union, of the Truman administration, of Britain, and even of French voters. 'French intellectuals are not charged with sustaining an atmosphere of devotion and panic nor with sustaining vague enthusiasms and terrors that give a mythical and almost puerile character to French politics, but to take stock of this century and the ambiguous forms that it offers to us. If, on the basis of information and facts, we no longer submitted to this equivocation but understood it, perhaps our political life would cease to be haunted by phantoms, perhaps it would again take on some reality.'[10] Merleau-Ponty ended his article with a conditional: if Marxism were still true, its truth would reappear in the structure of events.

This article and the interpretative strategy of *Humanisme et Terreur* suggest that the following considerations influenced his political writing during 1946 and 1947: we do not know, today, in 1945, what the Soviet Union is like. We do not know, therefore, how Marx's teaching, even as modified by Lenin and so no longer 'classical' Marxism, has turned out. Koestler has just published a very successful piece of anti-communist propaganda that claims to present the Soviet purges in a Marxist fashion. Moreover, there are the stenographic documents that recorded the words of the prosecutor and the defendants. It should be possible, therefore, to examine what really happened during the trial in light of a genuine Marxist understanding of violence, history, and humanism. Such an examination may tell us something about the present Soviet Union and, at the very least, will set the record straight by putting Koestler's arbitrary interpretation in perspective.

Koestler's was not the only interpretation of the Trials. To put his version and Merleau-Ponty's alternative into context, this chapter samples the now accepted explanations of what had happened; the effects of Merleau-Ponty's interpretation are discussed in the next chapter.

PROBLEMS OF INTERPRETATION

For some observers there were no problems of understanding, no ambiguities to be considered, no drama, and certainly no tragedy. The 'Bloc of Rights and Trotskyites' was indeed a conspiracy: guilty as charged.[11] If the accused were guilty there were no further problems. But if they were not guilty? This question was formidable, and consideration of it centred on the inescapable fact that those who were convicted confessed their guilt. In their own eyes they seemed to admit they were guilty; in the eyes of the prosecution they certainly were guilty; so who could raise questions? If we question the verdict we have to account for the 'error' of the accused in confessing their guilt and the 'error' of the prosecution in charging them. The first error has often been answered by psychology and the second by the political dynamics of Stalinism. The two explanations overlap in some measure, for, it is often held, Stalinism induced the psychological conditions needed for confession.

The question of the prosecution's error is simpler, and reference can be made to historical actions and documents. Isaac Deutscher in his biography of Stalin cited economic disagreements and fear of Nazis as leading to Stalin's action, which rid him of a conspiracy; George F. Kennan in 1962 used an equally persuasive argument to show that Stalin fully expected to come to terms with the Nazis, and Khrushchev's speech at the Twentieth Party Congress seemed to confirm Kennan. Leonard Shapiro and Trotsky suggested other policy matters; W.G. Krivitsky said in 1939 that there really had been a conspiracy. Others have seen the purges simply as a means for Stalin to eliminate competitors.[12] The main objection to these explanations, of course, is that, save for Krivitsky, they explained only Stalin's action, not Bukharin's. That is, it makes no sense to explain Bukharin's confession of guilt by Stalin's drive for power. Consequently, if we look at Bukharin's performance in the dock from the perspective of what he thought he was doing, a new complex of questions arises.

That the confessions of many who suffered through the purge were obtained by torture has, at least since Krushchev's speech, rarely been denied. So far as can be known, Bukharin had not been tortured.[13] In his final statement to the court,

Bukharin discussed some of the more bizarre explanations for confession, including Tibetan drugs, hypnosis, and a Dostoyevskian Slavic soul, all of which he dismissed as 'absolutely absurd.'[14] Even if we agree with Shapiro that 'the first point of importance to note is not that those who were put on public trial confessed but that it was those who confessed who were put on public trial,'[15] we are no closer to understanding why Bukharin confessed. The simplest explanation is that he was promised his life if he co-operated with Stalin,[16] but the only support for this contention is the argument that many people were not publicly tried and their not being tried is evidence that they refused to confess.[17]

If neither fear of punishment nor hope of reprieve inspired *Bukharin's* confession, what did? Both fictional and non-fictional explanations have had to rely on the evidence found in the transcript or upon participants' memories because Bukharin apparently did not leave any memoirs. The danger of imputing motives to Bukharin was obvious. The only solid public evidence was the transcript, but even that was not an unambiguous document. There was a difference in tone and style between the bulk of the testimony, which was in the form of a debate or interrogation between Vishinsky and Bukharin, and the final plea, which was spoken by Bukharin alone and covered only four pages. In some measure the evaluation of Bukharin's confession depends upon which section of the transcript is emphasized. Nearly all commentators emphasize the final plea and look to the bulk of Bukharin's testimony in order to corroborate points made at the end,[18] apparently assuming that Bukharin knew what his final plea would be and laid the groundwork earlier. If instead the final plea is read in light of what Bukharin said during the examination period, a different picture emerges.

Before presenting Merleau-Ponty's interpretation of the Trials and the significance they had for his understanding of the Soviet Union and for his criticism of Koestler, one additional line of argument must be noted. *Darkness at Noon* was neither the first, nor an original, fictional account. Shortly after the trials of Zinoviev and Kamenev, which took place in the summer of 1936, Charles Plisnier published a novel, *Faux passeports*, that contained a plot and argument nearly identical to Koestler's.[19]

In Plisnier's novel, Stefan, an itinerant international revolutionary, decided to quit the Party because of the Soviet policy in Western Europe and the liquidation of the opposition in the USSR. Iegor, a Russian agent, who later became Stefan's friend, sought to dissuade him by using arguments identical to those given to Rubashov, Koestler's protagonist. In 1936 Iegor himself was arrested and tried for being part of a terrorist plot. He admitted to having met Trotsky in Oslo on 11 August 1935, the same day that Stefan had eaten lunch with him 'in the restaurant of the Hotel Bristol in Salzburg.' Stefan, afraid that Iegor would 'smother himself in filth and die in despair,'[20] resolved to expose the lie. He received no co-operation from others who had been in Salzburg with the two of them, and he wondered if perhaps his exposure would not rob Iegor of his honour as a revolutionary, however misguided that desire for honour may have been: 'have I the right to rush in and try to prevent what I call the craziness of his suicide? If in his last hours he is seeking a self-endorsement, more precious, more important to him than fame – a harmony between his death and belief – can I, yes, can I try to cheat him of it?'[21] For Stefan, friendship was more important than political commitments because in the end it was the basis of those commitments. It was the crucial factor in his relationship with Iegor because it allowed him to respect Iegor's desire for honour. By forcing himself to recognize through his friendship that honour was admirable in itself, even when put to the service of a perverted regime, Stefan retained just enough faith in the revolution to nourish his doubts.

Iegor was shot in the basement of the Lubyanka. 'Iegor's death has broken me,' Stefan said, and yet he continued to write 'in order to breathe back a little life into people who like me had given their lives away to an earthly movement which far transcended them, raising them high above themselves.'[22] He wrote to preserve the memory of the men and women not unlike 'the illuminated figures which they held above us when we were children, to arouse our love.' Revolutionaries were not saints, 'though a sanctity may exist for which God has no name.'[23] But neither were they robots. Iegor's desire for honour, which (unlike a Hegelian master) raised him above himself, was pursued in service to the revolution. He was an embodiment of Kojève's 'post-historical' political actor. Stefan was left to reflect on Iegor's death, putting his political commitments behind him and relying for guidance only upon his friendship and his love, now in the form of memory.

I do not mean to give your histories. What have they mattered to you in any case, these memories of my days of faith, written in the form of a complaint?

Living? Or dead? Can I still tell? No, I will not give your histories. To have the courage to do that, I should need at least a spark of faith within me. That spark was put out with Iegor. The plane of vision, which for an instant became one with communist faith, is shifting.

Living? My love will always be with them.

Dead? May God keep their souls.[24]

Love and faith could no longer be extended to the party in the name of a future humanity; love was for living people and faith for God.

According to Merleau-Ponty, 'the role of a novelist is not to expound ideas or even to analyse characters, but to present an interhuman event, to make it ripen and burst forth without ideological commentary to such an extent that any change in the order of the narrative or in the choice of perspective would modify the *literary* meaning of the event.'[25] Plisnier's meditation on the life of revolutionaries and the priority of commitments to one's friends over commitments to the meaning of history brought him to reflect on a meaning above political life as such. Merleau-Ponty never mentioned Plisnier's book, though with the obvious exception of Plisnier's hints at a suprapolitical meaning *Humanisme et Terreur* dealt identically with many of the same themes. Plisnier and Merleau-Ponty had in common a sympathetic understanding of political ambiguity; the reflective, inquiring style they shared contrasted sharply with the vulgar, hammering certainty of Koestler's prose.

Koestler's novel opened with Rubashov in jail. The narrative consisted of Rubashov's memories of his career, particularly his revolutionary work in the west, and of his interrogation first by his old comrade Ivanov and later by Gletkin, a model New Soviet Man. It ended with Rubashov's reflections before he was dropped with two bullets in his head.

According to Koestler himself, Rubashov 'incorporated certain characteristic features of both Radek and Bukharin.' Specifically, 'his manner of thinking [was] modelled on Nikolai Bukharin's, his personality and physical appearance [was] a synthesis of Leon Trotsky and Karl Radek.'[26] Rubashov's last plea, 'with its emphasis on "rendering last service" and "serving as a warning example" was a paraphrase of Bukharin's confession at the Moscow trial of 1938.'[27] In short, Rubashov's reasons for confession represented Koestler's understanding of Bukharin's confession.

Rubashov's understanding of his own existence underwent a profound change as he thought of what he had done and what had happened as a result of his actions. On the day of his execution he voiced Koestler's own view: 'Looking back over his past, it seemed to him now that for forty years he had been running amuck – the running amuck of pure reason.'[28] In his diary on the fifth day of his imprisonment Rubashov wrote: 'We were held for madmen because we followed every thought down to its final consequence and acted accordingly ... We replaced vision by logical deduction.'[29] Indeed, his own actions were proof of a 'logic' that others had thought mad. In the west, a local communist once complained to Rubashov that the Moscow line on propaganda was 'rubbish' and that the Party leadership was 'mistaken.' Rubashov replied:

The Party can never be mistaken ... You and I can make a mistake. Not the Party. The Party, comrade, is more than you and I and a thousand others like you and I. The Party is the embodiment of the revolutionary idea in history. History knows no scruples and no hesitation. Inert and unnerving, she flows toward her goal. At every bend in her course she leaves the mud which she carries and the corpses of the drowned. History knows her way. She makes no mistakes. He who has not absolute faith in History does not belong in the Party's ranks.[30]

At one point Rubashov wavered, but then he relented and decided that a public confession was demanded from him by the 'logic' of events. Gletkin had by now replaced Ivanov as his interrogator and had drawn up a list of charges that 'surpassed his worst expectations in absurdity.' Rubashov replied to the charges with a veritable paraphrase of Bukharin.

I plead guilty to not having understood the fatal compulsion behind the policy of the Government, and to have therefore held oppositional views. I plead guilty to having followed sentimental impulses, and in so doing to have been led into contradiction with historical necessity. I have lent my ear to laments of the sacrificed, and thus became deaf to the laments which proved the necessity to sacrifice them. I plead guilty to having rated the question of guilt and innocence higher than that of utility and harmfulness. Finally, I plead guilty to having placed the idea of man above the idea of mankind.[31]

He elaborated his explanation that he was counterrevolutionary only in the sense that the policies that he had advocated in good faith would have had 'objectively harmful' consequences. But Gletkin read him his own words: opposition meant accepting civil war and foreign allies. Rubashov fell silent with the 'relief' of 'utter surrender.' Gletkin then enunciated the principle that 'Truth' was what served the interests of 'humanity.' Thus Rubashov's actual motives and actual activities must be subordinated and judged by that principle. Finally, Gletkin held out the promise that 'after the victory' Rubashov would be rehabilitated.

Koestler seemingly had touched on all major points of the Moscow Trials. They were a crude power play by Stalin, and the accused confessed after being convicted by the same 'logic' that would later rehabilitate them. He added a few of his own touches as well, which Merleau-Ponty discussed at some length. For example, following Rubashov's final plea we read his dying thoughts, which were Koestler's notion of Bukharin's final thoughts. The accused and now condemned man found refuge in a state 'which the mystics called "ecstasy" and saints "contemplation"; the greatest and soberest of modern psychologists had recognized this state as a fact and called it the "oceanic sense." '[32] Rubashov's 'refuge' was off the mark; it was most unlikely that Bukharin would have sought, or seeking found, solace with Freud. The emphasis on psychology, which Koestler shared with others, was to Merleau-Ponty a defective interpretative approach. The Moscow Trials were first of all political events, not psychotherapy sessions or rituals, so that the first level of understanding must be approached from the political side.

THE TRIAL

Bukharin denied he was a spy or an assassin, and yet, he said, he would have re-
lied upon espionage and assassination if he had been able to put his plan into operation. Was he, then, guilty of espionage? Not necessarily. Was he innocent?
There are those who say he was,[33] but let us consider the transcript of his trial.

Bukharin acknowledged that since 1928 he had been opposed to Soviet policy.
By 1933 he had considered the possibility of a 'palace coup' against Stalin, followed by an uprising with the support of the Kulaks, and then a coup d'état
proper. To this end Bukharin kept himself informed 'of Kulak Sabotage [in the
Caucasus] as a sort of preliminary stage preceding sharper forms of struggle.'
Rykov, also in the dock with Bukharin, knew Pivovarov, who was 'head of Soviet
state power in the North Caucasus.' Rykov knew that Pivovarov was in contact
with the Whiteguard Cossack League, but Bukharin did not.

VISHINSKY: Was it a fact, or was it not, that Pivovarov was connected with White-
guard Cossack circles abroad?
BUKHARIN: I cannot deny it. I can only conjecture that it could be so, since our
line was to make use of all force.
VISHINSKY: Including the Whiteguard forces as well?
BUKHARIN: That was not excluded.[34]

Vishinsky however, wished to establish the fact that Bukharin *knew* that the
Caucasus group had contacts with Whiteguard Cossacks. Bukharin continued to
insist that he did not know but that it was probable that contacts had been established.

VISHINSKY: Answer me 'No.'
BUKHARIN: I cannot say 'No,' and I cannot deny that it did take place.
VISHINSKY: So the answer is neither 'Yes' nor 'No'?
BUKHARIN: Nothing of the kind, because facts exist regardless of whether they
are in anybody's mind. This is a problem of the reality of the outer world ...
VISHINSKY: So ... you are unable to give a plain answer?
BUKHARIN: Not 'unable' but there are some questions that cannot be answered
outright 'Yes' or 'No,' as you are perfectly aware from elementary logic.[35]

In addition to Whiteguard Cossack support for an anti-Stalinist *coup*, there
had been discussions with the Germans concerning certain 'services' they were
to provide in exchange for territorial concessions. Bukharin knew of the negotiations from Tomsky and from the negotiator, Karakhan.

VISHINSKY: Did you endorse these negotiations?
BUKHARIN: Or disavow? I did not disavow them; consequently I endorsed them.
VISHINSKY: Did you [Rykov] endorse not only the fact of the negotiations but also the initiative, that is, the affair as a whole?
RYKOV: We are neither of us little children. If you don't endorse such things, then you must fight against them. One cannot play with neutrality in such things ...
BUKHARIN: Rykov has already stated that in such cases there can be no such thing as neutrality: if I did not put an end to them, then I endorsed them. But this is a paraphrase of what I said: if I did not disavow them, I endorsed them.[36]

Later, Bukharin acknowledged that, if necessary, the frontier would have been opened to the German army, though he was unaware of the specific plans. He allowed that if the coup was under way such plans would not have been objectionable.[37]

If we can argue that Bukharin was not guilty of the charge of espionage, it did not follow that he was simply innocent. His own words were significant: 'I regard myself politically responsible for the sum total of the crimes committed by the "Bloc of Rights and Trotskyites." ' In each of the specific charges Bukharin made similar statements.[38] Since he had belonged to the bloc from the moment it was formed, 'consequently' he was 'responsible as one of the leaders and not as a cog of this counter-revolutionary organization.' He repeated that he had 'no wish to disclaim responsibility for various practical things, for my counter-revolutionary crimes. But I want to say that ... as one of the leaders I play and answer in a far greater degree, bear far greater responsibility than any of the cogs.' Again, concerning the Ryutin platform, the Caucasus plans, or the negotiations with the Germans, after stating his ignorance of specific details Bukharin consistently added that it was he who was in large measure responsible for the detailed execution of the 'line.'

VISHINSKY: Do you bear responsibility for these criminal acts as one of the leaders of the organization?
BUKHARIN: Undoubtedly I do bear responsibility.
VISHINSKY: For the connections of your organization with Whiteguard Cossack circles and German fascists?
BUKHARIN: Of course I do ...
VISHINSKY: And so, accused Bukharin, you bear responsibility for these negotiations of Karakhan with the Germans?
BUKHARIN: Undoubtedly.[39]

Bukharin spoke, as did Koestler, about 'dotting the i's,' though with a distinctive meaning. For Bukharin, it meant facing the consequences of counter-revolution:

'restoring capitalist relations in the USSR,' 'the dismemberment of the USSR,' and, in Vishinsky's words, to which Bukharin agreed, 'outright rabid fascism.'[40]

Bukharin knew well that what was taking place was political, even if some western commentators did not. About the middle of his testimony he made a short speech on the plan to restore capitalism. He began by acknowledging that he was 'an accused person who must bear responsibility as a criminal, facing the Court of the proletarian country.' Since the trial was 'of public importance' and since the topic had been ignored, he wished to make a short disquisition in order to 'decipher one formula, namely what is meant by the restoration of capitalism.' Bukharin then explained in some detail how the 'logic of the struggle' had led to certain counter-revolutionary ideas which then redoubled the intensity of this logic. In particular, he wished to dwell upon the 'objective side of the matter.' The Right counter-revolutionaries began, he said, as a simple deviation from the Party line on industrialization and collectivization policy; their deviation was based upon the claim that 'industrialization was destroying [agricultural] production.' The Ryutin platform expressed these ideas just at the time that collectivization and industrialization had begun. They supported the Kulaks 'subjectively' by overestimating the importance of individual enterprise and then by 'idealizing' the individual property-owner. 'What was necessary was to develop rich property owners. This was a tremendous change that took place in our standpoint and psychology.' They 'pitied the expropriated Kulaks, from so-called humanitarian motives.' But they had not pitied the Whiteguards. Indeed, he said, pity for the Whiteguards 'would have sounded like frank and open treason.' Yet, Bukharin said, he had been led, through 'so-called humanitarian motives,' to pity and thus to support the counter-revolutionary and property-holding Kulaks against the proletariat. 'This meant that ideological and political platforms grew into counter-revolutionary platforms.' The 'objective' goal was 'the ideal of a Kulak agrarian country with an industrial appendage.' Thus it was that the 'logic of the struggle led to the logic of ideas and to a change of our psychology, to the counter-revolutionizing of our aims.'[41]

Some observers have taken this speech to constitute a subtle appeal to the Kulaks and a denunciation of Stalin's policy of collectivization and industrialization. Perhaps it was; but perhaps also it was a truthful reflection of Bukharin's thinking. He repeated substantially the same argument in his last plea,[42] and earlier in the trial two of his remarks confirmed that he meant what he said. Bukharin was giving testimony on the possibility of recruiting members of the Right counter-revolutionary organization:

VISHINSKY: With what object?
BUKHARIN: With the object of creating mass bases for the struggle against the Party line.

VISHINSKY: Cossack, Kulak circles for the struggle against the Party line?
BUKHARIN: Well, what of it?
VISHINSKY: For the struggle against Soviet power?
BUKHARIN: The struggle against the Party line is a struggle against the Soviet power.
VISHINSKY: But the struggle against the Party line finds expression in other forms.
BUKHARIN: I think that the Citizen Procurator, the Citizens judges and the whole country are interested in seeing how out of certain deviations monstrous conclusions are formed by the logic of the struggle.[43]

Later, when Vishinsky observed that the Prosecutor was interested not in ideology but in criminology, Bukharin responded: 'But ideology may also be criminal; actions are performed by thinking people.'[44] What Bukharin appeared to argue in the quotations cited was that his deviationist ideas became counter-revolutionary forces as industrialization and collectivization began and were resisted by the Kulaks. When the Kulaks resisted the Soviet policy, Bukharin's 'line,' as the expression of the Kulaks' action, became, as it were, part of the Kulak resistance and therefore counter-revolutionary, or at least anti-Soviet.

Merleau-Ponty's interpretation of Bukharin's defence remained close to the text of the transcript, and the quotations above have been selected by the emphases he made. He argued that Bukharin was responsible, as he admitted, for deeds about which he knew no details. Bukharin, said Merleau-Ponty, had been guilty of 'historical treason,' by which he meant that the logic of the struggle and the logic of Bukharin's ideas had led to counter-revolutionary consequences. Bukharin's policy and the tactics it entailed included support from Whiteguards, Kulaks, and Germans; 'to reckon *with*, is, in a certain way, to reckon *on*.'[45] If Bukharin were to have even a modest chance of success, he would have had to count upon anti-Soviet allies. In order to act against Stalin at all, a mass uprising was required because the time for a bloodless coup had passed. To have increased the troubles in the North Caucasus and to have inflamed Kulak discontent would have severely disrupted the country and perhaps paved the way for a 'reactionary' victory. Thus was Bukharin 'linked' to anti-Soviet forces.

There was a political complicity between Bukharin and the discontented peasantry that Bukharin had not created but that, since it would have worked to his advantage, nevertheless made him anti-Soviet.[46] Commented Merleau-Ponty, 'political man [*l'homme d'Etat*] defines himself not by what he does himself but by the forces he counts on. The role of the Prosecutor was to show Bukharin's activity on the level of history and objective activity.'[47] Politics is not the creation of a single man but a collective action; a political man leads, which is to say he orients around himself forces and vectors that are already in existence, what Merleau-Ponty called 'the movement of history.'[48] Bukharin's position in this movement was anti-Soviet, and his actions so defined him. Did this mean, if Stalin were in the dock and Vishinsky were Bukharin's prosecutor, that Stalin would have been a counter-revolutionary? For a Marxist, Merleau-Ponty said, the answer was ambiguous.

Merleau-Ponty's explication of the non-reversibility of roles showed reversibility to be a kind of historical residue or shadow that Bukharin dragged after him. It was a residue that had once constituted a real future, a projection and a project that once could have been accomplished and once was anticipated with the highest revolutionary motives. Merleau-Ponty's interpretation emphasized equally that Bukharin was a Marxist, and so acted from revolutionary motives, and that he acted politically. Marxist politics, he said, 'is not primarily a system of ideas but a reading of on-going history.' No reading of history is ever definitive, of course, because all the implications of a political action can never be fully known. There can only be more or less comprehensive perspectives, so that Bukharin's activity on the plane of history and objectivity must be open to interpretation. That is, Merleau-Ponty wished to distinguish between objectivity and definitiveness. Vishinsky did not. For Merleau-Ponty there remained something to be said after we have learned that 'objectively' or 'historically' Bukharin had been linked to the Whiteguard Cossacks.

Once again Merleau-Ponty invoked the 'harsh notion' of looking to consequences. Thus pity for the Kulaks, in a time of collectivization, was counter-revolutionary. But pity was not for that reason dishonourable. Rather, pity as such did not exist: there was only a certain attitude towards certain men that has particular consequences. Only one attitude was irreducible to its consequences, revolutionary honour. For Koestler's Gletkin, it was simply an 'old' attitude a bourgeois prejudice attributable to Rubashov's having lived in the decadent West, having had the privilege of education, and so on. But that was not Bukharin's understanding. If he were an accomplice of the Whiteguard Cossacks unintentionally, his intentions must count for something. Bukharin denied he was a spy; but he said he was 'no better' than a spy. He denied detailed knowledge of assassination plots or treasonable conspiracies but accepted responsibility and 'in a way' was a traitor. According to Merleau-Ponty, 'to Marxists of the future, these formulas preserve the revolutionary honour of the accused.'[49] Like Plisnier's Iegor, Bukharin faced death conscious that he deserved it. This was why he went to such lengths to explain his own competence and his motives. Policy differences held in good faith eventually entailed the defeat of one side. His self-recognition as an 'objective' traitor was not so remarkable, for it was no more than an acknowledgment of what he had in fact come to represent in terms of the policies he once had advocated. When he quoted Schiller's celebrated line, 'World history is the world court of judgment,'[50] he simply recognized that his deeds demanded, at that particular moment, that he, their author, be judged.

Bukharin's political position was complex. He recognized what he had earlier tried to do and what his failure meant in 1938 when he saw the 'new stage of the struggle of the USSR taking shape.'[51] However judged, he was not simply counter-revolutionary. In Merleau-Ponty's view the Trials were 'dramatic' and 'genuinely tragic' because 'the *same man* has understood both that he cannot disavow the objective pattern of his actions, that he is what he is for others in the context of history, and yet the motive of his actions retains a value for a man as he immediately experiences it.' The 'tragic' political actor exists in a kind of dialectical tension, 'a contradiction founded in truth, where the same man tried to realize himself on two levels.'[52] Moreover, the significance of the Trials transcended the details of Bukharin's biography: 'the personal pathos is eclipsed, and a drama transpired that is rooted in the most general structures of human action, a genuine tragedy, which is that of historical contingency.'[53] The same historical contingency that made commitment possible, that made God an illusion, and that made violence a necessary aspect of political change, also gave a meaning, sometimes brutal, harsh, and tragic, to political action. 'Man can neither suppress himself as freedom and judgment – what he calls the course of events is never anything but events seen by him – nor dispute the competence of the tribunal of history, since by acting he has committed others, and gradually more and more the fate of humanity as well.'[54]

I have already expressed reservations about the metaphysical and theological implications that Merleau-Ponty drew from his category of contingency. In the limited sense of political action, however, his understanding of contingency is indubitably valid. Contingency, whatever the constants that guide it, is the chief characteristic of political action in the strict sense. We cannot foresee all and thus cannot take precautions against what others will do to us; yet our actions reverberate throughout the world, and others whom we cannot control act against us. We cannot deny to others the power of action without destroying it in ourselves; if, as in a dream, we could foresee everything, know all, and thus control all others, we would no longer act ourselves but rather would preside over the smooth administration of the world. If we are going to act, we are going to act with and against others, and this means they will act with and against us. 'History's tribunal' is thus simply the issue of our interactions, and its verdict is only relatively final, for the boundlessness of our actions continues after we die.

SOVIET VIOLENCE

Merleau-Ponty criticized Koestler's interpretation of the Trials on the basis of not only Marx's teaching but especially his own understanding of political action. His remarks on violence situated Bukharin's actions in their revolutionary context, which in turn served as the basis for his critical analysis of Trotsky's interpretation and for his judgment of the USSR.

About a quarter of *Humanisme et Terreur* was devoted to an analysis of *Darkness at Noon*. Merleau-Ponty's criticism of the novel proceeded at two levels: Rubashov was a bad copy of Bukharin, and Koestler had an inadequate understanding of Marxism and politics. The two levels were joined inasmuch as the fictional character was simply the prefabricated illustration of Koestler's opinions.[55]

Summarizing the novel, Merleau-Ponty concluded that Rubashov lived in and sustained a world of bad faith by a dialectic whereby he 'could not obtain on the outside the realization of what he sensed himself to be on the inside, nor could he prevent himself from looking for [his sense of self] outside.' The result was a humanism that transformed itself directly into violence. If Koestler were right in saying that *Darkness at Noon* talked the authentic language of the Party then there was very little politics in the Party. The joy of action, which Rubashov and his comrades had experienced during the revolution, had been 'translated into a mechanist philosophy that disfigured it and is the origin of the inhuman alternatives with which Rubashov in the end is confronted.'[56] 'History' was the objective unfolding of events according to the iron logic of an idea known secretly only by Number One (the head of the Party). 'The logic Rubashov follows ... is the summary logic of the technician who deals only with inert objects, which he manipulates as he pleases.' The goal was clear: power to the Party. All else followed as a mere technical application of the required means. According to Merleau-Ponty, as we have seen, such an opinion had to be severely qualified to be compatible with Marx's teaching.

The other side of 'objective' history was Koestler's assertion that the individual can have but a 'subjective' view, which was worthless by comparison. Rather than reject the dichotomy as nonsense, Koestler projected a future when all is objective because 'science' will have clarified the subjective element into non-existence. The result would be not a political man but an executioner, who would do as he is told without trying to understand his actions and who, when about to be executed himself, would await the necessary verdict having 'worked it through to a conclusion' with a little help from Gletkin. His fascination with the death of others – one could almost say that Rubashov viewed himself as an 'other' – and the complementary passion for obedience as a way to avoid responsibility was, for Merleau-Ponty, a non-political position. It was the position of an administrator who simply applied the rules without thought or care about what they may mean or who wrote them. Rules were simply there and to be obeyed. In Koestler's metaphor, Rubashov was simply a cog in a large clock 'wound up for all eternity'; in Koestler's view, the Party would agree with Rubashov.[57] What Koestler forgot and what Merleau-Ponty insisted on recalling was that such objectivity was invented by Koestler himself.

In a later book, Koestler gave Rubashov's attitude a label: the ethics of the

Commissar.[58] From his autobiography we may learn that this was what attracted the young Koestler to the Party; the experience of jail was what turned him away again. The logic of the Commissar's ethics was valid only until it landed you in jail, then the Yogi took over. Koestler the author was less logical, and perhaps more real, than Rubashov his character. But the Yogi was also an example of bad faith, Merleau-Ponty said, because he desired the disembodied bliss of an 'inner life' while yet having a body. As Maritain said of Descartes, his was the sin of angelism. In his own way, Koestler had seen the necessity of transcending the bad choice to achieve what he called a synthesis.[59] It was a strange synthesis, however, preserving the worst of both the Yogi and the Commissar. The Yogi could forget about action and allow politics to be transacted over his head, thinking it none of his concern and thinking also that his hands were clean. Thus Koestler forgot the foulness of British imperialism while contemplating the glory of British constitutionalism.[60] The Commissar, impatient with the ambiguities of change and the slowness of revolutionary transformation, was much more comfortable with electrification than with Soviets. Koestler too was impatient with ambiguity and preferred the clear ideas of science. All else, we are assured, was madness or the nefarious doings of the 'old' part of the brain. As Rubashov, Koestler sought outside for what he knew was not there. His 'dialectic' of Yogi and Commissar was an irregular oscillation. The choice of a Yogi who acted as an 'inverted Commissar' (or vice versa) would never be overcome, Merleau-Ponty said, until Koestler sought truly to understand, even on pain of having to forgive, his present enemies who were once his comrades.[61]

Koestler was indeed a mediocre Marxist. The bad dialectic of Yogi and Commissar was his own invention and had no basis in Marx's teaching. But, Merleau-Ponty asked, 'is Rubashov just a fictional character and are his problems imaginary?'[62] Or, would not most Commissars, either real ones in the Soviet Union or prospective candidates in France, agree with Koestler's assumptions? In practice, the violence of the Soviet regime seemed to be at least partly intelligible in terms of Koestler's image. Merleau-Ponty denied this, though not by emphasizing but by ignoring the spiritual corruption of Stalinism and its origins.

In his analysis of the transcript, Merleau-Ponty concluded that a sense of revolutionary honour was the source of Bukharin's motivation. This account of Bukharin's 'drama of historical responsibility' had the great merit of considering directly the words of the accused without the mediation of Stalin. But what of the latter? According to Merleau-Ponty, the Moscow Trials were 'inconceivable' divorced from 'the revolutionary *Stimmung* [atmosphere] of violence.'[63] However, Merleau-Ponty, as we have seen, held a number of different theories of violence. He was silent here concerning the grand theoretical questions of process, incarnation, and the dialectic of contingency and necessity, and confined his remarks to the strictly political problem of founding a regime, discussed above in the context of his note on Machiavelli. One comment made by Merleau-Ponty, however, was redolent of Kojève.

For Kojève, one may recall, only the Leader of the universal and homogeneous state was 'truly satisfied,' but each citizen could become Leader on two conditions: that the risk of death implied in competition and political struggle be accepted and that the candidate take part in constructive activity of the society. The first condition, said Kojève, guaranteed the seriousness of the candidates for leadership and the second their competence.[64] Bukharin was in this sense serious and competent, and he lost the final struggle to one who was equally serious but more competent. This accounts easily enough for the fact of conflict between Stalin and Bukharin. What Merleau-Ponty called Bukharin's revolutionary honour would have been for Kojève only a token that referred to Bukharin's desire for universal recognition. As for the other victims of the purges, terror was for Kojève a 'metaphysical necessity' for the creation of universal human beings, purified by the dissolution of all stability through consciousness of death. Such dissolution, the Soviet experiment implied, could be obtained only by liquidating the bodies where consciousness lodged.

Unless Merleau-Ponty was persuaded by some elements of Kojève's thought, it is hard to see how he could have considered Stalin's terror as calmly as he did. His comparison of Bukharin's position with that of the heretic in the Church and his remarks on Bukharin's possible 'rehabilitation'[65] would be virtually unintelligible in the absence of Kojève's teaching that human beings could transform moral error into truth. Kojève illustrated what he meant by the example of one person who murdered a king and was arrested, tried, and executed: for this moral 'error' he was rightly condemned as a criminal. Another person also murdered a king but went on to lead a revolution: for this moral 'truth' he was rightly praised as a heroic liberator. Likewise, in time Bukharin's crime could be changed into a virtuous act.

The danger in Kojève's approach to truth and Merleau-Ponty's evident endorsement of it, as Hannah Arendt has pointed out, was first of all that it was inherently violent. As she said, 'when Trotsky learned that he had never played a role in the Russian Revolution, he must have known that his death warrant had been signed.'[66] Once the actions that preserved the name of Trotsky in the memory of his countrymen had been obliterated by the rewriting of Soviet history, the agent of those actions would also have to be eliminated as a witness. More important, when the liar believed his own lies, so that crime could be converted at whim into honourable action, the truth was not defamed, it disappeared. The image returns of Merleau-Ponty's traveller, wandering in the spaces of sheer potentiality, drifting from one mirage to the next; unable to find the way back to the real world.

As with other aspects of his political thought, on this question Merleau-Ponty may have borrowed freely from Kojève. His most persuasive arguments, however, and in particular his criticism of Trotsky's 'rationalism,' were indebted rather to Machiavelli's account of the violent foundation of all regimes. Merleau-Ponty's critique of Trotsky bore upon his judgment of the Soviet Union.

Trotsky's argument, to Merleau-Ponty, reflected his political failure. He too had been a member of Lenin's Politburo who ended up 'historically' or 'objectively' wrong. But he was not tried in Moscow and did not have to come to terms with the actual exigencies of confession. Merleau-Ponty considered Trotsky's situation crucial to Trotsky's argument. 'The Revolution at the time he created it was less clear than when he wrote its history,' which also meant that Bukharin's trial and its significance may also not have been as clear as Trotsky's declaration of a Stalinist counter-revolution.[67] It was of course true that by 1937 the Soviet Union was no longer the state Lenin founded, but 'the whole question is to know what this change is and if Trotsky interprets it aright.'[68] According to Trotsky, the Old Bolsheviks simply capitulated; since Trotsky had once 'capitulated' too, the odium of their action lay not in surrender itself but in surrender to the 'grave-digger of the revolution,' the instigator of the Soviet Thermidor, the head of the counter-revolutionary bureaucracy. Even granting that the 'triumph of the bureaucracy over the masses constituted a Soviet Thermidor,'[69] Merleau-Ponty argued, this simply introduced the ambiguity of history that Trotsky did not wish to recognize. For it remains a question whether, historically, Thermidor and Bonaparte 'destroyed the Revolution or rather consolidated its results.' Pursuing this possibility, Merleau-Ponty recalled Trotsky's own capitulation in 1926-7 and wondered whether there was not 'inevitably' a 'pause after each surge.' Such a pause, he said, 'is not a contingent fact, explicable by personal conceptions of one or several or by the interests of an established bureaucracy, but is a moment that has its place in the development of the revolution.'[70] From an abstract or rationalist perspective foreign to Marxism, said Merleau-Ponty, Napoleon or Stalin may appear as liquidators of the revolution. But even Trotsky described the Soviet Thermidor in such a way that it 'could represent, on the scale of universal history, a period of latency during which certain gains were consolidated.'[71] What counted, in Trotsky's own words, was that 'Stalin is a man of our times,' which meant that Trotsky was not.

The Moscow Trials and Trotsky's murder eliminated 'a generation that had lost the objective conditions of its political activity.'[72] Because Trotsky no longer was a political actor he had drawn up his 'rationalist' schemes based on a 'Kantian' ethics in order to account for Stalin's success and his own lack of it – but in such a way that he might present himself to the future as a beacon of Marxist truth. 'By seeing his life as having a meaning for the future rather than in his present actions, Trotsky gave in to the temptation of what Marxists have called utopianism.' Likewise, he idealized the past and forgot the arguments he used when he was in power. In his polemic of 1920 against Karl Kautsky, Merleau-Ponty pointed out, were arguments useful against the Trotsky of 1938. He did not reproach Trotsky with having used violence when in power, but using against a dictatorship to which he once submitted the arguments of formal humanism 'that appeared false to him when addressed to the dictatorship that he exercised.' 1920 was not 1935, but the transition was gradual: 'That is what we must start to see.'[73] In 1920 Trotsky recognized that politics depended 'upon the volition and audacity of men on specific occasions, that it contained an element of contingency and risk,' and that it necessarily included violence.[74] In this lay his superiority to Kautsky's 'formal humanism.' Fifteen years later this was still true. A possible interpretation of Trotsky's inconsistency, nowhere entertained by him even to be rejected, was that Kautsky was not wrong to oppose the interpretation of violence upheld by Trotsky (and Lenin) in 1920 and that by 1935 Trotsky had come to see the wisdom of Kautsky's argument.

The last years of Trotsky's life provided no relief from 'rationalism.' Trotsky's understanding of the conflict with Hitler, which he viewed as inevitable and in a way apocalyptic, was that it constituted a 'new and decisive test' of the proletariat: 'If the world proletariat should actually prove incapable of fulfilling the mission placed upon it by the course of development, nothing else would remain except only to recognize that the socialist program, based on the internal contradictions of capitalist society, ended as Utopia. It is self-evident that a new "minimum" program would be required – for the defence of the interests of the slaves of the Totalitarian Bureaucratic society.'[75] By fixing 'a due date for the historical proof of Marxism,' Trotsky courted the inevitable dilemma that sooner or later it would expire but the world would go on. Thus Merleau-Ponty wondered what Trotsky would have said had he lived until the fall of 1941: 'either to take the side of an abstract humanism and oppose the only country to date that had established a collective economy, or to take the side of collective production and the country that represented it. Either the USSR or counter-revolution.' Because neither alternative seemed likely and because the Soviet Union was being invaded, 'political life would have become *impossible* for him.'[76] Trotsky would have ended his days, said Merleau-Ponty, as a beautiful soul.

Much of Merleau-Ponty's argument against Trotsky appears strange today because we know so much more about Stalin's regime than was available at the time he wrote. Even so, it is difficult to agree with his view that the defeat of Trotsky in 1926-7 was at all comparable to the later defeat of Zinoviev, Kamenev, and Bukharin. Ten years after Trotsky was eliminated from effective participation in the rule of the Soviet Union, the possibility of a resurgence, of a 'new revolutionary thrust,' which Trotsky anticipated while making his retreat was even further away. The political situation of 1936 and the years following was less an ebb in the tide of revolution than the extinction of any revolutionary movement at all under the paralysing terror of Stalinism. But the post-war era had not yet made clear the situation under Stalin, nor could Merleau-Ponty neglect the tremendous appeal that Trotsky's interpretation had for left-wing intellectuals in France at that time, including many of Merleau-Ponty's friends. Yet there was something too easy about it. To be a Trotskyite meant that one could enjoy the fashion of a revolutionary Marxist heritage without the bother of understanding the problems of implementing it. One could deplore Stalinism, avoid unpleasant Party intellectuals, and praise the name of Marx, all with a good conscience. The price of admission to this genial company was that one subscribe to the orthodoxy and cease to look at evidence that, even from a Marxist perspective, was ambiguous. Merleau-Ponty conceived his own historical responsibility differently.

Stalin's terror was perhaps as a continuation of the violence that marks the birth of all new regimes. But Merleau-Ponty was unable, in 1947, to see (or foresee) the consequences of that terror and, not knowing what kind of regime would be born from it, was unwilling to pass judgment on it. *Humanisme et Terreur*, he said, was an attempt 'to take stock of this century and the ambiguous forms it offers to us,' and it could do no more than present the ambiguity for what it was – or rather for what it appeared to be in the light of Marxism and the declarations of the USSR. The politics of hope and resignation were translated into a practical commitment that refused to judge what was unknown. Waiting to see what events would bring, one could only tread the lonely *via media* between rival enthusiasms.

Merleau-Ponty's motives for writing *Humanisme et Terreur* were therefore mixed. Having made a commitment to Marxism, he wished to know what to make of the Soviet Union. As it happened, the success of Koestler's anti-Soviet book coincided with the trials of the major French Nazi collaborators. At one level, then, it was a *livre de circonstance*, best understood in terms of the surrender or opposition to tyranny. The conflict between Merleau-Ponty and Koestler was a consequence of their different understandings of political action. The superiority of Merleau-Ponty's version as a political interpretation did not mean that Koestler's obsessive pursuit of the arrow in the blue, his 'oceanic feeling' as he lay rotting in prison awaiting death by a Spanish firing squad, were unreal. It did mean that Merleau-Ponty had achieved a greater self-understanding of his own equivalent experience of war, violence, and armed political resistance and was able to bring it to bear successfully on the trial transcript, the only hard evidence available. Merleau-Ponty showed that Rubashov was a badly drawn portrait of Bukharin. The great omission from Merleau-Ponty's interpretation, explained, possibly by his Marxism, was any awareness of the spiritual disorder of Stalinism; in his gross fashion Koestler at least expressed something of this.

Merleau-Ponty's opposition to Koestler was deeper than their differences over the Moscow Trials. Koestler was passionately anti-communist. Merleau-Ponty insisted that this was a prejudice unsubstantiated by facts and unwarranted by events. Whether Merleau-Ponty was as informed as he might have been, especially from the numerous sources available in France hostile to the Soviet Union, may be doubted. In any event, he considered both Koestler and Trotsky to have committed a common error: they tore the subtle, complex, and ambiguous fabric of events into simple, loud, and distinct formular categories: reason running amuck, the Soviet Thermidor, the ethics of the Commissar, bureaucratic counter-revolution. For Merleau-Ponty on the other hand history consisted of composites, and he would not be forced into a hasty judgment.

We quoted earlier Merleau-Ponty's opinion that the truth of Marxism would appear through the structure of events so that one must attend to them. That it had not yet appeared did not seem to him sufficient reason to give up Marxism nor to foreclose the possibility that the Soviet Union was, as it proclaimed, on the way towards a society of humanism and mutual recognition. This attitude was intelligible only on the basis of assumptions that we have already had occasion to dispute. Within the limitations of those assumptions, Merleau-Ponty's arguments did not lack courage, especially when contrasted with the evasive dogmas of so many of his opponents who shared his metaphysical and theological views.

For most Frenchmen, eastern Europe and the Soviet Union were shadowy areas. Merleau-Ponty wished to distinguish the fog of ignorance from the darker gloom of a fatal conflict. Events soon forced him to abandon this attitude of 'Marxist waiting.'

4
The eclipse of
the middle way

Sartre called Merleau-Ponty's understanding of Soviet and world politics during the immediate post-war period 'one-eyed' while everyone else's was blind.[1] Yet his recognition of the hazy and ambiguous forces at work in the world only prompted vilification from blind men who thought they saw things clearly. *Humanisme et Terreur*, Merleau-Ponty's first extended reflection upon public affairs, provoked hostility from both left and right, a preview of how virtually all his political writings were to be received. Often, though, the criticisms of his contemporaries were the result of gross and perhaps wilful misunderstanding.

Communist intellectuals, it is true, reserved their most picturesque epithets for Arthur Koestler. Nevertheless, Merleau-Ponty received a generous share of calumny, of which the remarks of Jean Desanti may serve as a representative example. Intellectuals, he began, ask if we communists are on the right track. They wonder if we have a so-called philosophy of history. Often they lard their queries with quotations from the juvenilia of Marx, but 'the truth is that many intellectuals who have come from the bourgeoisie, having read Marx a little late in life, do not recognize the proletariat today. They maintain an abstract view of it and are quite astonished to find that reality does not conform to the monsters they have created.' What had happened, he said, was that the struggles of the working class have already created a new man, and intellectuals who clung to images of the 'old' man and the 'old' truth were understandably confused. When 'old' intellectuals insist upon sympathy with the Party, it is comic, for they also insist upon so-called philosophies of history, and these too have been surpassed. Abstract thinking was simply 'fooling around.' But to say this was to see the comedy in a different light, for the salvation of mankind was not a laughing matter. Hesitation was in fact not different from desertion and complicity with the enemy.

Merleau-Ponty, in particular, refused 'to see the Soviet Union as a socialist, proletarian state.' The communist reply to such doubts was simplicity itself: 'Take a look at the forces we are up against. They are under our very eyes, and surround even you. On one side, there is the working class and the Soviet Union. On the other, the imperialist bourgeoisie which finds its leadership in Washington. The working class is throughout the world. In France, it struggles for its life, and for yours too, petit-bourgeois intellectual. What are you going to do?'[2]

Trotskyite critics echoed the Communist Party regulars in calling *Humanisme et Terreur* the work of a petit-bourgeois intellectual but added that Merleau-Ponty had made two fatal errors: he had confused socialism and Soviet state capitalism and he had made light of Trotsky. Since the first mistake grew from the second there seemed to be nothing in Merleau-Ponty's remarks that spoke to Trotskyite preoccupations.[3]

The greatest criticism came from bourgeois liberals, however, and concentrated on the apparently odd statement of Merleau-Ponty that 'the appeal court of bourgeois justice is the past; for revolutionary justice, it is the future.'[4] Merleau-Ponty did not mean that Soviet courts could read the future and apply 'future precedents' to concrete cases.[5] What he meant, as the context indicated, was that politics is the realm of action, not the technical application of an externally valid legal norm. To be sure, Merleau-Ponty's language, which included terms unfamiliar or uncomfortable to liberals, was perhaps not the most acceptable to them, but he was talking first to an audience familiar with a Marxist vocabulary. For example, when he said that 'the Moscow trials were revolutionary trials presented as ordinary ones,' the emphasis must be placed on the dynamic, political, and activist connotations of the term 'revolutionary,' not on the legal form the action took; 'everything is clarified ... if we take the trial to be an historical act.'[6] Merleau-Ponty considered the trials an act of foundation, which was bound to be violent.

If emphasis is placed on the sheer form of the act, then a 'political trial' can only be a mockery of judicial procedure.[7] Merleau-Ponty agreed: 'For heaven's sake, it is not a matter of *judicial error!*'[8] Once this point is understood much of the furor that greeted his book seems quite beside the point. Indeed, a good deal of the cry against Merleau-Ponty's 'novel' kind of justice was simply window-dressing for anti-communism and pro-Pétain sentiments.[9] But one argument, advanced by Emmanuel Berl, was more subtle: 'Despite what M. Merleau-Ponty has said, there are not nor can there be two justices, one for calm periods and the other for storms. Political tension or reconciliation do not change justice and injustice; they can only change the attitude of power towards them.'[10] Berl understood justice as doctrinal, capable of being formulated exhaustively as an inventory of propositions on correct or right conduct. He did not interpret it, for example, as a Platonic idea, a symbol for an unchanging universal category for which there could be a number of different particular examples, some in calm periods, others in storms. But to Merleau-Ponty, Berl was open to an obvious objection, that a concept of such celestial splendour had nothing to do with ugly terrestrial events like the French and Soviet purges. At best Berl had not shown the connection between unchanging justice and political events; at worst he was no more than a beautiful soul.

The most widespread objections that were not thinly-veiled apologia for collaborators ignored the theoretical questions Merleau-Ponty raised and simply deplored the consequences of the book. Except for communists, wrote one commentator, nine out of ten who read Merleau-Ponty's essay would see it as 'a more or less disguised justification of the Moscow Trials.' As for Merleau-Ponty's reply, that he was justifying nothing, 'one would be tempted to call it bad faith.'[11] Another critic spoke for a number of readers by saying that 'a regime where all opposition is considered treason has a very precise name: it is called a totalitarian regime.' Bukharin's 'error,' thus was to have failed. ' "Death to the vanquished," such is the last word of this new philosophy of political police.'[12] Nor did the passing of time and of the immediate political issues increase public understanding of what *Humanisme et Terreur* was about; a quarter century later it was still seen as an apology for Stalinism and Soviet terror, and the expression of a 'religious' view of history.[13]

In view of such grand misrepresentation, it may be useful to recall Merleau-Ponty's understanding of what he wrote and something of the prevailing climate of opinion. The Bolshevik Revolution was not so purely proletarian as Marxists often remembered it, he said, and the 'counter-revolution' was not so impure. Consequently, 'the diagnosis is not so easy to formulate, nor the remedy to find.' We cannot begin 1917 all over again, nor believe that communism could be what it used to wish to be. Thus, it would be folly to exchange very real 'formal' liberties for the hope of a concrete humanism directed by Bolsheviks, who have so far succeeded only in 'suppressing' formal liberties without 'realizing' them. 'If this accomplishment [of a regime of mutual recognition] has become doubtful, it is indispensable to maintain the habits of discussion, criticism, research, and the instruments of political and social culture.' In practice this meant the defence of 'formal liberties' such as freedom of the press, habeas corpus, free discussion, and the like. At the same time one must guard against rhetorical excess and the use of libertarian slogans to cover the reality of liberal violence. 'True liberty ... takes others as they are, seeks to penetrate those very doctrines that negate liberty, and does not permit judgment to precede understanding.'[14] If the Moscow Trials, the Laval-Pétain trial, and the war against the Nazis were simply the murder of men, there would be no problem: but they were also the sacrifice of men for the preservation of certain specific hopes, truths, and, under some circumstances, homelands. The first thing to recall, therefore, was that violence may create a situation in which the only choices are bad ones.

In forming an opinion of the communists and the liberals, said Merleau-Ponty, the following points must be strictly observed. British and French imperialism was violent, police action against strikers was also violent, and if one excused them by the necessities of law and order the same argument would excuse Stalin. The communists could distinguish only adversaries, 'useful innocents,' and people under their command; they were so unused to debate, he said, they have no idea what an ally might be. 'In order to institute a genuine policy of union, it remains for them to understand one small fact: not everyone is a communist and, though there are many bad reasons for not being one, there are some that are not dishonourable.'[15] In the face of tacit agreement between communists and liberals to treat politics from the perspective of war and so render any unity impossible, 'one cannot be with either of the two present forces. We are called to choose between them. Our duty is to do nothing of the kind, but rather to demand, here and there, clarifications that are refused us, to explicate manoeuvres, and to dissipate myths.'[16]

Merleau-Ponty had no illusions that when men loved either the 'god of the East: or the god of the West' his own 'polytheism' would be either effective or popular. If the conclusion was that one cannot sacrifice formal liberties to Soviet society, did it matter how one arrived at the conclusion? Yes, he replied, because liberty was not exhausted by liberalism, and all evil did not adhere to the communists. If we habituate ourselves to see in communism only a menace to our life, we enter upon a struggle to the death, where all means are good; we enter myth, propaganda, and the game of violence. 'One reasons badly in these lugubrious perspectives. We must in good faith understand that these things can happen, and think like living men.'[17] Even so, perhaps it was already too late; perhaps men had become too accustomed to war and death. 'Many writers see themselves shot' by one side or the other. 'Our error, if it be one, has been to follow, pen in hand, a discussion begun a long time ago, with young friends, and to submit the result to every kind of fanatic ... They were simple, without reputations, without ambition, without a political past. One could talk with them ... Perhaps it will be allowed that they were individuals and knew what freedom was. Then it will not be surprising if, having to speak of communism, we try in mist and darkness to search for those faces gone from the earth.'[18] The experience of friendship and the memory of the sacrifice of friends were never far below the surface. If Merleau-Ponty had joined the men who knew clearly what was good and evil he would have betrayed those with whom he could speak. Even Bukharin could use irony to make the Soviet trials more than simply the mute and violent extermination of enemies.

We have seen that *Humanisme et Terreur* was motivated, among other things, by a desire to develop a Marxist interpretation of violence and to understand the practice of Soviet politics. It appeared to Merleau-Ponty that the three theoretical themes of Marxist politics, namely proletarian spontaneity, international proletarian solidarity, and proletarian control of the means of production, had in Soviet practice fallen apart. The important political question then became whether violence could force the restoration of the old political pattern. If no unequivocal reply could be found, what was to be said of the Soviet Union?[19] One thing at least was clear: 'we are not rid of communist problems by showing that contemporary communism is in difficulty because of them.' The criterion for Merleau-Ponty, as we saw earlier, was humanism, the recognition of man by man, as project if not yet as reality. Thus one could not invoke the actual problems of the Soviet Union as a practical refutation of Marxism.

Instead, Merleau-Ponty tried to see liberalism and communism as moving in the same direction. If one does not think that the power of the proletariat could be established, he said, or that, if established, it would do what Marxism expected it to do, then perhaps existing capitalist civilizations will appear to be less objectionable: 'Between them and the Soviet enterprise, the difference is not between heaven and hell or good and evil: it is only a matter of different uses of violence.'[20] Like liberalism, communism was an attempt to deal with 'the human problem,' not a pestilence.

The language Merleau-Ponty used here is worth noting. The common ground of liberalism and communism was a shared intention to find a 'solution to the human problem.' First of all, this problem-solving language is much less subtle than his earlier discussion of problematics. Second, compared with Marcel's notion of the mystery of humanity, which Merleau-Ponty endorsed before the war, this later position is shallow indeed. But the discussion remained severely practical on all sides. 'What to reply,' asked Merleau-Ponty, 'to an Indochinese or an Arab who makes us observe that he has surely seen our arms, but not our humanism? Who would dare to say that, after all, humanity has always progressed at the hands of a few and has always been lived by delegation, that we are that elite, and that the rest have only to wait. That would be the only frank reply.'[21] The implications of this frank reply which no one, including Merleau-Ponty, dared to make did not necessarily lead to the dead end of historical scepticism. But understanding western liberal imperialism and communism (or Marxist humanism) in terms of what they shared did mean abandoning one's faith in progress. Merleau-Ponty did not resist the heavily ideologized climate of opinion in pondering the questions he raised, but he did refuse to adhere unconditionally to one side or the other even while praising their common goal. This mild resistance to joining the partisan struggle, though it did not penetrate to the heart of the common modern ideology, was sufficiently attuned to common experience and common sense to scandalize his critics, who felt more comfortable with the simple and deadly clarities of war.

PROBLEMS OF COMMUNISM

We noted above in passing that according to Merleau-Ponty classical Marxism harmonized three analytically distinct themes: international proletarian solidarity, proletarian spontaneity, and proletarian control of the means of production. The first of these was most clearly no longer in existence. Indeed, it had ended with the disintegration of the Second International during the first world war. Lenin's response to this crisis, in his polemic with Kautsky, was to refuse to recognize the scope of the blow to proletarian internationalism and to retreat to the thesis of a saving remnant under whose direction all would be changed. Merleau-Ponty sided firmly with Kautsky. The German occupation had taught him the importance of nationality. During the war he had contrasted the terrible but lived reality of war experienced by the Russians and the British with the abstract threat the French suffered: 'we cannot *think* of war because we do not *make* war ... France does not await its self-deliverance.' The British, the Russians, and the Americans each had a purpose and a vision of what the post-war world might be like, but 'we are unable to preview our destiny, and even less, it seems, to make it.' Instead, 'we prefer to be assured that we will find our place among the great powers intact at the end of the conflict. But how can we think so? A place is not to be found again, it is to be taken. Even if, *per impossibile*, the Allies have kept it warm for us, we would not be able to hold it.' France would no longer be a great power. And yet, 'a second rank nation can still be a great nation provided it safeguards its freedom.' France could retain its independence as long as it conceived of itself as something more than 'a group of inert men inhabiting a bit of the earth,' as long as it was 'presented as a particular way of looking at present problems, as a unique effort at resolving them.' But the independence of France meant the rejection of 'two ready-made solutions: the return to pre-war capitalist democracy or the installation of state socialism in the Soviet mould. Persuaded, in effect, that our liberators carry the regime of their own choice with them, four years of occupation have given us a kind of laziness and fatalism. One often hears it said, with resignation, that if the Americans win, they will re-establish the Third Republic, and if the Russians are victors, they will Bolshevize us.'[22] Neither 'ready-made solution' would be acceptable to the men of the Resistance or to 'the great majority of Frenchmen.'

In *Humanisme et Terreur* the same theme was stressed: should the Russians and the Americans go to war they would not lack the necessary certainties to justify their endeavours. 'But the middle powers could not share in these certainties. There is no future in it for them and there will only be clarity in history through peace. The middle powers cannot be anything great, and their intellectuals matter even less. *Our role is perhaps not very important. But we must not abandon it.*'[23] In carrying out his role Merleau-Ponty developed a 'provisional political strategy' that contained the following three points. First, any discussion of Soviet and Western politics must consider all the circumstances involved; anything less was propaganda and evidence of an attitude of war. Second, humanism, even the formal humanism proclaimed by liberals, must exclude a preventive war against the Soviet Union. Third, we must remember that there has been neither a declaration of war between East and West nor Soviet aggression. Merleau-Ponty's three points appeared to be sensible enough, but a close inspection of the implications he drew shows the limitations in his thinking.

Anyone could see that the tendency of Western countries to resort to violence, as well as the economic backwardness of the Soviet Union and the devastation it had suffered at the hands of Germany were not mere propaganda. Furthermore, a selective reading of events could be propaganda for either side. If by mid-1947, when *Humanisme et Terreur* was completed, Merleau-Ponty still felt unqualified to judge Stalinism, to keep silent on such practical matters as a 'provisional strategy' would have been better. He must have been severely infected with what one political scientist has called 'Webbism' to have written, for example (at least with respect to the USSR), that 'in the Soviet Union, violence and deception are official, while humanity is in daily life; in the democracies on the other hand principles are humane, while deception and violence are found in practice.' In the same vein he wrote: 'The death of Socrates and the Dreyfus affair left intact the "humanist" reputation of Athens and France. There are no reasons for applying other criteria to the USSR.'[24] At the very least one would have thought that the difference in social scale between the vast purge trials of the Soviet Union and the trials of two men, Dreyfus and Socrates, would have had something to do with a 'reputation for humanism.'

The second principle, the exclusion of preventive war, was not based on the argument that the West had no business attacking the rest of the world or that aggression was in itself unjust and corrupting. On one hand was the perfectly legitimate fear of the kind of a regime Americans, who found 'reds' in the New Deal, might impose upon France, whose working-class population consistently elected a large contingent of Communist deputies. On the other hand was a not-so-reasonable assumption that the right-wing Republicans would attain victory in 1948 and immediately launch a drive to exterminate 'the principle of a socialist economy.' Merleau-Ponty seemed to assume that Americans were in fact willing to act on the basis of the ideology of a minority within a minority party. Again, this may have been an innocent misreading of events, but it nevertheless reinforced his first principle equating propaganda and war.

The third principle was more an empirical fact: Europe had been divided by agreement of the Allied belligerents. After the defeat of Germany, the Western members were reluctant to accept what they had agreed to under more strenuous circumstances. It may be true that Soviet aggression had been restrained out of weakness, Merleau-Ponty said, but concern with Soviet motives was a separate matter from understanding Soviet actions. If circumstances changed and the USSR grew stronger and threatened to invade Western Europe different principles would be needed. If one were forced to choose between the god of the East and the god of the West, polytheism would be absurd; until then, however, especially for a Frenchman, it would still be possible to retain an awareness of other options.

One may conclude that the first element of classical Marxism, international proletarian solidarity, was gone. Frenchmen, whether proletarian or not, had their own interests, which were allied to the ideals but not to the practice of Western humanism and to the socialist economy but not to the violence of the Soviet Union. Their interests were in humanism, and the pragmatic problem, as Merleau-Ponty saw it in 1947, was that it was impossible 'to commit oneself in confusion and outside of truth,' but the truth was that the world was dislocated. And yet, he concluded, this same dislocation was an opportunity, because the very assertion that humanism did not (yet) exist was itself an invitation to bring it into existence; it 'opens us to the other person.'[25]

Proletarian spontaneity had also suffered setbacks. As early as August 1945, Merleau-Ponty had noted that the retreat by the Soviet Union from the humanist politics Marx taught was complemented by the 'diversification' of the class struggle.[26] A few months later he spoke of how the class struggle was hidden, that 'other oppositions,' mainly nationalist oppositions based on the memory of war, had intervened between bourgeoisie and proletariat, and that one could only wait for events to unfold, without endowing them with the illustory meaning of proletarian action.[27] As in his concluding reflections to *Humanisme et Terreur*, the disintegration of the historical dialectic was an opportunity for action. It was 'even probable' that after a war the class struggle should reappear: 'We do not say that the class struggle will never again play an essential role in world history. We know nothing of that. Events, for example the American crisis, can bring it rapidly back to the forefront.'[28] In the absence of a crisis in the Anglo-Saxon countries, one ought frankly recognize that events were confused and followed no direction, that by default Anglo-Saxon power was in a position to crush any attempted proletarian revolution in France.

By 1947 it was becoming clear to Merleau-Ponty that the ideological confusion of French Communists and their forgetfulness of the humanist roots of their own actions was being translated into a policy that fragmented the fragile coalition emergent from the Resistance, a coalition that might have been able to sustain polytheism. The tripartite government of Communists, Socialists, and Christian Democrats that came to power after the Liberation and had earlier provoked his scornful comments about the degeneration and sterility of French political ideas had by 1947 become a firmly established political reality.

The Communists, whose control over the national trade union federation, Confédération Générale du Travail (CGT), was firm although not undisputed, used the unions in a bewildering series of tactical shifts. One day the Communist Party newspaper, L'Humanité, would denounce the 'Hitlerite-Trotskyist' agents provocateurs for counselling strikes; the next day it would demand 'direction action' and threaten to fill the streets with militant workers. By 1946, opposition to the Communists within the CGT was gaining ground, and a series of 'unofficial' strikes erupted, strikes that were almost welcomed by the bourgeoisie as showing the lack of Party control over the unions. Moreover, workers' demands for money wage increases could be financed through inflation. The 1946 strike of postal, telephone, and telegraph workers was denounced by the Party as being led by collaborators and reactionaries. Its obvious success, however, was a signal for further strikes by government workers, and cracks began to appear in the CGT monolith. In February 1946 an 'unofficial' printers' strike left Paris without newspapers, and Party strikebreakers engaged in pitched battles with striking workers in the offices of L'Humanité itself. By spring, the power of the CGT was on the downswing: CGT candidates lost in elections to union councils and were unable to control the thirty thousand workers at Billancourt who stopped work at the giant Renault factory. The Party, in an attempt to regain control over the 'anarchically' inclined workers, resigned from the Government, reversed its policy of 'Stakhanovite discipline,' and began to fight for higher wages.

At best the new Party line made a virtue of necessity. Following local elections in the fall of 1947, France appeared to be split along the lines dictated by the strategy of the Cominform: the 'party of peace' was face to face with the Gaullist 'party of war.' In the National Assembly Blum's attempt for a 'third force' between communism and 'Caesarism' fell flat, and Schumann formed the government, which Gaullists and their sympathizers in the Assembly thought would preside over the dissolution of the Fourth Republic. But Schumann and his cabinet of technocrats stood firm. Jules Moch in particular rendered singular service to the 'forces of order' by the formation of the Compagnies Républicaines de Securité (CRS), which took on a major police role when it was obvious that the regular police were riddled with Communist and Gaullist 'cells' and hence unreliable. Order was guaranteed by Moch and his CRS, and René Mayer, the finance minister, with a drastic economic policy beat the French economy into a condition where Marshall Aid could be effective.

After the CRS had been organized and French economic recovery had begun, the Party used the CGT to implement a general strike. By no stretch of the imagination could the winter of 1947-8 be called a 'revolutionary situation.' If Schumann's government were to be overthrown by violence, the victors would be on the right, not the left. What the Party succeeded in doing was to deprive itself of all chance of gaining power, whether legally or illegally. On 12 November 1947, the Party issued a 'manifesto to the working class of France,' and the same day their carefully orchestrated plans went awry as trade unionists in Marseilles rioted against a Gaullist city council that had increased tram fares. On 17 November the coal mines shut down, and Billancourt again ceased production. On 19 November a general strike was called with no warning or prior negotiation with the employers. The Palais Bourbon and *L'Humanité* were again the vehicles of communist histrionics, but to no avail: the CRS and the army began to clear the factories, and by mid-December the strike was over. The CGT had been split, and the Force Ouvrière, long smouldering within the CGT, was born. The utter defeat in the 1948 coal strike showed that the power of the CGT had been broken. Four years later, the spasmodic 'action day' that was to greet General Ridgeway as the new NATO commander was a failure. Henceforth the French Communist Party could be counted among the forces of stability rather than of revolution, despite the perennial election appeals of the centre and right. In this context must be understood Merleau-Ponty's remarks on the 'dubious combat' that the Party invited.

The Communists, he began, said the strikes were not political, as if a general strike, which combined all the work in the country into a single action, was not by itself political. The government said they wished only to prohibit the political exploitation of the strikes, as if trade unions could be maintained in the absence of an ability to strike. Whatever the intentions of the strikers, the general strike was political, and whatever the intention of the government, repression of the strike was social and economic. Of itself, he went on, the general strike had always been a major weapon in the arsenal of the working class: 'Those who attribute themselves rights over the world, who believe themselves born to be masters, suddenly find themselves helpless and learn that their rights fall to dust if others do not consent to them ... For once, it is no longer princes, ministers, comedians and writers who are on the front page, but miners, metalworkers, glass workers, and electrical workers. It is necessary to please men who have never sensed this greatness.'[29] But an understanding of the general strike as a version of Hegel's dialectic of master and slave was not enough. However 'sacred' it may be, a strike never occurs in isolation but is deeply embedded in the tissue of pragmatic events.

The 1947 strike ended in disaster for the strikers. It was foolishly undertaken, thought Merleau-Ponty, and the foolishness stemmed directly from confusion and ineptness of the Communist Party.

L'Humanité for some time declared that the choice was between freedom and fascism, but, because it attacked all other coalitions or positions without exception, what they wished to say plainly was that one must be a fascist or a Communist. To use such language at the moment when the elections attested to popular belief in the [Gaullist] RPF and to the relative decline of communism, is precisely to push all the undecided non-communists toward the RPF. An adventurist politics in a period of change and flux is a provocation. To declare war on the 'American party,' which 70 per cent of the citizens, in their confusion, support, is to call down repression upon oneself. To give the order for the general strike when it is known (some say for as long as three years) that an attempt at revolution will be broken, by foreign intervention if necessary, is to exhaust the working class instead of defending it. To say, 'we will be masters or we will be nothing,' at the moment when the battlefield is lost, is to choose the political annihilation of the working class along with that of the Communist Party.[30]

The Communists' actions in 1947, he concluded, were simply a continuation of the stupidities and lack of courage so evident in the period immediately following the Liberation. 'Lacking principles and lacking clarity, it prepared itself to lose on the field of class struggle after having lost on the field of coalition politics.' He ended his lament for the decline of proletarian action with a question: 'In the middle powers of Europe, is there room for anything besides the skirmishes of Great Armies?'

Early in 1948 Merleau-Ponty used the occasion of the re-publication of his essays in *Sens et Non-sens* to draw attention to mistaken hopes he had entertained at the time they were written. 'Just after the war,' he wrote, 'one could hope that the spirit of Marxism was going to reappear, that the movement of the American masses was going to carry on the Russian revolution.' But America turned to 'Red-hunting,' and the Soviet Union accepted the division of the world into two camps as inevitable, embraced military solutions, and placed no hope at all in a restoration of proletarian action, 'especially when it risks national proletariats in sacrificial missions.'[31] In a note to 'Pour la Verité' he repeated the theme:

It used to be possible to imagine (and necessary to hasten, through friendly discussion with Communists) the formation of free and innovative social structures in Western Europe, which would have spared Europe the alternative of 'peoples' democracy' or reactionary politics, of Stalinist politics or an anti-Soviet Crusade. Since then, while the West was cranking up its war machine, the USSR returned to pessimism, pure authority, and compulsion, placing the non-communist left, under pain of being mystified, under the necessity of saying clearly why it was not communist but would not in any circumstances play the role of liberal apologist for the system. This does not mean that, at the time and within the framework of possibilities of the day, the attitude expressed here was not justified as one that had a chance at saving both socialism and freedom.[32]

Later that year in an editorial note to an article by his Trotskyite friend, Claude Lefort, Merleau-Ponty registered, for the last time, his faith in the practicality of a middle position. For Lefort, he said, 'the USSR is *accused*. For us, with its greatness and its horrors, it is an enterprise that has had a breakdown. It is necessary to say if one is a communist or not, and we say no. But the prosecutor's tone appears to us to be misplaced in a world that nowhere is innocent and nowhere appears to be governed by an immanent rationality.'[33]

All that remained of classical Marxism was proletarian control of the means of production. That prop was not called into doubt until the scandal of the labour camps broke, and even the Soviet camps could not dislodge the critical importance of Marxism. Humanism therefore became for Merleau-Ponty a standard by which a critical appraisal of both East and West could be undertaken, and was used in this way by him until the outbreak of war in Korea, after which he felt further talk to be in vain.

FRENCH AND INTERNATIONAL POLITICS

A similar evolution of Merleau-Ponty's political thinking occurred in the domain of French foreign policy and in the international activity of the United States. The traditional date marking the onset of the cold war was 2 July 1947, the day the Soviet Union walked away from Marshall Aid. In France, division of the country into pro-American and pro-Soviet factions had begun in earnest a full seven months earlier, in December 1946, over Indochina, when the returning French army clashed with the Viet Minh. The initiative for hostilities on this occasion came from the pro-American side, not to say from the Americans themselves. In an editorial hastily inserted while the December issue of *Les Temps modernes* was in press, Merleau-Ponty wrote his first impressions of a crisis that remained unresolved for another quarter-century. Faced with censored news and a style of newspaper reporting whose common feature was 'the sadistic taste for sensational information,' he said, one could only reply with indignation. Frenchmen were both 'hangmen and victims,' and this was bad enough. What was worse was that 'the militarists of 1940 ... still try to gratify their rage at no longer being as powerful as before by fighting the Indochinese.' The argument that the war was defensive was clearly spurious: 'To remain in Indochina by force of arms would be ignominious of itself; to remain there because we have, in our own degeneration, found them in the end weaker than us, would be the worst kind of mockery.' It was 'the most ignoble war of all, for it is thoroughly impossible to justify by anything other than nationalism: it is a colonial war.' Lack of information should not be used as a pretext for not taking a stand on principle. 'It is unimaginable that after four years of occupation, the French did not recognize the face which is today their own in Indochina; it is astounding that in reading the newspapers, which speak of cowardly thugs killing our soldiers, they did not recognize a style that was familiar to them.' In Indochina 'we are Germans.' Consequently, the militarists had no right, in order to justify shameful deeds that sent Frenchmen to death, to invoke the memory of other Frenchmen who had died in the Resistance. 'We do not deceive ourselves about the strength of this protest,' he concluded: 'by formulating an impotent indignation, we no longer hope, as they say, to get out of a scrape. We will repeat it as much as is necessary and we will say, as soon as possible, all that must be said, all that can be said. To those elsewhere, who would reproach us with an exasperated moralism, we must reply that we still prefer this attitude to an opportunism fully in the service of interests that are clear enough.'[34]

Reproach came quickly, but not in the form he anticipated. In *Le Figaro* François Mauriac wrote a front-page criticism. He complained not about the expression of dissent, for he too thought the policy 'stupid,' but about the attribution of vengeful motives to French generals. 'But there is worse. Our philosopher dared to write that he saw no difference between the French in Indochina and the Germans in France.' Such assimilations would be understandable only if they come from an enemy: 'one need not be a philosopher to see at a glance the essential difference between the French presence in Asia, which dates back more than half a century and which has been the manifestation of a beneficent civilization, and the organized extortion of Europe by Germany.' Of course there was no question of defending nineteenth-century imperialism, but France had an obligation to continue the 'partnership' founded with the Indochinese; anything else would constitute a betrayal of French history. There were in addition, Mauriac said, two other questions all Frenchmen must answer: if France were to leave Indochina, would not the Viet Minh take over? And was it not true that what happened in Indochina would influence the destiny of 'the whole of overseas France?' To counsel withdrawal, he concluded, was to repeat the mistake of the sincere collaborators who thought France was 'finished,' and 'that its destiny was closed as an independent and sovereign nation charged with a mission of education for the lesser people (*les petites*). It is up to us to discover new bases of co-operation and understanding with those to whom we have been united for half a century of History, before it is too late.'[35]

Merleau-Ponty's reply to Mauriac came in an introduction to the series of articles on Indochina promised in the December editorial.[36] He summarized his earlier remarks and allowed that it was incomplete for having gone beyond an expression of moral outrage to define a policy. The one pragmatic observation that even censorship could not deny was that France in Indochina is a poorly tolerated occupying authority. What Mauriac and numerous other Frenchmen seemed to have forgotten was the meaning that 'great "ideas" ' had for the oppressed. 'But the war is over, the Germans have gone, and everything has returned to order. We are in power now, so it can only be honourable.' Such an attitude was nothing if not that of nineteenth-century imperialism: it could justify any violence and viciousness that colonialists and the French army imposed upon the Vietnamese in the name of abstract principles such as the famous *mission civilisatrice*. Perhaps it was to be expected that cynics and politicians should partake of the corruption of power, 'but what to say to those beautiful souls who are associated with it without having the courage to call Terror terror? Our times have this incomparable advantage over others for having given the public a glance behind the scenes of history and brought to light some of its more gross deceptions. It is up to us to defend this privilege.'[37]

Mauriac was a Catholic of the left, and in Merleau-Ponty's view he had been lucid on other occasions. 'What has happened to him, then?' The answer was found in a parenthetical comment: 'Is it or is it not true,' Mauriac asked, 'that another power (the same whose spirit animates the Viet Minh) would substitute itself for a faltering France?' 'There we have it,' Merleau-Ponty commented, no need for any further analysis of French policy, of Soviet policy, or of the actual spirit of the Viet Minh. 'It suffices for Ho Chi Minh to be communist and for François Mauriac to understand. Nothing but a tentacle of the USSR is there.' Mauriac had been infected with the virus of nominalism: so long as you knew what to call your enemy, the old conservatism that dispensed its disapproval upon all things communist had no need to question events. Mauriac could once judge the powerful when French patriotism opposed them in the name of humanity, he continued, but it has always been difficult to distinguish the legal and the just: 'Let us forget these horrors, he thinks. Do not reopen old wounds. What offends him is not the Indochinese affair but the dishonour of Vichy. Blood may well flow out there the moment our own wounds are closed.'[38] If such a decline in thinking had overtaken a man such as Mauriac, what was to be hoped for the many who feed upon myths?

Shortly after the polemic with Mauriac, Merleau-Ponty was again embroiled, along with Sartre and even Aron, Benda, and Camus, with communist intellectuals, though not this time over matters of foreign policy. The Comité nationale des Ecrivains, with Henri Lefebvre at the head, had posthumously accused Paul

Nizan of having been a traitor. Nizan had quit the Party in 1939 over the Hitler-Stalin pact, and everyone could decide for themselves, said his defenders, whether such action was treason. But Lefebvre had implied that even before 1939 Nizan had been in the pay of anti-communist police agents, which was more serious. Prove it, they said, and if we receive no satisfaction silence would confirm Nizan's innocence.[39] There was no reply, and the incident passed. It illustrated once again the difficulties that Merleau-Ponty's attempt to steer a middle road encountered. As Sartre said, the Communists did not believe in damnation, they believed in nothingness. 'The annihilation of comrade Nizan was decided. He had already been hit with a dum-dum bullet, in the back of the neck, among other places, but this liquidation satisfied nobody; it was not enough that he had ceased to live; he must never have existed at all.'[40] Some of Merleau-Ponty's darkest fears, it seemed, were coming true.[41]

Not all his activities before the Korean war were so bitter or so grim. In October 1947, Merleau-Ponty, Sartre, Simone de Beauvoir, along with two friends of Sartre and Merleau-Ponty, Pontalis and Bonafé, and Chauffard, a comedian, appeared on the 'Programme Parisien' of the French radio network. The *'Temps modernes* team,' as they were called, were scheduled to broadcast three discussions of current political affairs. They were sent off the air by Maurice Schumann, however, after only two broadcasts. The second one, on 27 October, was billed as a discussion of anti-communism, and consisted of attacks on the Communists and the Socialists for betraying the interests of the workers, criticism of their lack of revolutionary élan, and so on. It was the first broadcast, on Gaullism, that had caused the scandal and, after due bureaucratic delay, led to their being silenced.

In that first broadcast Sartre had begun by noting that nearly a third of the electorate had not voted in the recent elections, and he found in this a good sign. The Gaullist reply, read by Chauffard, was that 'France is a miraculous country; every time it teeters on the abyss, a man of providence emerges to save it.'

SARTRE: We have already had a man of providence, I forget quite when ...
CHAUFFARD [in imitation of Pétain]: The number one man of providence was Pétain; the number two is De Gaulle. Both are good Catholics; both are brilliant orators; both maintain the principle of sovereignty ...
SARTRE: They don't intend war, do they?
CHAUFFARD: Don't tell me you think the marshall would double-cross us!
SARTRE: But you called De Gaulle a traitor yourself, in 1942.
CHAUFFARD: Only because I double-crossed myself!

Chauffard went on to say that De Gaulle knew Stalin would declare war on Christmas Day, that the Americans would pull out the day after, and the Asiatic hordes would soon be bathing in the fountains of the Tuileries.

SARTRE: Then it's too late to join the RPF?

CHAUFFARD: Oh no! If the General takes power, he will stop the Russians.

SARTRE: But how?

CHAUFFARD [in imitation of De Gaulle]: With the French Army, of course! ... No Frenchman has the right to refuse. Above all and especially you intellectuals who are always talking about committing yourselves. An no! This is not a matter of literature; the time is at hand and we must seize it by the hair!

After this banter, doubly annoying to loyal Gaullists for being spoken by such a well-known buffoon as Chauffard, the discussion grew more serious. Sartre gave a lengthy speech deploring Gaullist propaganda that assumed war to be inevitable. The more often such fatalist propaganda was repeated, the more confused people would become, and the more likely they would be to believe it. When enough people believed war to be inevitable it would actually become so, and when it did the fatalists could say they were right. 'In other words, you would be right at the price of being wrong.' Merleau-Ponty continued where Sartre left off, and pointed to a speech that De Gaulle had recently delivered which presented only the familiar two alternatives: 'I wonder if the United States would be very thankful to General De Gaulle for offering them a military alliance they need not at all. I wonder above all if a French nationalist can seriously imagine as a possible policy one that includes war.' The chief problem now, it seemed, was to avoid those fatalist attitudes that turned a possible war into a real one.

De Gaulle sought to bridge the growing abyss between the Soviet Union and the United States with his notion of a Third Force. Earlier Merleau-Ponty had spoken of an intermediate way that a middle power might take. If Merleau-Ponty ever meant what De Gaulle did, it was clear that by 1947 he rejected the measures De Gaulle proposed. 'This Third Force,' he said,

would, I suppose, unite an appreciable number of men, but it would also unite only worn-out countries, only exhausted countries that lack the war potential of the other two. In the end, all Third Force policies in this sense are fantasies. What must be done is quite different. A real French policy consists not in choosing one of the two blocs and even less in trying to create in a perfectly artificial way a third one equal to the other two. A French policy consists in appealing to whatever forces hostile to the policy of war and the policy of blocs there may be within the two great countries concerned ... It is necessary to appeal, I would say, to all forces within the US and even within France that could weigh against war and against the crystallization of blocs.

In order to prevent this crystallization three things, none of which seemed likely, would have had to occur: a more profound political understanding in the

USSR as well as the USA and France would have to develop; communism must be treated in less summary terms than is done at present; 'and perhaps also a generosity of character must replace the dominant attitude of the present, which is one of contempt.'[42]

Merleau-Ponty found some reasons for hope in the gradual dissolution of blocs in Marshall Aid. In June 1947 the American secretary of State, George Marshall, announced his plan to bring 'order' to the chaotic economic and social situation in Europe. But actions, precisely because they introduce something new, are always unpredictable. We know today that some of the architects of the Marshall Plan hoped to use it to facilitate the penetration of American-based multinational enterprises into Europe and to a degree were successful. But other factors were also responsible for *le défi americain*, and other intentions lay behind American aid.

It is understandable that Merleau-Ponty read events as he did in 1948. His article was an editorial introduction to an analysis of Marshall Plan by Pierre Uri.[43] Again Merleau-Ponty denounced 'the confidence of sleepwalkers' who refused to recognize opportunity and saw only fate. Such confidence was particularly inapposite regarding the Marshall Plan. It was impossible to find a single meaning to it because it was not the consequence of a single intention but 'the confluent result of both economic conditions and human volition ... In the circumstances themselves, there is no effective essence to the Plan that destines it for war rather than peace.' Specifically, Marshall Aid was incomprehensible in terms of both the Leninist notion of imperialism and the free trade doctrines of liberalism: 'We must confront a situation wherein classical concepts leave us helpless.' The United States was trying to re-establish trade links with Europe so as to improve its own ability to export, but the effects would also restore the ravaged European economies and thereby eventually undermine the Americans' privileged financial position. 'Imperialism with its rivalries was not, therefore, the final stage of capitalism. The phase when the history of capitalism can no longer be written in the plural comes next.' In place of national exclusiveness was to be found something like an international community.' The Marshall Plan is beyond generosity and avarice, it expresses a situation where our juridical and moral superstructure is inapplicable.' One could see, in outline at least, suggestions by Merleau-Ponty that the economic basis of humanism, namely an integrated world economy though not its ideological superstructure, was being restored. These hints explain the otherwise curious remark in the preface to *Sens et Non-sens*, quoted above, that 'the American masses were going to continue the Russian revolution.' The importance of ideology, or consciousness, or superstructure was not to be minimized, however, which was why Merleau-Ponty fought so tenaciously against the simplifying psychology of blocs, and why most of his analysis of the Marshall Plan was an ideological critique.

Because the United States had not sought to create a colonial empire in Europe, conservatives had attacked the Plan as the last gasp of the New Deal. Yet the Plan did establish an *imperium*, he said. Countries that accept annual aid could only with difficulty neglect the advice of the State Department. In Congress the internationalist flavour of the Plan was diluted with heavy injections of Americanism and anti-Soviet measures. Moreover, the Plan was passed with a rider that extended military credits to Greece, Turkey, and China. Soviet non-participation, Merleau-Ponty said, was almost inevitable: 'If Russia accepted, it meant the necessity of declaring that by itself it could do nothing, and of renouncing its zone of influence.' The Marshall Plan was ambiguous not only because of Congressional amendments to an otherwise internationalist document, and not only because of the shattering of classical Marxist politics. In addition, Lenin's formula of imperialism as the highest stage of capitalism did not apply. The very intention to make the Plan a universal instrument, which justified the United States in liberal eyes and formally decided the question in favour of the Americans, was in fact a reason for Russia, reconstructing in the midst of poverty and with nothing to contribute, to reject it.

In order to break the deadlock of tension, more than clarity about ideological factors was needed. A real detente could be attained, he said, with a genuine socialist policy. 'In America as in Western Europe it would make American aid the business of the proletariat. It would engage the battle not against American aid but against the imperialist use of this aid; it would seize upon an opportunity for socialism at this moment when classical capitalism has recourse to means that go beyond it. It would be a difficult, dialectical policy, a matter of breaking the shell without crushing the kernel within. But it is also an optimistic and convincing policy, and in the end the only one that gives us hope.' European workers need not thank generous American capitalists but their fellow workers in America; the political representatives of Europe's working class, therefore, were charged with the task of preventing capitalist blackmail on the pretext of American generosity. Likewise, they were obliged to reject the Soviet simplification, which saw only tricks and manoeuvres. 'If, in one way or another – and first in Western Europe, since the maximum political consciousness is found there – a regrouping is not made in order to accept the aid by combating the imperialist sabotage, by defending the progressive direction and explicating the objective complicity of the Truman policy with the policy of the Kremlin, then the American aid *will have been* only an element of the Truman policy, the popular movements but an element of Soviet power, and the world will find itself, once again after the American initiative, yet a little closer to war.'

To understand Merleau-Ponty's attitude from the 'optimistic' or perhaps naïve days when he could write that the summary of the policy he advocated was that of the Communists[44] through the ever more circumspect distinctions between his own position and that of the Party, we must recall that a wait-and-see attitude, *la politique d'attente* as he called it, could not last forever. It is true that he joined with Sartre, Rousset, and Rosenthal in the spring of 1948 in the Rassemblement Democratique Révolutionnaire, but, as Sartre has said, probably less out of conviction, for he never attended meetings of the executive although he was a member, than out of an unwillingness to repudiate his friend.[45] It is obvious enough in retrospect, and Merleau-Ponty probably knew at the time, that practical action by way of institutions such as the RDR was unlikely to succeed.

Merleau-Ponty's article on the Marshall Plan, which advocated a 'genuine socialist policy,' was the high point of his hope for practical co-operation between East and West and the last of his policy recommendations until the mid-1950s. Henceforth his writing was concerned with explication and critique, the tireless repetition of his convictions that history had not yet been written and that war was not inevitable. Indeed, Merleau-Ponty ended his analysis of 'objective complicity' with a reaffirmation of the principles first articulated in 1945. 'In the west,' he said,

we must act from the perspective of peace and search for the means of free coexistence with the USSR. As long as the USSR does not show that it wants war, we maintain that it is necessary to take the Soviet view into consideration with respect to each problem, to ask if, and under what conditions, the Marshall Plan is acceptable to the Soviet Union, to see the communism of today in the evolution that, piece by piece, has produced it, and, in a word, to try and understand the Soviet Union and observe towards it a challenging posture, which is not that of war. But the USSR will continue to be the devil if the USA plays the role of God. Thus, we must speak of racism or of American proto-fascism. Progress will be made if the Europeans and the others are able to understand and admit that there is nothing sacred in the political apparatus of today, nothing that merits being blindly followed or blindly hated. Let us keep to the rule we set down in the first issue of this review: 'We have to hide no truth if we tell all the others.' Let us refuse the [presented] alternative, and work to move beyond.[46]

The quotation from the first issue of *Les Temps modernes* was intended, no doubt, to suggest continuity. In earlier days he could decide neither for the USSR nor for the USA, although for practical purposes he followed the policy of the communists. In 1945 he did not choose because he was ignorant of both sides; in 1948, knowing what realities they represented, he could choose neither. The proletarian movement, he said, had decayed into violent and sordid national societies. American workers saw themselves as Americans; Russian workers were victims of their own dictatorship, a state apparatus 'heavier and more imperious than any other.'[47]

From the summer of 1948 to the winter of 1949 Merleau-Ponty was silent about politics. These were the days when the Palais Bourbon was the scene of fortnightly crises and when the lofty figure of De Gaulle was promising to 'pick the Republic out of the mud' once again. Perhaps disgust with this unedifying spectacle lay behind Merleau-Ponty's silence; perhaps he was simply too busy editing *Les Temps modernes.*[48]

In any event, it was not until December 1949 that Merleau-Ponty published anything political, a prefatory note to a study of Georg Lukács.[49] What he said of Lukács was uncomplimentary. The issue, broadly speaking, was a Marxist understanding of the relationship between cultural enterprises and society. Merleau-Ponty quoted Marx's words on the 'eternal charm' of Greek art, and concluded that Marx at least 'recognized a domain of art (and no doubt of literature) where anticipations or even "eternal" acquisitions were possible.'[50] Such 'optimistic communism' was absent from the contemporary world, which behaved as if there were no longer any intrinsic criteria in matters of culture, as if literature and science were merely one means among others of immediate political action, itself understood simply as the defence of the USSR.[51] With these prefatory remarks, Merleau-Ponty turned to Lukács's 'auto-criticism.'

In 1946 Lukács had once again repudiated his earlier work in terms of a fundamentally sound principle, that a writer may always go beyond what he had previously written. Of course, Merleau-Ponty said, one may doubt that Lukács's subsequent writings show he has matured since the days of *History and Class Consciousness*, but at least the theory was sound. In 1949, however, even the theory was jettisoned: there could be no eternal charm in anything save the home of the Revolution. Defence of the USSR was as pressing in the field of the novel as in that of diplomacy; it was not a revolutionary duty, it was the *only* one: 'The rest is westernism.' In 1946 Lukács's autocritique, however judged, had at least in principle affirmed the value of culture; in 1949, it was the negation of culture. Just as there was a difference between Bukharin, who accepted responsibility for his opposition but denied he was a spy, and Rajik, who, contrary to all that was known about him, confessed to being an American agent as well, so Lukács was required to make a fool of himself and declare his esteem for Goethe and Tolstoy to have been a hasty blunder. 'Thus does communism pass from historical responsibility to naked discipline from autocriticism to repudiation, from Marxism to superstition.'[52]

THE SOVIET CAMPS

By October 1949 the RDR was officially dead. A month later *Le Figaro Littéraire* published an enormous headline: 'An Appeal to those Deported to Nazi Camps: Help those Deported to Soviet Camps.' Merleau-Ponty's former comrade from the RDR, David Rousset, had given the alarm.[53] The right-wing press made a great deal of propaganda from the news, going so far as to employ old Nazi photographs with captions identifying the trains and the camps as Soviet. They could, moreover, breathe a sigh of relief: the colonial massacres, the Indochina war, the Algerian poverty, and the prisons of Greece and Spain were all justified by the Soviet camps. In January 1950 Merleau-Ponty wrote an editorial that tried to place the camps in some kind of perspective.[54]

He began by quoting the Russian 'Code of Corrective Labour,' which established the legal basis for deportation without trial and the administrative independence of the NKVD. He said there were probably millions of people in the camps, most estimates falling between ten and fifteen million. With these facts, it was time to look at the USSR in a new light. 'What we are saying is that there is no socialism when one citizen in twenty is in a camp.'[55] One could not explain this anomaly by an appeal to the comfortable notion that every revolution has its traitors or that industrialization was impossible without violence; such alibis were invalid when so many people were involved a generation after the revolution. There was, he said, something within the Soviet system that created opposition, with the result that the forces of repression, rather than having been absorbed by the system, were on the contrary made independent of it. The real problem was to discover why this was so. Merleau-Ponty recalled that two years earlier he had written that the Soviet system was an ambiguous enterprise, that he had found signs of progress and signs of regression; by 1950, quantity had changed into quality and the whole system had altered its meaning.

Merleau-Ponty dismissed the argument that Soviet party members, like the Nazis, were 'neurotic,' for there was no 'religion of death' as in the extermination camps. Nor was it simply a question of bureaucratic interest, for naked interest would never have clothed itself with convictions, and the Soviet law had been public since 1936. Rather, he said, it appears probable that the evolution that led from October 1917 to ten million slaves and, beneath the permanence of forms or of words, little by little changed the meaning of the system took place by degrees, without deliberate intention, from crisis to crisis, from expedient to expedient. 'Its social significance was beyond the control of its creators: faced with the ever more painful alternatives of aggravating [the direction of events that led to the camps] or of disappearing politically, they continued without understanding that the enterprise changed beneath their hands.'[56] Merleau-Ponty did not entirely absolve Stalin and his followers from the charge of being 'neurotic bureaucrats,' although he did not reflect deeply on some of the implications he drew. 'The survivors of 1917,' he said, rather than name Stalin outright, 'are not the best minds of Marxist humanism.' Like Koestler's Gletkin, human feelings and human beings counted hardly at all: 'Undoubtedly the best communists are deaf to ten million prisoners.'[57]

Not considered was what Camus later called 'logical murder.' Merleau-Ponty stuck to his principle that the 'difficulties' of the Soviet Union could not be adduced as evidence for the untruth of Marxism. Marxism belonged to the second reality of Merleau-Ponty's ideological imagination, whereas the camps existed in the first reality of real life. Nevertheless the humanist ideal in Marxism ought to have been present in embryo even in Stalin's regime. To reflect upon the possibility that somehow or other the camps were the logical outcome of Marx's teaching meant abandoning the standard of mutual recognition and humanism, and that was something Merleau-Ponty was not prepared to do. And so, for example, having noted the deformation of Stalinist Russia, he proceeded to accept at face value the Soviet statement that the institutions were labour camps, not concentration camps.[58] The debate could then be joined on the familiar ground of distinguishing between communism and facism[59]:

If one concludes from this that communism is facism, one would submit, after the fact, to the fascist wish, which has always been to hide the capitalist crisis and the humane inspiration of Marxism. Never has a Nazi been encumbered by ideas such as the recognition of man by man, internationalism, the classless society. It is true that these ideas only find an unfaithful bearer in today's communism and that they serve it as décor rather than as motor. Yet they always remain part of it. That is what a young French or Russian communist is taught, whereas Nazi propaganda taught to its listeners the arrogance of the German people, the arrogance of the Aryans and the *Führerprinzip.*[60]

Merleau-Ponty's position on the humanist fringes of communism was growing ever more exposed. He fastened on the obvious differences between fascism and communism and ignored the elements of equivalence in the two ideologies that lay at the heart of their shared institutions, the concentration camps. Thus he was forced to rely on the feeble argument that the bureaucrats did not appreciate the significance of their own compromises.

A more serious question lay in justifying his own Marxist humanism in the face of Soviet communism. Here his argument turned toward the question of practicality, but it was suffused with a desperate faith in the humanist ideal. The difference between Nazis and communists, which he had just elaborated, meant 'that we have nothing in common with a Nazi and that we have the same values as a communist.' Such a statement would, of course, have satisfied only those who shared his faith in humanism. Merleau-Ponty knew the weakness of this opening, because he continued immediately with an obvious objection[61]: 'it will be said that communists do not have values, that there are only loyalties.' In response he made the most astonishing assertion: 'We reply that the communists try hard not to have any values, but, thank God, no one can live without breathing. Communists have values *in spite of themselves*.' Perhaps they were not found in Russia, where 'the camps dissolve the humanist illusion, the lived facts drive out imagined values the way bad money drives out good.' When he spoke to a communist from the colonies about colonial affairs, however, they found themselves in agreement; a French worker told him that whatever happens in Russia it was the Communist Party in France that did the most for him. Thus, whatever the nature of present Soviet society may be, across the world in the equilibrium of forces, the USSR was found beside those who struggled against the forms of exploitation known to us who lived outside the Soviet Union. There was no question of showing indulgence toward communism, Merleau-Ponty said, but at the same time one could not make a pact with one's adversaries. 'Thus the only sane criticism is one that deals with exploitation within and outside the USSR. Every political position that is *defined* in opposition to Russia and localizes criticism within it is an absolution given to the capitalist world.'[62]

One direction that his argument could have taken would have been the radical examination of premises shared by liberal imperialists and Soviet Marxists. By confining the argument to the level of adversaries and struggle in light of the ideal, nothing but an increasingly unconvincing restatement of the necessity of a *via media* was possible. There was no awakening sense, such as overtook a man of impeccable leftist credentials such as Dwight Macdonald about this time, that radicals were not the same as progressives, that progressives were part of the problem, that liberalism and Marxism were brothers in their faith in history, and most of all that 'the difficulties lie much deeper ... than is assumed by the Progressives, and the crisis is much more serious.'[63]

There was, as always, brilliant rhetoric in Merleau-Ponty's statements, but also a certain deviousness. Against Americans who boldly declared that they lacked such European oddities as a class struggle and who invited the rest of the world to join them in prosperity, Merleau-Ponty had recourse to principles. 'When we explain to them that they are in the process of sacrificing all political evaluation to this uncertain fact, and that, all things considered, the recognition of man by man and the classless society are less vague as principles of a world-wide politics than is American prosperity, that the historic mission of the proletariat is, in the end, more precise an idea than the historic mission of the United States, they reply, as did Sidney Hook in *Partisan Review*, that it was urgent to send us a few masters of thought of his calibre.' Against Western politicians who compared the camps to their own colonies, Merleau-Ponty replied that the colonies were the camps of the liberal democracies.

Against Rousset, for whom the camps illustrated the falseness of Soviet Marxist principles, Merleau-Ponty replied with an argument of prudence. If colonies and camps were equivalent, he said, one must try to avoid both. Rousset, however, was silent about Greek and Spanish camps, and 'with even greater reason he will not think to implicate diffuse or hidden forms of slavery: forced labour in colonies, colonial wars, the condition of American Negroes.' Then for whom did Rousset write? For a public tormented by camps or prisons only when they are Soviet. 'The holy alliance (*l'union sacrée*) against the Russian system solicits here all those who detest it for bad reasons as well as good ones; it will take aim and attack all socialist ideas by way of the system of concentration camps.'[64] Rousset in other words had based his politics on the single principle of opposing the greatest evil, while Merleau-Ponty forsook discussion of principles and pointed to the reality of lesser evils in order to show the soundness of his prudence. To fight enemy number one one must either forget about enemy number two or turn him into an ally. Since the only allies were capitalist, added Merleau-Ponty, Rousset must have taken leave of Marxism. Moreover, one could not rely simply on Rousset's conscience, however sincere; if he spoke for Soviet prisoners in the name of one who had for a time dwelt in *l'univers concentrationnaire*, he kept his silence well enough when it came to Greek and Spanish inmates. Even the experience of an absolute such as the horror of concentration camps could not determine a policy. 'The days of our life are not the days of our death ... Death is always forgotten when we live.' Both Rousset and the communist Pierre Daix, who said the camps were the greatest of Soviet achievements, had forgotten certain groups of men and so held the lives of these men cheaply. 'They would only be faithful to themselves by seeking a policy that did not oblige them to choose *their* deported persons.'[65]

Quite apart from the soundness of comparing colonies to concentration camps, the arguments varied according to the presumed interlocutor. Against principles Merleau-Ponty counselled prudence and took issue with tactics; against factual evidence he had recourse to Marxist principles. This inconsistency betrayed, perhaps, an unease he was unwilling to acknowledge. The time when it made sense, even theoretically, to advocate a middle road was drawing rapidly to an end.

'This article displeased nearly everyone,' wrote Simone de Beauvoir.[66] Pierre Daix replied, on behalf of the Communist Party, with the usual riposte: 'Which side are you on? With the Soviet peoples who are building a new society? Or with their enemies, with those who, even in the USSR, are sabotaging this effort?'[67] In such circumstances dialogue was becoming difficult and persuasion impossible. Merleau-Ponty provided what was, in effect, a reply to Daix in his response to J.D. Martinet, a Trotskyite. Martinet had written to *Les Temps modernes* a letter critical of the editorial on the Soviet camps; it was not published at the time it was received and subsequently appeared in *La Révolution prolétarienne*.[68] Merleau-Ponty republished Martinet's criticism and gave his own reply.

Martinet's first two points stressed rather more strongly than did Merleau-Ponty that Spanish and Greek concentration camps, because they did not constitute a coherent system of exploitation, were not comparable to the integral exploitation and servile labour of the USSR, and that the Soviet camps were an important element in the Russian economy. Then he asked: 'How could you have waited until 1950 to interest yourself officially in this problem?' Martinet had known of the camps during the 1930s and had refused to oppose either the Nazis or the Stalinists for fear of aiding the other. Finally, he asked: 'In practice, what does your contemporary political position of equilibrium between the two imperialist blocs, American and Soviet, signify?' His own answer was that it lacked realism because it spoke not of actual conditions in the USSR and the United States but of what they might become.

Merleau-Ponty passed over Martinet's first two points as being of minor importance. He had not spoken of Soviet camps earlier, he said, because he had been ignorant of their extent and purpose. For a long time it had been possible to regard the camps as a cruel and regrettable aspect of revolutionary violence.[69] But Martinet 'knew everything: you were sure that Nazism would be ephemeral, and that the Communists brought the People's Democracies to hell. Perhaps we understand too late. Perhaps as well, you are right *too early* ... Perhaps it would not have been fatal for the USSR to subdue the People's Democracies had American policy been different.' Martinet's attitude before the war, which saw the alternatives in terms of Stalinist or Nazi victories, was appropriate for the Baltic peoples, the Hungarians, and the Poles, but not the French. The source of Martinet's thinking was exactly that of the Stalinists: 'you have taken on the habit of treating all political questions from the angle of support for the USSR.' Moreover, Martinet still thought in terms of abstract blocs 'to the point of distorting our position because you have seen it in terms of your own categories.'

To begin with, Merleau-Ponty said, neither the Soviet expansion in Eastern Europe nor American aid to Western Europe could be understood properly as varieties of imperialism. Nor did it make much sense to compare Soviet and American political forms. 'Never have the editorials, at least, spoken of American fascism. We have explained that it was more agreeable to live in the United States than the Soviet Union, adding only that this did not suffice to condemn the USSR, if the Soviet system was truly on the road to socialism.' Obviously, he said, the truth was not to be found in America or in the Communist Party. If war broke out, such a position would become absurd, but if, as seemed possible, 'the cold war lasts twenty years, broken by pauses and détentes, we will have done our part to conserve and uphold the instruments of political discussion during an era which knows less and less how to serve them because it is haunted by blocs, and thinks only of geography when it is necessary to think of society. We do not waver between two blocs; we think that blocs have only a diplomatic and military existence.' Such a view was ambiguous and open to abuse, but it was untrustworthy 'only in the eyes of generals or ambassadors. Perhaps one day they will be the only ones who have words. In our view that would be a day of misfortune, because the victor, whoever he is, would carry everywhere his evil along with his good. It would certainly be enough, if the events took place, to have to undergo this confusion. It is not necessary to anticipate it. We must do everything to avoid it.'[70]

On the crucial point concerning the 'actual conditions' in the USA and the USSR, Merleau-Ponty and Martinet spoke past each other. For Merleau-Ponty conditions in the United States were contingent on the future of capitalism as understood through Marx; the Soviet Union was to be judged on other, non-Marxist, grounds. For Martinet on the other hand Soviet and American realities were contingent too but had differentiated into two blocs. Merleau-Ponty and Martinet both appealed to the contingency of events and emphasized that injustice in America could never justify Soviet camps, nor the camps American injustice. The sole difference between them, it would seem, was that Merleau-Ponty objected to Martinet's schematizing, while Martinet thought it was naïve of Merleau-Ponty not to have recognized the reality of blocs. As it happened Martinet was proved right, though perhaps not for his own reasons, when the North Koreans crossed the armistice line late in June 1950, making the editorial recording the debate, when it appeared in the July issue, already obsolete.

Sartre recorded Merleau-Ponty's reaction to the outbreak of war:

'We have nothing more to do but keep quiet.'
'Who is "we"?' I said, pretending not to understand.
'Well, us. *Les Temps modernes*.'
'You think we ought to close up shop?'
'No. But we won't breathe another word of politics.'
'And why not?'
'They are fighting.'
'Okay. In Korea.'
'To-morrow they'll be fighting everywhere.'
'So even when they are fighting here, why should we keep quiet?'
'Because. Brute force will decide: Why speak to what has no ears?'

I climbed aboard the train; leaned out the window, waved good-bye as one should; I saw that he waved back, but I was dumbfounded for the rest of the trip.[71]

A final comment from Merleau-Ponty came in the October 1950 issue of the review in the form of an editorial preface to an article that analysed American manoeuvres prior to the outbreak of war. It provided 'an interesting analysis of factors that went into American policy,' he said, but 'we are astonished at the fact that the author concentrated all his attention on American acts of diplomacy and never *exposed* the initiatives of the other bloc, which sometimes followed these acts but sometimes preceded them as well.' Even if one thought that the Americans started the war, it was odd to present the circumstances as if their adversaries were wholly imaginary. One might ridicule hysterical journalists who prophesied a succession of coups in the West following the one in Prague, 'but after all, there *was* a coup d'état in Prague.' To argue that Soviet actions in Eastern Europe and Korea were simply a response to the American monopoly of atomic weapons and that Soviet possession of an atom bomb would re-establish an equilibrium was an 'astonishing optimism. The very least it implies is that Soviet diplomacy ceased to be a simple reaction from that happy day when Mr Truman made public Russian atomic experiments. Henceforth there was a Soviet foreign policy.'[72] But such an interpretation was untenable. Korea and the events in Eastern Europe showed Merleau-Ponty that American nuclear blackmail was only a contributing factor, not a cause. Stalin sought to overcome the Soviet nuclear inferiority by obtaining a conventional strategic superiority.

Merleau-Ponty's counsel of silence, therefore, was not simply that the voice of *Les Temps modernes* would not be heard: Stalin's diplomatic and strategic moves showed he considered war inevitable. Therefore the Russians were no longer concerned with preventing war but with winning it, for it only took one side to view the future as fatal for it to become so. If the West had attacked, Merleau-Ponty reasoned, the world would perish, but with a meaning: socialism was trying to be born. Nevertheless it was the North that had crossed the Korean De-Militarized Zone. Consequently, if war were to destroy the world, it would be in utter meaninglessness.[73]

AFTER KOREA

The silence of *Les Temps modernes* did not go unnoticed.[74] Sartre was unhappy with silence, and Merleau-Ponty was unhappy that their views of Korea and Soviet manoeuvres were not the same. With the Chinese intervention in Korea and MacArthur's plans to strike north of the Yalu, the prospect of direct Russian intervention and war in Europe appeared. For two years the right and centre parties had been talking of the inevitability of Cossacks marching through the Arc de Triomphe unless the Americans prevented it. Thus was the Atlantic Pact signed in April 1949 and the long-term division of Europe ensured with the creation of the Federal Republic of Germany. The deterrent value of NATO ground forces was nil: east of the Elbe there were 175 eastern block divisions, west of it ten: two American, two British, and six French. Moreover, the French divisions were of poor quality, the best being engaged in Indochina, while the British and American ones were underequipped. NATO deterrence lay in the American superiority in nuclear weapons, which was, with the flood of horror literature that inundated France at the time, a prospect hardly any more appealing than a Soviet conquest. In July 1950 the Americans announced the strategy of arming West Germany. The French government, understandably, objected, and it was not until the spring of 1952 that the European Defence Community was formed. As a Frenchman and as a 'man of the left,' Merleau-Ponty was in an intolerable position. NATO protection meant shelter beneath the American nuclear umbrella: French interests, to say nothing of the possibilities for revolution, were badly served by dependence on foreign arms. But neither did he welcome the prospect of Russian troops in Paris. With some public attention, Etienne Gilson had accepted a post at the University of Toronto, so that there was always the possibility of exile. Indeed, Sartre reported that Merleau-Ponty made some half-serious remarks about becoming an elevator-boy in New York.

The years between 1950 and 1952 constituted an important watershed for Merleau-Ponty. On the left, Russian pressure on Tito, the new purge trials, the camps, and finally Korea reinforced the feeling of futility that must have descended even before the RDR episode. Small comfort was to be had in the knowledge that his analysis of the Marshall Plan and the 'American challenge,' Vietnam, and peaceful co-existence were to prove sound ten and twenty years later.

Merleau-Ponty turned away from politics. As Sartre said, he took refuge in his 'inner life,'[75] but it was with a sense of failure. The first loss, as we said earlier, came with the Liberation. During the later post-war years, the prolongation of his memory of action, which had been expressed in his political analyses, appeared to be in vain as well. For such a man the return to the banality of a purely private existence, the abandonment of the public realm to ambassadors, generals, and the spokesmen for blocs, was a bitter loss and deprivation. Merleau-Ponty's inner life was of course his academic career at the Sorbonne and then at the Collège de France; but he had also become, through the pages of Les Temps modernes, a public man, and to his readers silence was understood as a kind of abdication, whatever private integrity he retained and confided to his friends. Even in terms of interpersonal relations, he could not long keep silent while differing with his friend Sartre, who was also official editor of the review, over an issue as fundamental as war.

Events settled the question when Sartre broke the political silence of the review with a series of articles entitled 'Les Communistes et la Paix.'[76] Sartre was motivated to speak out because of the arrest of a Communist Deputy, Jacques Duclos, despite his parliamentary immunity, following an abortive demonstration organized by the Party to greet General Ridgeway, fresh from Korea, who was about to replace Eisenhower as NATO supreme commander. The 'forces of order' had been preparing for a showdown with the Party for some time, and Duclos was clearly framed.[77] One reason why the anti-Ridgeway demonstration failed was because the Parisian workers had refused to turn out as the CGT and the Party urged them. Failure on the part of the communists caused unconcealed glee among their opponents, including those of the non-communist left, some of whom argued that at last the good workers were awakening to the truth that French communism was simply a tool of Moscow; evidently they hoped to gain what the Party had lost. Sartre, who had recently been a leading protagonist in *l'affaire* Henri Martin,[78] lashed out at non-communists and anti-communists alike as *rats visqueux*, slimy rats.

Merleau-Ponty was amused rather than offended with the first instalment of Sartre's polemic.[79] The second part of Sartre's article, originally scheduled for August 1952 and then promised for September, was not published until the October-November issue. In the meantime occurred the celebrated clash between Sartre and Francis Jeanson on one side and Albert Camus on the other, centred on Jeanson's biting review in *Les Temps modernes* of Camus's *L'Homme révolté*. Late in 1952 Sartre became engaged in yet another polemic, this time with Claude Lefort over the first two parts of 'Les Communistes et la Paix,' and Merleau-Ponty was called upon to mediate and soften the tones of both men. In this exchange Merleau-Ponty was clearly on the side of Lefort: what he thought of Sartre's treatment of Camus is unknown.

Simone de Beauvoir has said that the years of Merleau-Ponty's silence, 1950 to 1952, were the years when Sartre most emphatically repudiated his bourgeois heritage and sought accommodation with the Communists[80]; Sartre allowed that Merleau-Ponty may have distrusted his own zeal: 'if I should start talking politics, where would it end?'[81] In consequence of Merleau-Ponty's silence, Sartre had replaced him as the de facto political voice of *Les Temps modernes*. Sartre's zeal directed the review further and further from the radical but limited or moderated critique that Merleau-Ponty was beginning to express. The break between the two men was occasioned by an editorial formality: Sartre supported Jeanson in removing a prefatory note by Merleau-Ponty that had expressed certain reservations about an article by Pierre Naville.[82] This triviality was the efficient cause of the break between Sartre and Merleau-Ponty but as we shall see other and deeper motives sustained it.

During the first period of Merleau-Ponty's public career as a political thinker he was involved in the major political events of the day through his polemics and his commentaries. After the war in Korea, after the disappearance of nineteenth-century colonial empires, after the war in Viet Nam, Merleau-Ponty's relations with his fellow Frenchmen might seem trivial and unimportant only because of the accumulated weight of intervening events. At the time his statements were anything but second-rate, and even today one can admire his courage.

5
A reappraisal
of dialectic

Merleau-Ponty's doubts about classical Marxism were nourished by his integrity and the seriousness of his commitment to humanism. Proletarian internationalism and proletarian spontaneity had ceased to be effective factors in politics, and proletarian control of the means of production was grotesquely distorted by the Stalinist regime. Nevertheless the pressure of events compelled him, not to abandon Marx's teaching, but to reinterpret it. Sartre was right to note that Merleau-Ponty had returned to his inner life, but his refuge was no more than a strategic retreat. In his lectures at the Collège de France he was undertaking an intellectual overhaul that resulted in the publication of *Les Aventures de la Dialectique*. Not until the problems of reinterpretation had been worked through, some time in the autumn of 1954, did Merleau-Ponty speak again on public matters, this time it was in the pages of *L'Express*, a weekly magazine of considerably broader appeal than *Les Temps modernes*.

Les Aventures de la Dialectique is a complex work, difficult to understand from within. Again, the subtleties of the argument are best approached indirectly, by way of the crude external criticism that greeted it. The book appeared in 1955, within two weeks of the publication of Raymond Aron's *L'Opium des Intellectuels*, and not surprisingly the two were often discussed together. For some commentators both books were occasions for rejoicing at a resurgence of French political thought following so many years of intemperate and personal polemic. Others were less impartial. Because Merleau-Ponty criticized the Communist Party, he received the praise of the right for his late rediscovery of truth. Communist intellectuals denounced the book, along with those of Raymond Aron, Thierry Maulnier, Etiemble, Herbert Luthy, and Albert Camus, as further evidence of petit-bourgeois treason. But Merleau-Ponty was singled out for separate treatment because he had based his argument on texts from Marx and followers of Marx.[1] The first Communist replies appeared in the late spring and early summer of 1955. The Party must have felt the book's impact because in November they called a public meeting in the Mutualité in order to denounce it again.[2] Because it took issue with Sartre's position developed in 'Les Communistes et la Paix,' Simone de Beauvoir responded in defence of that position and was joined for a time in a qualified way by Jean Kanapa.[3] Finally, the non-communist left, perhaps not fully understanding what Merleau-Ponty was trying to argue, was cautious and rather cool.[4] In short, *Les Aventures de la Dialectique*, like *Humanisme et Terreur*, displeased nearly everyone.

The hostility *Les Aventures* provoked cannot all be ascribed to the heavily ideological climate of opinion into which it was thrust. Merleau-Ponty's intentions were provocative. This 'bulky pamphlet,' as it has been called, was intended to present 'samples, surveys, anecdotes of philosophical life, the beginnings of analyses and finally the continual rumination upon readings, discoveries and events.'[5] It was a meditation, not a vigorous textual exegesis. 'It ceaselessly mixes literal exposition and personal commentary. This is a dangerous game: if we are strict, he can be accused of plagiarism (for example, of Weber, of the early Lukács, of Mannheim); if we are personal, he can be accused of misrepresentation (for example of Marx by some, of Sartre by others).'[6] Merleau-Ponty knew the risks he ran. As with Sartre's 'Les Communistes et la Paix,' it was a *livre de circonstance*, 'as personal and as general as possible, it is philosophic.'[7]

There were other reasons too. The book was intended to be a theoretical study rather than a political weapon; yet it presented reflections upon events as well as upon texts. It was a kind of voyage of discovery, complex and composite, where events of the twentieth century overlapped with textual interpretations. 'We do not wish,' said Merleau-Ponty at one point in the book, 'to present as a syllogism what has appeared to us little by little, in contact with events; but the event has been the occasion of a clarification, and not at all one of those accidents that confuse without clarifying.'[8] *Les Aventures*, in other words, was the product of Merleau-Ponty's understanding of events, where as much emphasis must be given to the theoretical significance of historical action as to the practical and personal activities that Merleau-Ponty undertook in the wake of his reflections.

Aron interpreted Merleau-Ponty's remarks on the Korean war as a kind of revelation. In contrast, Aron himself claimed to have seen the truth about the Soviet Union shortly after the close of hostilities in Europe. Merleau-Ponty no doubt would have considered Aron's wisdom premature, or even retrospective. To Merleau-Ponty, even in 1955, Marxism continued to express the truth that where the proletariat is nothing, there is no human history. Because he thought that joining the Communist Party was impossible, an attitude of sympathy, upholding the chances for a new revolutionary upheaval, was imposed. He had said it was not necessary to choose between Communism and its adversary and quoted from *Humanisme et Terreur*: 'If tomorrow the USSR threatens to invade Europe and establish a regime of its choice in all countries, a different question would arise and would have to be examined. It does not arise at the moment.'[9] But between 1948 and 1950, he now conceded, the conditions for maintaining that position had disintegrated, because the 'different question' was raised. 'We know all that can be said about the regime in South Korea; we do not pretend that the USSR wished or unleashed the Korean war: but since it put an end to it, no doubt it could have prevented it, and since it did not prevent it but instead turned to military action, our attitude of sympathy ... becomes disguised adherence ... Marxist waiting would become communist action.' Just after the war, Marxist waiting had been possible because of 'objective conditions,' specifically the neutral zones across the world in Czechoslovakia and Korea. When those neutral zones disappeared, Marxist waiting turned into a suspicious dream.[10] But if practical affairs had a theoretical significance, more was involved than concessions to political expediency.

For this reason Merleau-Ponty had to raise a far more formidable issue: could he retain the same favourable prejudice towards a Marxist philosophy of history? Or was the Korean episode a crucial practical experience whose theoretical consequences had to be brought to light? Could he continue to think, with all conceivable reservations towards Soviet solutions, that the Marxist dialectic remained negatively valuable, and that history must put the proletariat into perspective even if it did not put it into power? The Korean war, he said, recalled the identity of praxis with theory. He implied that the refusal to choose between eastern and western blocs must also find a platform and enter the public arena if it is to be anything more than a suspicious utopian dream. To say, as Merleau-Ponty recognized he had done, that Marxism remained true as negation no matter what happened positively in practice 'would be to place us outside history and, more particularly, outside Marxism.' One then would be a Marxist for wholly un-Marxist reasons because, in history, Marxist criticism and action are a single movement. Consequently, 'if we affirm that revolution does not keep its promises as action, we cannot conclude from this that we should maintain criticism and forget about action. *There must be something that prepares for the defects of action, even in criticism.*'[11] The significance of these remarks would seem to be something like the following: Marxism could remain 'true' and an attitude of sympathy was possible only under certain conditions. Just as it took the war and the occupation to bring the specific conditions of French life to his attention, so it took the post-war communist manœuvres, which culminated in Korea, to bring the conditions for sympathy into perspective. In both instances the events that made former attitudes visible as perspectives destroyed their viability as ways to live. The destruction of the everyday world of peaceful and contented France was necessary in order to see it as peaceful and contented; the destruction of sympathy and Marxist waiting was necessary in order to see it as a prejudice.[12]

The war and occupation, as we have seen, taught Merleau-Ponty 'history,' in the sense of the Hegelian regime of mutual recognition and authentic intersubjectivity. With Korea there was another lesson, 'the identity of praxis with theory.' Whatever such a phrase may have meant for Marx, for Merleau-Ponty it meant that both Marx's understanding of history and communist action based on that understanding, however vulgarized, would have to be reinterpreted. That was the double objective of *Les Aventures de la Dialectique.*

The structure of the book is centred on the chapter entitled 'Pravda,' 'truth,' a title not wholly ironic. The Preface announced the question to be explored: 'Each political act involves the whole of history, but this totality does not provide us with a rule to which we could be reconciled because it is never anything but an opinion.'[13] The Epilogue restated an enriched variation of the question as a conclusion. Between were chapters dealing with the ascent to 'Pravda' and the decline through Party discipline to wholly external sympathy. The subsidiary theme, presenting Merleau-Ponty's own political position and preparing the way for his subsequent activities, emerged in his account of the genesis of 'ultra-bolshevism.'

MAX WEBER

Merleau-Ponty began his analysis of the vicissitudes of a dialectical understanding of history with Max Weber because, he said, Weber was concerned with grasping the conditions under which a historical dialectic, an 'action that invents itself,' was possible.[14] Weber's notions of truth and freedom were both exacting and vague; he knew the importance of contingency and creative action but formulated the most rigorous rules for understanding history. Yet he also knew his own methodology to be in part a product of historical chance, personal audacity, and invention. The impossibility of Weber's division between historical contingency and historiographic strictness was exposed by a consideration of his juxtaposition of historical violence and historical truth. Truth in history, according to Weber, could be known through quasi-Kantian rules of construction. The historian asked his own questions, and so could never fully know the reality he interrogated. But he did so according to procedures that minimized his subjective involvement. On the other hand historical violence was a matter of present existence. In Gabriel Marcel's words, it was suffered rather than understood. In the present we cannot suspend our judgment because the present is what we must judge. And we must judge because we are responsible. Knowledge and practice confront the same infinity of historical reality, but they respond to it in two opposite ways: knowledge responds by multiplying views, by provisional, open, motivated, conditional conclusions, whereas practice responds by absolute, partial, and unjustifiable decisions. Such dualism made no sense, Merleau-Ponty said, for tomorrow I can contemplate today's deed. More broadly, the past too has been lived, so that history is action and action is history, whether contemplated or assumed as a responsibility. 'The condition of the historian is not so different from that of the man of action ... Knowledge and action are two poles of a unique existence.'[15] We would not be spectators if we were not involved in the past, and action would not be serious without some sort of finality. Thus, Merleau-Ponty concluded, Weber must move beyond the contradiction of objective understanding and unjustifiable moral feeling.

In his historical studies Weber surpassed the methodological strictures he formulated as an inoculation against the ideological confusions of the early Weimar regime. In his famous study of Protestantism and capitalism, for example, Weber began with abstract ideal types that took their meaning from a specific logical structure; this logical complex led to other facts not apparent in the original empirical basis of the ideal types. Weber's writing, a practical action, which began as an awareness 'of a certain style and diffused, though never completely, so as to grasp the structure of events,' cut through 'the appearances that enclosed understanding, moved beyond provisional and partial perspectives by re-establishing the anonymous intention, the dialectic of an ensemble.'[16] Here Merleau-Ponty slightly Hegelianized Weber's formulation: with the dogma of predestination, the expulsion of the sacraments as mediation between man and God, the atrophy of brotherhood in the face of the overarching significance of divine wrath, the depoeticization of the cosmos into material at hand, all these familiar Weberian themes, according to Merleau-Ponty, meant that 'the only way left we have to bring the reign of God to earth is to regulate the world, to change its natural appearance and to rationalize life.' But, he went on, Weber distinguished the motives developed by the spirit of capitalism after capitalism had been crystallized in the world by the Protestant ethic from the original motives of Calvinism itself. That is, he 'did not believe that capitalism is the truth of Calvinism.' Indeed, Weber said exactly the opposite, that the transition from Protestantism to capitalism denatured religion and then sustained itself according to its own motives.[17] For Weber, capitalism and Calvinism were interwoven in a dialectical ensemble; there was no progression and no development, as with Hegel, of an Idea. History was ordered and there were meanings, intelligible nuclei of sense, but the structure of events was embedded in empirical history.

Merleau-Ponty pushed Weber's analysis in a Hegelian direction. 'The course of circumstances makes the errors and contradictions of the fundamental choice [of Calvinism] explicit, and the historical failure is proof against the truth of Calvinism.' Again, Merleau-Ponty affirmed that 'history eliminates the irrational' and no situation was final. Thus, 'there are only advances. Capitalist rationalization is one of them because it resolves our given condition through knowledge and action, and it can be shown that the appropriation of the world by man and demystification are better because they face difficulties that other historical regimes avoid. But this progress is purchased by regressions ... Demystification is also depoeticization and disenchantment. We must retain the capitalist denial of an external sacrality but renew in it the claims of an absolute, which capitalism abolished.' In short, the elimination of God was an 'advance,' a historical acquisition, but it must be distinguished from the abolition of all absolutes because this later abolition has the unfortunate consequences of depoeticization and disenchantment.

Now, in order to conclude that the elimination of God was an advance, whereas depoeticization and disenchantment were not, one must have a standard of measurement. Once again it was supplied by Hegel and Kojève. The historical goal of a regime of mutual recognition placed both events, the elimination of God and the disenchantment of the world, into the sought-for context. God must be abolished, but the realities of disenchantment could hardly be applauded. Thus they are deplored as unfortunate by-products, the 'regressions' by which 'progress' is purchased. Likewise, Hegel lay behind the otherwise odd statement that 'capitalism is the truth of Calvinism' inasmuch as 'truth' here must be taken to mean 'historically revealed reality.'[18] Accordingly, the next historical questions concerned the 'truth' of capitalism, that is, the result that capitalism would engender as Calvinism had engendered it. That there would be a 'truth' of capitalism was ensured by the contradiction expressed in the phrase 'progress purchased by regressions,' which fairly cried out for resolution. But once again, both the statement of the question and any attempt at resolution demanded that the whole of human existence and history be understood within an immanent Hegelian field.

Merleau-Ponty's ambivalence toward Weber can be summarized as follows: Weber was wrong to judge the Russian Revolution as a military dictatorship in alliance with a group of intellectuals parading as politicians. That was the judgment of 'a provincial German bourgeois' and was unworthy of him. At the same time Weber had shown that a philosophy of history was not a waste of time or an exercise in imaginative system-building but rather 'a meditation on the circle of knowledge and reality.' What remained to be done, therefore, was to apply Weber's dialectical philosophy of history to the present and employ our historical understanding to the benefit of political action. 'It is only after Weber and this Weberian Marxism that the adventures of the dialectic during the past thirty-five years can be understood.'[19] After *Weber* because he raised the most important historical questions; *after* Weber because he did not resolve the questions he raised.

PROBLEMS OF 'WESTERN MARXISM'

The third representative of 'this Weberian Marxism' to emerge from the 'contradictions' of Weber was Georg Lukács, or rather, the Lukács who was the author of *Geschichte und Klassenbewusstsein.*[20] The central problem with Weber's analysis was the question of relativism, of nihilism. Weber's ideal type concepts, according to Merleau-Ponty, provided a 'glimpse' of the road beyond relativism. They provided an access to the meaning of history because they were not arbitrary but part of history itself, namely the process of capitalist rationalization. A radical relativism, therefore, would take into account the historical context of Weberian understanding and the contextual significance of meanings. Weber was unwilling to go so far, Merleau-Ponty said, because he was still captive of the Kantian dream of unconditioned truth. 'But would not a more radical critique, the unrestricted recognition of history as the unique milieu of our errors and our verifications, recover an absolute within the relative?' The recovery of this absolute would outline, Merleau-Ponty said, 'a kind of totality,' a 'totality of the empirical,' namely 'the coherent assembly of all the facts known to us,' including the self-reflective knowledge of the historian.[21]

Numerous implications followed. Henceforth one might analyse consequences as well as fundamental choices. Thus, if it were possible to understand the transformation of the Protestant ethic into the spirit of capitalism there was no reason why it ought not be possible to analyse the transformation of the spirit of capitalism, since the 'totality of the empirical' was 'coherent.' In principle, therefore, there was but one knowledge, the knowledge of our world in becoming, and this becoming embraced knowledge itself. 'But it is knowledge that teaches us this: that there is a moment when knowledge returns itself to its own origins, takes up again its own genesis, compares itself as knowledge to what it was as event, collects itself together in order to totalize itself, and tends toward self-consciousness.' The same ensemble is, under its first aspect, history, and under the second, philosophy. History was realized philosophy as philosophy was formalized history, history reduced to its internal articulations and intelligible structure. Such was Lukács's understanding of Marxism, which 'is, or must be, this integral and undogmatic philosophy.'[22] Moreover, he said, Marxism thus understood must be a revolutionary philosophy exactly because it refuses to be dogmatic. There is an infinite succession of moments as the interrogation of history produces a philosophical meaning and as reflection by the philosopher on his own present informs history as political action.[23]

Merleau-Ponty's account of this self-conscious totalizing ensemble is not at all clear and perhaps not even coherent. But let us try to analyse what is involved. If one is to speak of the 'totality of the empirical,' one may do so either if one were God or if one were to transfer the context from historical description to eschatological evocation. That is, in the second instance one expresses within a historical idiom a symbolic transfiguration of existence at an 'end-time.' Thus we find the unusual imagery of the apocalypse of Daniel or the revelation of St John. Here the 'totality of the empirical,' that is, the whole of existing history, is transfigured and its true meaning revealed. The transfiguration is to be accomplished by God; all men can do is evoke its presence by means of myth and symbol.

The modern, secular apocalyptics endow man with the role previously accorded to God. The term generally used is 'totalizer.' It is clear that a totalizer is needed, since events by definition do not form a totality. One such totalizer, of course, was Hegel (as interpreted by Kojève): the end of history, the synthesis of absolute power and absolute knowledge, totalizes all empirical events by exhaustively comprehending their meaning. We have seen that Merleau-Ponty followed this line of speculation at least to the extent of postulating a regime of mutual recognition as the ideal of historical action. In *Les Aventures* he followed a variation of this theme in connection with his explication of Lukács. Totality arises, in its strictly Hegelian or Kojèvian form, from history under that aspect of history called philosophy; philosophy is a self-conscious totalization of history under that aspect of history called empirical events. Hence, events give rise to philosophy, which in turn grasps or totalizes events as its own contents: history *is* philosophy. Or rather, the ensemble 'history-philosophy' is a revelation of itself. This doctrine is at least logically consistent and systematic. However, if both the religious-eschatological and the strictly Kojèvian end-of-history notions are rejected, then the totalization can only be provisional; in other words it is not a totalization at all, since it may fall apart through its own internal instability. This was Merleau-Ponty's reading of Lukács and Marx, and it amounted to a notion of a detotalizing totalization or a totalizing detotalization, that is, to an unresolvable (self-) contradiction.

Merleau-Ponty did not attempt to overcome this apparently self-cancelling theory through discursive argument. Instead he adduced a historical example, the exchange between man and nature that sustained capitalist productivity as described by Marx and Lukács. Pointing to the actual course of events and the truth of them as expounded by Marx and Lukács, Merleau-Ponty evidently felt he had overcome the (merely) theoretical incoherence of a totalizing detotalization. The problem and his evasion of it were identical in structure with his earlier dismissal of Kant's criticism of progressives.

Merleau-Ponty began with a consideration of Marx's concept of alienation.

Whatever its psychological and historical complexities, insights, or inconsistencies, it was for Merleau-Ponty the principle of historical Darwinism in concrete operation.[24] What capitalism had achieved by its destruction of feudalism was a society unmediated by family, religion, or nationality. 'All those who live in capitalist society are placed under the common denominator of labour, and in this sense it is homogeneous.' Against the ground of this real homogeneity, it is possible to perceive the figure of ideology, expressive of a Hegelian inconsistency between a homogeneous reality and a heterogeneous actuality. But not all 'pre-capitalist' societies are the same, and while one may be justified in judging capitalism as a 'more integrated' society than the feudalism it replaced, it is not at all necessary that all non-capitalist societies pass through the capitalist phase of homogenizing. That is, we are not justified in identifying non-capitalist society with pre-capitalist society. The reason, of course, is that capitalist society is not the end of history, and in order to arrive at the entire truth one must pass beyond the limits of present capitalism.[25] If 'it is only in the structure of the whole that there is progress,'[26] then capitalism is only *one* way of traversing the gap between a hierarchic society and a homogeneous one. By implication one may be tempted to conclude that until history is actually over and the regime of mutual recognition is an empirical phenomenon, we shall be unable to judge which transitional society was absolutely progressive, which society most efficiently bridged the gap between a hierarchical society and humanism. Otherwise, the 'structure of the whole' might never appear, and one could never decide whether any particular regime was 'progressive,' since tomorrow it might change and, in changing, alter yesterday's meaning.

Yet somehow Merleau-Ponty agreed with Marx that capitalism was progressive. Capitalism, he said, has produced subjectivity. In non-capitalist societies, which lack the transparency of homogeneous market relations and the radical differentiation of subject and object, of men and things, there can arise no universal mediation but only, as Hegel taught, the particular mediations of family, blood, Church, and so on. In short, there is no *history*.[27] But since consciousness is not a thing, there can be no end to history. If there is progress in capitalism over precapitalism, and even if this progress is only relative because other non-capitalist societies may overcome the problems of capitalism more efficiently, the progress of capitalism 'is only an acquisition if it is followed by further progress; it cannot maintain itself as it is.' The fact that progress has occurred will change the situation, and in order to remain progressive the new situation must be faced. If, on the other hand, the achievement were immobilized, it would already be lost. 'All progress is therefore relative in this profound sense, that the same historical entry that establishes it introduces the problem of decline. The revolution that has become an institution is already decadent if it thinks itself accomplished.'[28] Thus, Merleau-Ponty concluded, everything is true because it once existed or presently exists, and everything is false because it is passing away.

Within this unstable realm of pure genesis, so aptly suggested by Merleau-Ponty's earlier image of the traveller, there is but one privileged act, the travelling itself, which is to say, the action of historical change oriented towards the final regime of authentic intersubjectivity. That is, the revolution alone is privileged. 'The revolution is the moment when these two perspectives [of past and present truth] are united, when a radical negation delivers the truth from the whole of the past and allows us to undertake the recovery of it.'[29] According to Marx, consciousness, as both the product of history and the source of history, as the apprehension of the universal mediation between man and nature, must distinguish between the moment of negation and the moment of recovery. The two will coincide in the ever-progressive process of 'a homogeneous society, where the situation no more constrains life than life imprisons our vision.'[30] This means, as just noted, that in the present a truly homogeneous society appears as a nonexistent ideal extrapolated from the meaning of capitalism – namely partial homogeneity. Now the partial homogenization of capitalism is what made the ideal of a homogeneous society intelligible, and by being partial or incomplete ensured that history was not over, so that capitalism can be both progressive and regressive. If one notices, however, that the 'progress' involved is on the plane of real empirical history and the regress is in terms of the ideal of a homogeneous society, and if one were to doubt that a common calculus could ever unite the two (at least in the absence of divine wisdom), then one must be referred once again to the revelation of necessity that the ensemble of an empirical totality is said to provide.

This 'philosophical reading of history,' which revealed that 'history was philosophy,' must be deepened 'by showing that philosophy is history.'[31] The philosophical significance of the homogeneity created by capitalism is the existence of the proletariat. The argument may be summarized as follows: capitalism is revolutionary in so far as it has created a world of commodities, including the proletariat; but the proletarians, that is, factory labourers, etc., are not commodities but human beings. Second, capitalism has as its premise homogeneity; but the proletariat is not part of society, so the premise is false. Third, the proletariat discover they are human but are treated as commodities and so discover as well that production is a human process. Fourth, the proletariat take up again the revolutionary capitalist premise of homogeneity. The proletariat are the true homogeneous ones whose action with things is true history since they exist as a 'class' only in virtue of bourgeois society. Thus history by itself has secreted its truth through its own operation, that is, through the interstices of capitalist production and its premise of homogeneity. To the obvious objections that Marx, who discovered the truth of history, was not a proletarian, that the proletariat, which existed only by reflection in bourgeois society and not at all in homogeneous society, was the most unreal of phenomena, a 'negative idea,' the answer given by Marx was that such objections existed only for a theorist and that in practice, 'which is not subjected to the rivalry of consciousnesses,' there would be no problem.[32] The proletariat thus could carry the meaning of history in their existence without it having to take the form of an 'I think.' The dilemma therefore may be overcome in so far as the 'theorist' can translate proletarian experience into 'theses,' and the proletariat can receive these theses as the expression of their experience.[33]

At one level Merleau-Ponty was simply reiterating a commonsensical sociological observation first made in the *Phénoménologie*, that one lived such-and-such a role before being conscious of it.[34] One exists, for example, as an exploited, miserable labourer, perhaps accepting one's condition as fate, perhaps not; the 'theorist,' whether a community organizer, a communist functionary, or a priest, can clarify to an individual the reasons why he is exploited and what he can do about it. If the 'theorist' is truly concerned with clarification of the situation that the exploited individual suffers, and is not concerned with proselytizing an external dogma, then persuasion is the only means at his disposal, so that communist doctrine and Marx's teaching are understood as possibilities to which one may or may not be committed. What is involved is not an imaginary marketplace of ideas but the legitimation of one's adversary.[35]

For Lukács, however, the implications of the relationship between 'theorist' and exploited must be confined to the Party and the proletariat. In the end only Marx's notion of the historical self-actualization of man through the self-suppression of the proletariat is admissible 'theory,' or better, the self-suppression of the proletariat is truth or reality not (yet) accomplished. In Merleau-Ponty's words, the '*Stimmung* of Lukács, and, we think, of Marxism, is therefore of being not within the truth but on the threshold of truth, which is at once wholly close, as indicated by the entire past and present, and at an infinite distance from a future yet to be made.' Lukács's efforts, Merleau-Ponty said, were to show that the empirical proletariat 'retains an implicit totality and is in itself the universal subject that will only become for-itself by the indefinite development of classless society, because it is autocriticism and suppression of itself.'[36] This may mean, as Lukács said, that the meaning of Marx's teaching changes after the revolution because beforehand the context is polemical while afterwards not. But it may mean one of two other things as well. First it may mean that autocriticism, when practised by an entire society, amounts to an argument among antagonists who respect the right of the other to hold their errors for truth even while trying to persuade them away from their folly. By courtesy we may wish to call this autocriticism Marxism, but there is no compelling reason to do so, especially if it has the odd result that there are many more such 'Marxists' than follow Marx's teaching and that some of his most assiduous pupils are not at all 'Marxists' in this sense. Or second it may mean that Lukács's understanding of Marx's teaching is as protean as historical circumstances. The first alternative is more than a nominalist quibble. Genuine autocriticism can question the premises of Marxism, such as proletarian self-actualization, premises that for a Marxist must be accepted before discussion can begin. The second alternative may express a mood of hope, but it gives no *reason* why one should be hopeful.

Merleau-Ponty's argument did not explore the critical by-ways that Lukács's speculations opened upon. His criticisms of Lukács, even where explicit, always passed by way of Lukács's thought. 'The becoming of truth [is] the core of history,' man is 'dialectical,' 'truth is of another kind than the positivity of being, it is elsewhere; it is to be made': such phrases are Merleau-Ponty's own and express well the Hegelian heritage shared by him with Lukács and at times even Marx.[37] For Merleau-Ponty, Hegel had clearly been able to show that the problem of knowledge had been overcome because the question of atemporal relations of being and thought had been replaced by relations of man with his history or of the present with the future and the past.[38] Whatever else may be said of it, the dialectic, so understood, is open: it is a fundamental awareness of contradiction and of limits, of knowledge that in the end knows itself to be personal and provisional; it is 'a principle of universal disputation that deepens human questioning rather than stops it.'[39] If the principle of disputation is universal, and if the 'theorist' is constrained to persuade individuals to recognize their suffering and perhaps to alter its meaning or extent, and if one's adversaries are given the right to be right as well as to be wrong, then in practice, all the rhetoric about totalization, progress, the ensemble of history and philosophy, was superfluous. All that remained of Marx's dialectics was a willingness to ask questions. That is, Marx's dialectics have become Socratic.

THE CONCEPT OF INSTITUTION

Whether this was a legitimate reading of Lukács's book or of Marx we need not inquire. It was Merleau-Ponty's reading, and would seem to suggest that the basic premises of Marxism were questionable. At this point in the development of his thinking Merleau-Ponty was not willing to be so radical and introduced, as a kind of holding action, the concept of 'institution.'[40] By means of this concept he was able to combine the philosophical residue of questioning, which was for him now the most important element in the legacy of Hegel and Marx, with the insights directed against Lukács's book by those whom Merleau-Ponty called 'the orthodoxy.' The latter, including both German social democrats and Russian communists, were in their turn not above reproach, because they ignored or suppressed genuine problems that Lukács's arguments raised.

By 'institution' Merleau-Ponty meant 'those events of an experience that en-

dow it with durable dimensions, in relation to which a whole series of other experiences will make sense and form an intelligible succession or a history.' As the
title of his course at the Collège de France indicated, the concept could be applied
to both personal and public history.

Simultaneously there exist decentralizations and recentralizations of the elements
in our own life, a movement of us toward the past and of the reanimated past toward us; this labour of the past against the present does not culminate in a closed
universal history, a complete system of all possible human combinations of an institution such as kinship, for example, but results rather in a tableau of diverse,
complex possibilities, always tied to local circumstances and burdened with a coefficient of facticity so that we can not say that one is *more true* than another,
although we can say that one is more false, more artificial and is less open to a
less rich future.[41]

At the theoretical level, analyses on the basis of the concept 'tend toward a revision of Hegelianism, which is the discovery of phenomenology, of the living, genuine, and ordinary relation between the elements of the world.' Unrevised Hegelianism, he said, placed these real relations in the past so as to subordinate the
world to the system, and 'the vision of the philosopher.' Such a phenomenology
'remains alien to the adventures of experience,' whereas a revised phenomenology or a revised Hegelianism would remain 'entirely within philosophy' and
would 'take into consideration the mediation of being. We wish to outline here
this development of phenomenology into a metaphysics of history.'[42]

Merleau-Ponty took up the question of 'elements of the world' and the development of phenomenology into metaphysics in subsequent courses at the Collège de France and in his posthumous work *Le Visible et l'Invisible*. In *Les Aventures* he elaborated the more obviously political or historical implications of the
concept of institution: durability of complexes of meaning, the remembrance of
things past and the meaning of the past for present action, the significance of local circumstances, and the coefficient of facticity. Merleau-Ponty did not develop thematically this concept of institution much beyond the sentences we have
quoted, and yet it formed the basis not only of his criticism of Lukács but also
of his account of the adventures of the dialectic in the years after Lukács's book
was condemned. If this interpretation is correct, the concept also appeared to be
a significant element in guiding Merleau-Ponty's more practical observations and
actions in the years following the publication of *Les Aventures*.

Institution in public history was not just a pattern. Merleau-Ponty no longer
considered satisfactory concepts such as a 'Soviet Thermidor' or a 'pause' that often followed a revolutionary 'advance.' To observations of patterns Merleau-

Ponty added those of self-interpretation: the Moscow Trials appeared in *Les Aventures* as revealing 'a revolution that no longer wished to be a revolution ... an established regime that mimicked the revolution.'[43] This mimicry, which expressed the decadence of the Russian Revolution, was not simply fortuitous. 'Local events,' the public memory of the peoples who presently comprise the Soviet Union, a public memory that could not serve as a model for Western European countries, imposed its own weight. The concept of institution referred both to the stability and durability of the sense of a regime or a culture, what is sometimes referred to as its character, and also to the modifications, erosions, and restorations of sense exemplified in action. That is, it referred to a dimension beyond what was evident. In the light of this hidden, or as he later said invisible, source, the alternative tableaux of 'diverse, complex possibilities' could be judged in terms of the more or less artificial and more or less impoverished future that they opened upon. Institution implied equally the weight of public memory and the possibility of search insofar as human beings have been charged with carrying forward those memories and adding to them, which is to say, modifying them through persuasive criticism. In short, institution had an aspect of tradition to it that could serve both as a guide through the myriads of past events and a fetter that bound the understanding of each generation to pre-established patterns of meaning.

Merleau-Ponty's concept of institution thus served as both the theoretical and practical ground for his criticism and action. Because of the textual nature of the material, the first contention is easier to document. The ironic meaning to the title of the third chapter of *Les Aventures*, 'Pravda,' was that Lenin's crude doctrine elaborated in *Materialism and Empiro-Criticism* had become an anthropological 'truth.' As Merleau-Ponty said, Lenin wrote his book in order to reaffirm that dialectical materialism was a materialism; it presupposed a materialist scheme of knowledge and simply added the dialectic on to it. All Lenin succeeded in doing was 'to annul everything that had been said of knowledge since Epicurus.' This 'new dogmatism,' he said, 'removes the duty of autocriticism, exempts Marxism from applying its own principles to itself and installs dialectical thought in a massive positivity, which is denied by its own movement.' Making all possible allowances for tactics, Merleau-Ponty concluded that Lenin's use of expedients in philosophy hid an internal difficulty of Marxist thought.[44]

Ever since the discovery and publication of Marx's early manuscripts a good deal of effort has been expended in reconciling (or denying the possibility of reconciling) the early with the later works. By and large the controversies have in fact been concerned with disputing the most fundamental aspect of Marx's work. For example, if one considers the division between humanists, that is, atheists, and theists to be fundamental, the changes between the formulas of 1844 and

1867 are relatively trivial. If, however, one works within the context of human-ism in Marx's sense (as Merleau-Ponty did), there would indeed appear to be a contradiction in Marx's thought between dialectical and naïve realism, between the 'concrete dialectic' of the young disciple of Hegel and the 'scientific socialism' of the old economist.

According to Marx's later doctrine, praxis was understood as 'a type of tech-nical action like that of an engineer who constructs a bridge.' The fundamentalist reductions of Lenin, 'that mélange of dialectic and the positivist spirit, transports into nature the modes of human being: precisely, it is magic.'[45] The absurdities of a 'dialectic of nature' were felt in politics as well, since if nature could receive the modes of human being men could receive the modes of natural being. That is, men could be treated as things. Neither the young Marx nor the young Lukács developed a means of expressing a middle way: there was simply a change of mood from 'revolutionary optimism' to a desperation that was badly covered by 'merciless voluntarism.' Both lacked 'the means of expressing the inertia of infra-structures, the resistance of economic and even of natural conditions, the founder-ing of "personal relations" when they strike upon "things." The history they des-cribed lacked depth and they allowed its meaning to appear too quickly; they had to learn of the slowness of mediations.' The notion of dialectic developed by Lukács, therefore, was 'too agile, too conceptual and did not express the opacity or at least the depth of real history.'[46] Since historical depth existed only in virtue of public memory, Merleau-Ponty's criticism was that Lukács's dialectic was ab-stract in the sense that it was no more than an idea and did not consider or ac-count for the specific traditions and configurations of meaning to which human cultures have in fact been committed.

Lenin and Lukács both sought to understand the logic of history, which meant both its 'true' direction towards a concrete humanism and its detours, 'its mean-ing and what in history resists its meaning.' But in order to do so, he said, they needed

to conceive of the appropriate milieu, the institution, which is developed not ac-cording to causal laws like another nature, but never independently of what it signifies, not according to external ideas but by more or less taking account of fortuitous events and being changed at their instigation. Torn by all these contin-gencies but restored by the involuntary gestures of men who are caught in it and wish to live, this web merits neither the name of spirit nor matter but precisely that of history. This order of 'things' that informs 'relations among men,' sensi-tive to all the cumbersome conditions that link it to the order of nature, and open to everything that personal life can invent, is in modern language the milieu of symbolism, and Marx's thought must find its way out through it.[47]

Marx's teaching was unable to transform itself by taking into account changes in historical reality. It ceased to be a dialectical philosophy and decomposed into consciousness and history, with consciousness understood as simple reflection, in accord with Lenin's formulas (and so besieged constantly with the spectre of radical doubt), and history understood as a 'second nature,' not in Burke's sense of the term but rather after the fashion of Engels' 'dialectics' of nature (and so endowed with a brute opacity never completely to be grasped).

Consequently, consciousness could no longer provide any criteria for distinguishing by itself what was knowledge and what was ideology, and naïve realism, as ever, ended up in scepticism. If realism were to avoid this consequence, it could do so only by force, by an unwarranted approval by some external source such as an imaginary social process 'in-itself' or the Party. Henceforth, all the products of thought would be measured by this standard, and judged true and false according to whether or not they conform.[48] Such a result was incoherent or absurd, but for this very reason was significant: 'Orthodoxy does not accept that one think it, even if it is in order to base orthodoxy in reason and in dialectic; it does not wish to be true at the second remove and for reasons that are not its own; it claims for itself the truth of the thing itself.' In the end, no one could possibly be satisfied, and communists were left with a system of philosophical double talk, which disarmed the dialectic by refusing the subject the ability to judge history and the intrinsic appreciation of literature as well as politics, but which led one to believe that the dialectic continued to function underground, in a mysterious future the economic and technical infrastructures were preparing, 'which honoured the dialectic from afar without practising it and without disavowing it, which annulled it as an instrument of critique and conserved it only as a point of honour, a justification, and an ideology.'[49]

Further evidence of the decomposition of Marxism into a set of antinomies without a unifying principle could be found on the side of action. Merleau-Ponty chose the example of Trotsky, whose philosophy, he said, was 'the most banal naturalism' but whose reflections on ethics or literature or politics were both precise and supple and indeed were the basis of many of Merleau-Ponty's own ideas. His concept of historical selection and his understanding of the two-way communication between the Party and the proletariat expressed a fine dialectical theory. In his practical struggle with Stalin between 1923 and 1927, however, Trotsky made no attempt to institute any dialectic between the Party and the proletariat: in Politburo meetings he read French novels and in public he submitted to the principle of Party discipline and the rule of 1921 prohibiting inner party groupings.[50] Merleau-Ponty pointed out that Trotsky's excuse, that 'history' decided against him, was lame: the truth was that he did not seem to know what was going on.[51]

Trotsky's blindness was not just a personal failure or the result of certain deficiencies in Soviet practice but was inherent in Marx's teaching. No one ever denied that the Party could deviate from the dialectical theory without *clearly* betraying the Revolution; it would always be a question of proportion. So long as the Party were the party of the Revolution, and even though it did not act like it (but could), differences might simply be 'personal.' But when Trotsky associated himself with lies and deceptions by the Party of the proletariat? Why obey the rule of discipline when the Party was not obedient to the rule of democracy? Did such a situation mean that the spirit and style of the Revolution had evaporated and that Trotsky alone was revolutionary? Trotsky could see no way out of the dilemma, because Marxism had taught him that truth could not be placed outside the Party and in principle could not dwell elsewhere than the junction of the proletariat and the organization that embodied it.[52] An absurd orthodoxy found an appropriate incarnation in an unquestionable party discipline.

The problem lay deeper than Bolshevik fundamentalism or the Scythian character. According to Marx, a Thermidorian reaction was always possible in a bourgeois revolution. But he had nothing to say about a regime without property that was not directed for the benefit of the proletariat. To consider such a regime 'would have been to admit that the revolution could betray itself and to renounce the immanence of truth.'[53] Thus, Merleau-Ponty concluded, it was Marxism and not Bolshevism that justified Party actions on the basis of allegedly already existing social forces. That is, Marx's own 'scientific socialism' taught that the homogeneous socialist society was already present within capitalism. 'The mélange of extreme objectivism and extreme subjectivism, the one constantly supporting the other, which defines Bolshevism, is already present in Marx when he allows that the revolution is present before having been recognized.' In short, Marx too had postulated what Daniel Guérin called an 'internal mechanism' to history, and, Merleau-Ponty said, this amounted to creating a third order beyond that of historically objective conditions and human will.[54] In this way, while there could be deviations, in the end the internal mechanism would set matters right. Both Trotsky's notion of permanent revolution, the more orthodox dogma of unequal development between substructure and superstructure, and Guérin's notion of premature revolution assumed the existence of this occult and hidden reality. The only hypothesis to be excluded, the only one to prevent Marxist disputation from being 'universal,' was 'that a party born of the proletarian movement and carried to power by it could not only have degenerated but could have turned itself against the revolution.' Such a hypothesis was excluded by materialism, by the idea that the classless society was inscribed in the processes of capitalist production, that it was already there and as soon as the barrier of private appropriation were raised the future would press with all its weight upon a revolutionary policy that sooner or later could not fail to set it right.[55] Such a hypothesis expressed but could not mend the fractured dialectic.

The dogma of the internal mechanism, even with its auxiliary variations of permanent revolution, unequal development, and so on, could only postpone the genuine problem of action. If Trotsky believed in the dogma, how could he ever abandon the Party, let alone undertake such odd activities as founding a Fourth International? How could he ever have abandoned such a guarantee? The question was a bad one, and Merleau-Ponty reformulated it along the following lines:

> dialectical materialism holds that the dialectic resides in the material of the social whole, that is to say, that the ferment of negation is carried by an existing historical formation, the proletariat, from which comes the idea of the proletariat as *Selbstaufhebung* [self-suppression, self-transcendence], as well as the idea of permanent revolution, that is, the idea of a continuous negation, immanent to the internal mechanism of history. When realized in the world in this way, negativity can be illegitimately invoked as a source or a subtle material. The Party that labours to put the proletariat in power can pride itself on it, and the society it prepares is, as by definition, permanent autocriticism, classless society, or true society. *Unfortunately, a government and a party, even revolutionary ones, are not negations; they must exist positively.*[56]

In short, Merleau-Ponty recalled an earlier lesson, that the acts of all governments were not provisional but, at least for the present, absolute. The 'subtle material' of a self-suppressing proletariat was the fantasy of a communist theoretician. In truth there are only real human beings who have particular desires.

Lacking a conception of institution, abstract mediations of the greatest complexity and charm were transformed into non-mediated real entities: the proletariat is the revolution, the Party is the proletariat, the leader or the leaders are the Party. Only at the 'sublime point' of a genuine revolution could the internal mechanism of history appear and negativity be truly incarnate in history. Then there are no mediations, but there is also no regime. Trotsky erected the memory of this moment, in 1917, into the myth of permanent revolution. In the absence of a genuine revolutionary flux and in the presence of a real regime, the revolution is represented by bureaucrats, which led Merleau-Ponty to formulate the following paradox: 'The revolution as continuous autocriticism needs violence in order to be established, and ceases to be autocritical to the extent that it exercises it.'[57] Such a dilemma never worried Marx, because he conceived of capitalism as an absolute Other, but men who have seen a Marxist revolution know better. Nothing would be achieved by returning to a pre-Marxist theory and turning the homogeneous society into a limiting case. Such a course, Merleau-Ponty said, would be either a declaration of non-political utopianism or, worse, would sustain the existing non-dialectical pair of truth as an idea and violence as the technique for realizing it. Marx felt that the split between the Revolution as present achievement and the Revolution as ideal could be overcome by the participation of the proletariat in its Party and by its growing self-consciousness. The result, however, was that this self-consciousness actually appeared as dogmas of 'socialist' literature and 'socialist' science, that violence was justified in the name of necessity and excused in the name of a future 'truth.' Purge succeeds détente, and the 're-sult is that each of these attitudes becomes the simple mask of the other.'[58] Marx's ideology was modified by the adherents to his ideology: they forgot of the weight of social factors, which Merleau-Ponty partly recovered in his concept of institution, and they situated the dialectic in things or in the future. This crude theory was complemented by brutal action, violence, and 'terror exercised in the name of a hidden truth.'[59] In Bolshevism the adventures of the dialectic in action had clearly come to a dead end.

If taken seriously, Merleau-Ponty's notion of institution would remove any prejudice in favour of a Marxist totalization of history, and this could not help but alter the meaning of the rhetoric used earlier in the book concerning the empirical totality or the ensemble of philosophy and history. In other words, Merleau-Ponty's thinking in Les Aventures de la Dialectique was forced, through its own rigour, to modify some of the untenable elements that served as its original foundation. One may say, therefore, that the development of Merleau-Ponty's argument illustrated its own dialectic and so moved beyond the problems it documented.

ULTRA-BOLSHEVISM

Whitehead's declaration 'modern philosophy has been ruined' found an echo in Merleau-Ponty's judgment that the theory of the dialectic had been ruined by modern thinkers.[60] In political affairs it was significant therefore that Sartre provided an analysis of Communist action that was entirely denuded of dialectics even as ideology or point of honour. 'Here for the first time we are told what a communist must say in order to defend communism in all clarity and without appeal to the presuppositions of the tradition.'[61] Sartre 'understood' Communist politics according to his own principles, not according to those of 'the orthodoxy.' Merleau-Ponty discussed both the significance of attempting to justify Communist actions while remaining outside the Party and the peculiar contours of Sartre's argument.

Les Aventures de la Dialectique contained the most serious critique Merleau-Ponty ever made of Sartre's philosophy, though it was not the only one he had made nor even the most significant aspect of a long and sometimes repetitive chapter. In addition to two early reviews,[62] Merleau-Ponty's earlier comments on Sartre had been presented in the *Phénoménologie de la perception*, which contained some mild disagreements between the two men. The only explicit differences were found in the concluding chapter of the *Phénoménologie*, and even there it was only one of emphasis. Whereas Sartre's account of fatigue and motive tended to emphasize the importance of the individual's ability to choose to become tired, for example, so as to live through his fatigue and so 'conquer' it by appropriation, Merleau-Ponty emphasized the 'sedimentation' of past existence that conditioned one's freedom and so made one's past never quite as translucent to consciousness as Sartre argued. One might find there a primitive rendering of the concept of institution.[63] Again, in *Sens et Non-sens*, articles dating from the 1945-7 period drew attention to Sartre's 'truncated' dialectic, his overemphasis on antitheses, his lack of an awareness of the importance of passivity and 'sedimentation,' and his tendency to derive social phenomena from the radical contingency of the individual.[64] Keeping these intellectual differences in mind, two things must be recalled. First, in many respects, and certainly at the secondary level of common philosophical concerns, Sartre and Merleau-Ponty were in agreement. Second, the differences between the two men, as Merleau-Ponty understood them, were intellectual rather than personal. Merleau-Ponty was surprised and dismayed at the bitter personal tone of Simone de Beauvoir's review of *Les Aventures* and for some time afterwards held Sartre, as editor of the journal, responsible. Merleau-Ponty's criticism of Sartre was both philosophical and limited. The title of the chapter was 'Sartre and ultra-Bolshevism,' not 'Sartre the ultra-Bolshevik.' Moreover, the term 'ultra-Bolshevism' must be understood in the context of what Merleau-Ponty understood by Bolshevism and the dogmatizing ruin of dialectics that the Bolshevik enterprise implied.

Merleau-Ponty summarized his argument against ultra-Bolshevism in four points: Sartre's justification and its implications, Sartre's substitutions for Marx's concepts, the origin of Sartre's concepts and their consequences, and the pragmatic question, what to do when the dialectic dies? Sartre's study, 'Les Communistes et la Paix,' was, Merleau-Ponty began, first of all a factual account of the anti-Ridgeway demonstration and its disastrous consequences both for the French Communist Party and French workers. During the period when the demonstration was orchestrated and suppressed, opposition to the Communists meant opposition to the workers, and yet to change the policies of the Party one must do so in the name of the proletariat of tomorrow. Such was the very stuff of politics: there would always be equivocation and always the risk that the idea of tomorrow's proletariat would not be recognized by today's workers. But such a commonsensical understanding of the Party's fortunes could not be found in Sartre, though both men agreed, pragmatically, that the Party and the workers had been badly bloodied.

For Sartre, the Party would always be justified because it was a pure and absolute negation of the bourgeoisie. Now the notion of a pure and absolute negation was Sartre's understanding of consciousness. Consciousness could not be committed externally unless it found an appropriate or resonant 'vehicle' of negation, and for Sartre 'the party is the double of consciousness.' The militant worker, likewise, was a pure will to refuse: 'The sting of duty or of nothingness upon being, freedom that Sartre once called "mortal" is what constitutes the militant.'[65] Because the Party was pure negation it could constitute a resonance with the negation of consciousness, but it was, like consciousness, a constituting, or creative, or active negation as well. As pure negation the Party would destroy the bourgeoisie, but as pure action it would create the proletariat. Thus there was a single act of creative annihilation. Pluralism therefore meant the dissolution of the proletariat because it meant the corruption of Party purity. Thus, 'if there is a proletariat, it has confidence in the Party,' and consequently a real worker lacking confidence in the Party was not a proletarian but a traitor to himself. There could be no popular control of Party leaders; minority factions must be liquidated in the name of a unified will; workers could say nothing to their leaders; and their only task was to obey. To judge the Party was to be less than the Party; therefore there could be no control. By definition, obedient workers would find themselves reflected in Party actions on the basis 'of an oath exchanged outside of life.'[66]

There could be no 'objective conditions' in Weber's sense, no questions of probability to mediate between the 'pure fact' and the 'pure act' that endowed it with meaning, for the proletariat only existed by resisting and negating the facts. For Marx, consciousness, like the Party, was one pole of dialectical tension: the observer and the observed existed in an ambiguous situation, 'two signposts on the same road.'[67] Sartre's consciousness, like his Party, Merleau-Ponty said, was an absolute that provided all meaning, with no external appeal to facts, 'which say neither yes nor no.' In place of Marx's notion of praxis and the elaboration of praxis in Merleau-Ponty's concept of institution, Sartre substituted his own concept of freedom. True politics, for Sartre, was pure creation, and 'preparation' was simply a retrospective illusion. Since praxis was a matter of will, there could be no external constraints on what was possible. Praxis 'is the magic power we have of making, and of making ourselves what we must be.'[68] When Sartre did not give totally novel meanings to Marx's words, he took at face value the meaning given them by contemporary communists. The two were often in agreement and equally distant from Marx. The Party as well as Sartre used the revolutionary rhetoric of 1917 as a myth, an incantation to conjure an instant, voluntarist transformation at the hands of a non-existent neo-proletariat. Indeed, Sartre's conception of a neo-proletariat, which owed its existence not to its role in the process of production but to its wretchedness, was derived directly from his study of the 'gaze.' The 'look of the most wretched' provided, in the end, the principle of judgment. But it was not a judgment properly speaking but simply a response of sentiment or will: who do you sympathize with? Who do you will for? The only authentic response to the look of the most wretched must be pure negation and pure action.[69]

In order for negation and action to be conceived as 'pure,' the acts of a plurality of men, which in reality condition human existence in a quasi-anonymous fashion, must be transformed into the explicit doings of a single imaginary actor. What Myrdal called the 'communistic fiction,' the auxiliary hypothesis that invented the notion of a harmony of interests and made possible the science of economics, reappeared, suitably Hegelianized in the last classical political economist, as the 'postulate' of a community producing and consuming like a huge Robinson Crusoe.[70] The notion reappeared as well in 'Les Communistes et la Paix' with its attendant problems. 'The "social" is a scandal for the "I think" ' was the way Merleau-Ponty indicated the necessity of obliterating human plurality. The scandal was only enlarged when the *cogito* became the Party. Then the actions of men were obliterated, and the gap between intentions and consequences was no longer the result of an act of liberal deception. It was nothing other than a clear and distinct implication of Sartre's own allegiance to his private intellectual invention. 'For Sartre, as for the anarchists, the idea of oppression always dominates that of exploitation. If he is not an anarchist it is because he passes suddenly from the poetry of the subject to the prose of the world at the same time as from the for-itself to the for-another. But the other is still a subject and magic is enough to ensure he remains one: behind the prose and discipline of the Party we have seen sorcery expand.'[71] As a result of Sartre's sorcery, history was turned into a single, monotonous struggle, unbroken by truce, where the Party gathered all the virtue of history and the bourgeoisie all its crimes.

In the closing pages of third part of *Les Aventures*, Merleau-Ponty emphasized again the eclipse of the dialectic. There was no need for an exchange between the leaders and their followers, for there was no way that the leaders could be judged wrong. One could be wrong and one could judge (in an ambiguous fashion, to be sure) if there were a road for which the Party and the proletariat could be 'signposts.' But 'the road chosen is the only possible one, and a fortiori the best.' Between the leaders and the proletariat there was by definition a strict identity. If there were only consciousnesses and things, and if each consciousness desired the death of the other, then only the devotion of the proletariat to the Party and the creation of the proletariat by the Party as the incarnation of historical negativity could prevent the carnage of competitive individual negativity. Such a magical creation out of nothing was 'a long way from Marxism.'[72] The only proof of being on the road to communist society, according to Merleau-Ponty's reading of Marx, was proletarian participation in politics. For Sartre, such empirical criteria as bureaucratic rule or workers' democracy could mean nothing, because 'true' democracy, which was Party rule and worker obedience, must always be there.

'What distinguished Sartre from Marxism, even in this recent period, has always been his philosophy of the *cogito* ... Many times in these articles one finds a movement of thought that is Cartesian.' Either there is meaning or there is not, and if there is it must come from somewhere, from the gaze of the most wretched and their prosaic incarnation, the will of the Party. Consciousness intervened in the world 'as sovereign legislator because it gives the world meaning, because meaning is neither more nor less than it gives, because it is undivided, because it is total or it is nothing. We recognize the *cogito*, and that is what gives the Sartrean nuance to violence.'[73] The purity of the *cogito* and the unconditional freedom of Sartre's speculation bridged the gap between intentions and consequences. In the context of his polemic against Claude Lefort, the Sartrean nuance to violence took the form of a personal vindictiveness that by all accounts was uncharacteristic of his real personality. If Lefort had the same understanding of history as Sartre and yet disagreed about the real Communist Party, it could only be for base motives. 'But is Lefort Sartre? There is the question Sartre forgets. Is what he thinks so true that any disclaimers must be impure?' As if there were no ambiguities and contradictions in Marx! In the end, Sartre reproached Lefort for not joining the Party, and Merleau-Ponty drew attention to the 'high altitude' thinking involved: 'You who are Marxists, says Sartre, you must join the CP. As for me, who instruct you so well in your Marxist duty, but who by happy chance am not a communist, I retain all my freedom.'[74]

Violence, even when genuinely creative and achieved the founding of a new regime, could never be pure. It is brutal. As Merleau-Ponty noted, 'what is completely lacking in Sartre's studies to date is any confrontation between terror and the humanist perspective.'[75] For Sartre, violence was pure, it was what constitutes the proletariat as meaning, much as Descartes' *cogito* magically constituted its meanings. 'Is violence Sartre's last word? Surely not, and for a reason of principle: pure violence does not exist.' It was not pure for the Bolsheviks; it was the brutal backdrop to Bolshevik truth, and, as we have seen, it rendered that truth implacable. Ultra-Bolshevism, in fact, got rid of this pretext: truth and reason were for tomorrow, and today's action must be pure. 'But that is to say that one agrees only with the principles of communism, with its will to change the world.' All of which, Merleau-Ponty said, is purely or abstractly 'philosophical' and has nothing to do with politics. The pure will to change the world was so much a matter of internal life that we were never told how to go about it, and it was so pure that if Sartre were ever assailed with doubt he would instantly become one of his own 'slimy rats.' 'Sartre's conclusion is no longer pure action, it is pure action contemplated at a distance; in other words, it is sympathy.'[76] Sympathy, like the gaze of the most wretched and the voluntarism their gaze must evoke, was as labile as events themselves because it lacked weight and responsibility.

In addition to the internal critique of Sartre's attitude, Merleau-Ponty discussed it from outside. This change in interpretative strategy was legitimate because, as he said, Sartre's position on its own terms was not a political one. If the attitude of 'Les Communistes et la Paix' was to have any political significance it could only be discovered from a perspective greater than its own. Sartre's sympathy for the non-existent 'essence' of the Party, attained through the sorcery of his imagination, could never issue in action or collaboration. Action in history was an ambiguous enterprise, sympathy was not, and the price of Sartre's clarity was inaction.[77] 'When the Party is judged from the outside and is given an absolute respect, one dreams of a constructive opposition that is recognized in other respects to be impossible. A Marxist and dialectical Communism has room for an opposition. Sartrean Communism tolerates none of it, not even that of Sartre for his own "reasons." The same reasons that oblige him to respect the CP prevent him from joining it.' This did not mean, however, that there was any contradiction involved. 'Simply, it is a thought, not an action, and there is not a great deal of sense in dealing with Communism, which is an action, by pure thought.' Sartre's faith in true action as a consequence of true thought was the dream of a mandarin who united the fantasy of total knowledge and pure action. To be sure, action and knowledge were mixed with each other, modalities of the same existence, but it was a serious mistake to think that an external vision could overcome the difference between seeing and doing.[78]

The most serious flaw in Sartre's position, however, was that it could be a solution only for someone who lived in the capitalist world. Sartre never wondered why Communists never have written what he has, although they apparently did what he said. What Communists thought made no difference; there were no periods of greatness or decline, no founders or epigones. The real essence of Communism, as revealed by Sartre, was found in the categorical violence of the proletariat that would create what never has been. If Sartre were right in what he said, the Communists were wrong, and one could question what kind of regime really existed in the Communist world and what kind of ideological distortion the Communists really had made. Such an inquiry could never be held outside the capitalist world. 'At the limit, if Sartre were right, Sartre would be wrong. Such is the situation of the single man who incorporates Communism into his universe and thinks without regard to what it thinks itself.'[79]

The fracturing of the dialectic into consciousness and things and its pretended restoration by ultra-Bolshevik sorcery also had a meaning. Sartre's magically pure violence was an expedient, the expression of a widely held allegiance to an amalgam of extreme realism and extreme formalism. No clearer evidence of a crisis within Marxism could be desired. 'But expedients, products of the crisis they attempt to hide, will not put history back onto a Marxist course.' Sartre described a communism of pure action that no longer believed in truth, the revolution, or history. To Merleau-Ponty the 'reasons' of Sartre were in fact opposed to those of Marxism, and indeed, he said, it was *because* the dialectic has had a breakdown that Sartre defended Communist politics. 'It remains to know what must be concluded from this.'[80] When history, which was supposed to sustain the dialectic that expressed its structure, was abandoned in favour of 'theatre,'[81] when the dialectic was moribund, that too had to be understood and new questions posed.

CONCLUSION

The conclusion Merleau-Ponty drew from his study of the intellectual adventures that ended in ultra-Bolshevism divided his earlier political thinking from his later. There were, of course, continuities, but there was also a genuine and fundamental change. It was no longer a question, for example, of judging Sartre wrong from a correctly interpreted Marxist perspective, of showing him to be a 'mediocre Marxist,' as with Koestler. Merleau-Ponty's perspectives now were broader. Marx's tests and the proper understanding of them were for the first time themselves to be questioned in light of their contributions to the confusions of the contemporary world and not simply as authoritative recipes for ridding it of illusions and errors.

The first theoretical problem was to recognize that the restoration or the reinstitutionalization of dialectic was a critical task. This was why, as Pierre Aubenque pointed out, 'in the single passage where he treats it *ex professo*, M. Merleau-Ponty proposes nothing other than a kind of *theologia negativa* of dialectic.'[82] In the text to which Aubenque referred, Merleau-Ponty discussed certain paradoxical formulas in terms of a more basic and fundamental experience, 'the conjunction of a subject, of being, and of other subjects' where, he said,

there is room, without magic, for relations with a double meaning and direction, for reversals, for contrary and yet inseparable truths, for surpassings, for a perpetual genesis, for a plurality of levels or orders. Dialectic exists only in this kind of being, where the junction of subjects is made and which is not simply a spectacle that each one of us is given for his own advantage but is their common residence, the place of their reciprocal insertion. Dialectic does not procure, as Sartre said, a finality, that is, the presence of a whole in what by its nature exists by separated parts, but rather obtains a global cohesion, primordial on a field of experience where each element opens upon the others.[83]

This double meaning of thought applied especially to the topic of his book: the adventures of the dialectic in recent times were errors, but of a kind that invited a critical reader to pass through them and beyond them.

There was a dialectic at work even within the history of its own apparent self-destruction. Once the elements in this history were made thematic for the primordial field of experience, whose mode of being embraced both genesis and order, one could establish more clearly the meaning of the adventures of the dialectic and the logic that bound Sartre back to Lukács, Lenin, and Marx. With Sartre the adventure reached its end, 'the world and history are no longer a system with many entrances but a bundle of irreconcilable perspectives that never coexist.'[84] But to conclude from this that the dialectic was a myth would be wrong, precisely because the illusion had a history of successive interpretations the combined effect of which was to make the master assumption ever more clear and ever more impossible. The dialectic that stretched from Marx (and behind him, no doubt, from Hegel) to Sartre was predicated on the reality of an historical fact, namely the genesis and development of the proletariat into a '*true*, homogeneous and final society.' Such a 'fact' did not exist, and Sartre's magical operations were simply the most carefully developed consequence of its non-existence. 'What is decrepit therefore, is not dialectic but the pretension of terminating it in an end of history or in a permanent revolution, in a regime that, being the confrontation of itself, has no need of being challenged from outside and, in sum, no longer has an outside.'[85]

In his later years Husserl was said to have remarked: 'Philosophy as a rigorous science? The dream is all dreamed out.' Merleau-Ponty might have said the same. As an explicit reference to Kojève was doubtless intended to suggest, the dream of an end to history, to the story of the disputes and conflicts, the actions, passions, and thoughts of human beings, was over. It was not to be revived.

When the end of history is no longer conceived as meaningful, even as an idea, 'the concept of revolution is found to be relativized.'[86] In order to sustain the dialectic historically, there must be an authentic opposition to the revolutionary regime, an opposition that is bound to appear to the men of that regime as a threat to the revolution itself. In principle, Merleau-Ponty observed, 'power ignores its truth, which is the image that those who do not exercise power have of it.' Power was justified to itself by its intentions, while its truth, to be found in its effects, was suffered by others. The result was that action and truth fell apart.

Truth and action will never communicate if there are not, besides those who act, those who look at them, showing them the truth of their action and claiming to be able to replace them in power. There is no dialectic without opposition and without freedom, and opposition and freedom do not last long in a revolution. It is not accidental that all known revolutions degenerate: as an instituted regime they can never be what they were as movements, and, exactly because it has succeeded and ended up as an institution, the historical movement is no longer itself; it 'betrays' itself and 'disfigures' itself while under way. Revolutions are true as movements and false as regimes.[87]

Later, with respect to the French Revolution and Daniel Guérin's Trotskyite interpretation, Merleau-Ponty wrote: 'The failure of the French Revolution, and all the other ones, is not an accident that shatters a logical development, for which it is necessary to impute to the peculiarities of the rising class and which will not take place when the rising class is the proletariat: the defeat of the revolution will be the revolution itself. The revolution and its defeat are but one.'[88] It would be hard to find a clearer and more honest example of a genuinely courageous autocriticism.

In summary: *Les Aventures de la Dialectique* was a subtle and complex book not only because it was, as Merleau-Ponty said, a series of disparate meditations and reflections but also because in it we can trace an alteration in Merleau-Ponty's attitude towards Marx and Marx's account of capitalism and revolution. In the earlier sections of the book Merleau-Ponty raised objections to Max Weber's analysis of capitalism. By following the road from Lukács to Sartre he showed that Marxist writers grew successively less empirical and more abstract, ending in what he called 'magic.' At the same time, particularly in the chapter on western Marxism, Merleau-Ponty still appeared to show a fundamental commitment to a regime of mutual recognition. His later argument drew increasingly away from the 'dream' of a homogeneous society. With the concept of institution Merleau-Ponty opened perspectives that led him back to the empirically rich themes of Max Weber, unencumbered by the theoretical restrictions of Weber's methodology. The concept of institution indicated a more concrete and commonsensical, less abstract and apocalyptic, turn in his political thought. As we shall see, no melancholy resignation to political impotence was implied.

6

Virtù without resignation

What attention has been paid to *Les Aventures de la Dialectique* has shown little appreciation for its structure or its significance. Understandably enough, philosophers have tended to direct their concern towards the essays in *Signes* and the limpid but indirect prose of his two posthumous works. For example, Claude Lefort, who has devoted as much attention to the texts of Merleau-Ponty as anyone, traced the line of thought indicated initially in *Titres et Travaux* through its successive incarnations first in *La Prose du Monde*, a manuscript from the 1951-2 period, then in his lectures at the Collège de France, and finally in *Le Visible et l'Invisible*. He noted in passing that Merleau-Ponty was at the same time working through the problems that were set forth in *Les Aventures*. But he was most circumspect in suggesting inferences to be drawn about the 'other direction' in which Merleau-Ponty's thought moved.[1] I have argued that *Les Aventures* was a watershed so far as his political thinking was concerned and suggested that it may also have been a turning point for his philosophy as a whole. Evidence in support of a more significant place for *Les Aventures* may be found in the courses given at the Collège de France after 1952-3 in which, apart from a single course in 1953-4, Merleau-Ponty took up themes elaborated in *Les Aventures*. Even his lectures on passivity may have grown from his reading of Sartre.[2] After 1956 the themes that appeared in *Le Visible et l'Invisible* seemed more prominent in his courses. Nevertheless, *Les Aventures* was the last full-length and integrated study Merleau-Ponty presented, and the estimation presently accorded this work would increase if its pivotal philosophical significance were appreciated.

The present task is more modest than a reinterpretation of Merleau-Ponty's philosophy in the light of his discovery that the historical dialectic was dead and the theoretical dialectic remained a task. Our purview is confined to the political dimension of his thinking, first with respect to the implications he drew from his analysis of the adventures of dialectic and second with respect to the political judgments he made on the basis of those implications.

POLITICS AND CULTURE

What had killed the dialectic, in the end, was purity. Even though the genuine sy-namics of thought and action had hardened into the dogmatic recipes of prole-tarian action, there was still the possibility of thawing dogma through an appeal to interpretation. In principle, dogma may remain close enough to the reality of our experience in the world that its inherent tendency to sclerosis may be ameli-orated through persistent appeals to our common sense of the world's shape and to argument based on the internal inconsistency of deeds and doctrine. When the already half-dead dialectic had been purified and embalmed, however, the sharp features of contradiction and the hazy background of partially repressed common sense reality disappeared within the second reality, a uniform, homogeneous whole. Rather than Hegel's grey on grey, which permitted one to judge contrast if not colour, one is reminded of the night when all cows are black. Equally dis-astrous, although apparently less sinister, was the obliteration of Gestalt by pure white on white. The analogy with perception is not misleading: just as figure and ground are equal elements of the perceptual field, so contrasting elements are necessary even for there to be a social field. The poetics of our participation in the world, to use Merleau-Ponty's metaphor, are experientially prior to the artic-ulate prose of the world. Sartre's prose of politics tried to obliterate the poetics that gave it sense; if pure prose could ever replace the ambiguity of poetics, there would indeed be nothing more to do or say, because poetics, and the variegated texture of its sense, reveal the ambiguous reality of our participation.

Merleau-Ponty applied the metaphors of prose and poetry to the political realm when considering the relations between politics and culture, and specific-ally the reduction of culture to a province of politics. *Les Aventures* may be seen as an argument against a symmetrically opposite reduction, which was equally destructive of the historical or political dialectic, namely that politics can be re-duced to a province of culture. This prejudice was no more than the 'dream of mandarins' and not even a political position. In fact, however, it made little differ-ence from which side one approached the question because the results were iden-tical: the attempt to remake the world after the mandarin's image is as senseless as obliterating all independence because it might be critical. 'If it is true that all action is symbolic, then books are also actions in their own way, and they deserve to be written according to their own rules, with nothing in the way of their duty to unmask.' Likewise, politics, which 'consists in tracing a line in the obscurity of historical symbolisms,' has its own methods and its own technique. The worlds of vision and action, culture and politics, are different, and yet they are linked, not because they are immediately superimposable or because they are both glued to events, but 'because the symbols of each order have echos, transfers, and induction effects in the other.' To keep the two worlds distinct, Merleau-Ponty said, may be the only way of being faithful to either. If politics and culture must be both separated and joined, that is, dialectically related, it is certain that the contact between the two cannot be maintained by politics. There can only be a 'delegation' of power to the political man by the writer, who ever must guard his ability to say so and to judge otherwise. Politics and literature were joined in virtue of their being two strata of single symbolic or historic life. If the conditions of the age are such that this symbolic life is shattered, such that one cannot at the same time be a free writer and a communist or a communist and a member of an opposition, the Marxist dialectic that unified the two would be replaced by an enervating oscillation between them. 'They will not be reconciled by force. It is necessary, then, to correct oneself, to approach in an indirect way what we have been unable to encounter directly, and to search for a mode of action other than the communist.'[3]

We can see more clearly now why Sartre's position of sympathy was to Merleau-Ponty so futile. In order to retain the tension between politics and culture, between poetics and prose, between the city and the philosopher, separation or deflection was necessary. Otherwise the tension would collapse into the mandarin's dream or the tyrant's brutality. With respect to the communists, who were to incarnate the dialectic, who were to exist as the critical tension between action and thought, the collapse into authority and obedience meant that the man of culture must be outside the Party. But this position was impossible too, because from the point of view of the Party it was already too much to have reasons, and one could never be loyal enough from the outside.[4] As Merleau-Ponty said: 'Whether he judges for or against, it doesn't matter; the sympathizer is out of the action.'[5] Moreover, one cannot be part of the action and be a communist as well, because action is not the same as giving or taking orders; action, like criticism, is the actualization of one pole of the dialectic, one pole of the tension. In short, action and criticism are a pair, and Sartre's 'direct' attack on the crisis of a fractured dialectic, his attempt to force a junction, could only be 'enervating.' The most generous evaluation, therefore, would hold Sartre's posture to be one of courageous desperation.

Like the cripple who exposed his deformation by trying to hide it, Sartre's declarations, which expressed his reckless hope that a dogmatic shell retained the vitality of an earlier day, succeeded only in pointing to the fracture. 'Sartre said: since there is no dialectic we can keep the *aura* of the revolution from escaping from communism.'[6] The language Merleau-Ponty used was important: in 1946 he had said exactly the same thing about Communist rhetoric, and his subsequent analyses of the behaviour of the French Communist Party dwelt at length on the stupidity of preserving an 'aura of revolution' the result of which was only to justify the fears and propaganda of the right.[7] 'We will say,' he continued, 'if there is no dialectic, Communism must be secularized.' If there were no dialectic, the constituent elements must be judged as they are, and, most important, the prejudice in favour of the nostalgia of communism must be extirpated. Again, just as in 1946, Merleau-Ponty said that about the only thing of which one could be certain was that the way of the Master was a dead end, and that attempting to start the entire social enterprise over again from the beginning by destroying what presently exists would attain, not the sought-for authentic intersubjectivity, but only another State. Nothing could be learned from placing one's hope in the intentions of leaders, because leaders change, and the hopeful sympathizer must always say yes, although leaders may disavow what their predecessors had done. 'It seems to us, therefore, that one can only draw an agnostic conclusion from these analyses.' Such an agnosticism, Merleau-Ponty said, was a positive conduct, a task, just as sympathy was an abstention.[8] The next task was to make precise the political position that could be deduced from it.

The first step in defining a political position was to reaffirm the notion of commitment that, he said, was the basis of his early writings in *Les Temps modernes*.[9] We noted above the restatement of commitment in his inaugural lecture at the Collège de France in 1952.[10] Later, in the spring of 1956, Merleau-Ponty and Sartre met again at a week-long conference in Venice, and their discussion illustrated well their diverging views of commitment. On Monday morning Stephen Spender remarked that, in light of the fact that communist intellectuals from Eastern Europe were present, one should avoid using provocative language such as 'freedom' or 'peace,' and introduced the theme that not everyone needs be committed; in the afternoon, Merleau-Ponty replied. To begin with, he said, if we agree to talk only about what we agree upon, then the conversation can only be vague and dull. We are all very happy with the 'thaw,' he continued, but what does it mean to each of us? Does it have a philosophical as well as a political meaning? At the very least it puts into question 'the intellectual formula of the cold war, according to which intellectual life is not a dialogue but a battle.' If political events were to have repercussions in the domain of culture, it must be acknowledged that some aspects of culture may attain greater perfection in non-communist countries, in which case one must make room for a new kind of universalism. Such a new universalism would not be bourgeois philosophy, the abstract universalism of liberal ideology, but 'the idea that if one places oneself at the level of living men, it is possible, in non-communist countries, that living men express what they live in complete autonomy and that they find themselves overcoming the limits of their class or their society. It is a question of a man who would be more than his class on the condition that he places himself at the level at which he lives and not at the level of abstract principles.'[11]

Raising the possibility of a new universalism led Merleau-Ponty to the significance of commitment. A committed writer was not simply responsible for his books but for all that he did in life, including his participation in the injustices of events; even so, he must still do something of his own in writing and in his speech. Consequently, the correct idea of commitment is quite distinct from that of Marxists who place the writer in a category, and within that category consider the writer as someone respectable. Commitment was more than simply also being a citizen. In writing one rooted oneself in one's human being and in one's way of being. As a result, there were two different meanings to commitment. The first was a pessimistic conception, a product of the cold war, according to which the writer must keep silent or even lie rather than be unfaithful to the institution and the apparatus that, in his eyes, will someday win. Such a writer must accept the dilemmas of action and decide, even if it means following a lie or, what amounts to the same thing, not saying what he knows or not expressing it fully. But there was also a more optimistic alternative, where the writer does not have to choose between political action and silence, where instead 'there is an immanent convergence between the values of culture and those of action,' where the two were distinct but writing would be related to politics in the contents of what was written. Now, Merleau-Ponty asked, is the thaw a step toward this kind of commitment and this kind of dialogue? It was possible, he said, but 'only at the cost of a very profound and substantial change in the Soviet regime.'[12] But that was not the topic: questions about the Soviet regime and the extent of the thaw would be evident, in any event, if a practice of truth and of culture emerged. Such a practice would make obsolete any speculations about the Soviets.

Following benign remarks by Spender and Umberto Campagnolo, and a misinterpretation by Ignazio Silone, Sartre replied. Merleau-Ponty had asked the wrong question, or at least an incomplete one, Sartre said. 'When it is so cold that a part of humanity is frozen, it is certainly necessary to consider that the other is as well,' so that the question of a western thaw must also be posed. Moreover, he added, it is also badly put to wonder if a socially superior people such as the Soviets could learn from an advanced cultural phenomenon such as American social science because this latter is not dialectical but ideological. The Soviets could, Sartre said, integrate whatever insights were to be found in American social science into their own way of thinking, but no more. 'Here we arrive at the basis of the cultural problem: cultures are also ideologies.'[13] Hence the culture-ideology of the west must also thaw.

To this Merleau-Ponty answered that it was not a matter of common cultural contents nor a question of clarification of our own prejudices and ideologies. In fact, he said, from the point of view of ideology the very conference they all attended was held under the auspices of the superstructure of the western bourgeoisie. But that fact is not sufficient to condemn what goes on at such conferences, especially as they are attempts to practise a genuine universalism. Sartre agreed, but only 'because we have representatives of the other side among us as well.' Merleau-Ponty pointed out that the Eastern Europeans had kept silent, 'and even if they do not speak, I do not think we will have wasted our time, for from the moment we begin to discuss as we have been doing we certainly move beyond the conceptions of ideologies.'[14] There followed a series of exchanges in which Merleau-Ponty argued that Sartre's demand to integrate the insights of social science into a Marxist framework amounted to a 'transsubstantiation' of both Marxist and 'bourgeois' social sciences. Sartre ended by saying that 'rather than reach a coexistence that Merleau-Ponty seems to ask for, with one idea here and another there, we admit that coexistence can only be a dynamic movement of integration.'[15] The dynamic movement of integration, as Sartre soon made clear, was Marxism. Merleau-Ponty replied that what he had in mind, however, was not an integration in Sartre's sense, and certainly not a juxtaposition of ideas, but a lived communication between human beings. Even communists accepted in conversation the insights of psychology or sociology, but they abandoned them in application. A new universalism and a genuine commitment unemcumbered with ideological predispositions would move a little further along the road of application as well.

Merleau-Ponty was to repeat his understanding of commitment and the persuasive task of the philosopher a number of times in later years. 'It is by writing that dialogues are held today.' 'Intellectuals are not here to take sides; they are here to shed light, if they can.' 'Our role is to understand what has just ended and what is beginning.'[16] Toward one side of the 'task' of commitment was philosophy, at once a 'long-term action' and at the same time 'provincial and almost clandestine' because the 'sacred fire is transmitted from man to man.'[17] But if that were all there was to it, as he asked in the Preface to *Signes*, is it not an incredible misunderstanding if all or nearly all philosophers thought themselves obliged to have a politics, since politics arises from the practice of life and escapes understanding? 'The politics of philosophers is that which no one *does*. Is it then a politics? Are there not a good many things they could speak of with greater assurance? And when they outline wise perspectives, of which interested parties wish to know nothing, do they not simply admit they know nothing of politics?'[18]

There is, however, a kind of speech that is turned into action by the circumstances under which it is uttered. As Hannah Arendt has emphasized, the liar is by definition an actor, while 'the truthteller, whether he tells rational or factual truth, most emphatically is not.'[19] But this observation holds only for the intentions of the truthteller: when everyone else is telling lies the consequences of telling the truth may be indistinguishable from intentional action. At the very least, the philosopher wished to persuade others, his readers or his interlocutors, of the truth of reason, or in our day to remind them of what is a fact and what is 'transubstantiation.' In this doubly ambiguous realm, of words about public deeds whose sense is at first never clear, Merleau-Ponty tried to forge a political position from what, without paradox, was a committed agnosticism.

Genuine commitment that was also agnostic, Merleau-Ponty said, amounted to an 'accord not on principles but within an action that one is called to elaborate, not an accord on particular points but on a path that ties them together, relations that are, therefore, differentiated at the same time as being continuous.'[20] Consequently, the very least to be expected is that this 'a-communism' would deal with genuine problems rather than living with one eye fixed on the USSR and the other on the United States.[21] Whatever benefits the communists or their adversaries may gain through a frank analysis, the intention was to resist the drift of circumstances and expose the tricks of men. The non-communist left would not avoid speaking out about the communists or simply fight its enemies. To deserve the name, it must arrange a terrain of coexistence between communism and the rest of the world. Such a task was in principle conceivable only in the absence of an adherence to communism because communists refused to recognize any principles beside their own as legitimate.[22] More precisely, two rival and symmetrical manœuvres were to be avoided: the one, which presented communism as the heir of Marxism, and the other, which tried to hide the problems of the 'free world' under the pretext of an anti-communist defence; on one side was the attempt to allow communism to rest in the shadow of Marx, and on the other the attempt to eliminate the problems Marx raised in favour of an anti-communist defence.[23] There was, clearly, a continuity in Merleau-Ponty's position, which, refusing to accept the inevitability of blocs, attempted to understand their significance and so move beyond them. Just after the war, he felt such a policy was 'historically,' 'pragmatically,' or 'objectively' justified by 'neutral zones' and by the hope that the dialectic had not evaporated completely. When the nostalgia of communism was purged and the blocs seemed permanent because they had equipped themselves with self-justifying ideologies, Merleau-Ponty saw that inevitability could be avoided only by a creative intellectual mediation between the two that was not simply a compromise between unsatisfactory dogmas. Circumstances had changed, and his response had changed as well; the meaning of his position, and in the most fundamental sense his motive, had not changed.

Merleau-Ponty sought an active as well as an intellectual mediation. Both followed directly from his analysis of the adventures of the dialectic. In the previous chapter we noted Merleau-Ponty's argument that inherent in the course of establishing a revolutionary regime was the betrayal of the movement that gave it life. 'There is no dialectic without opposition and without freedom, but opposition and freedom do not last long in a revolution.' This empirical observation was formulated as a theoretical principle: 'Revolutions are true as movements and false as regimes.' If, as Merleau-Ponty argued, the notion of permanent revolution were a parody of the revolutionary movement, the pragmatic implications were clear: the question is whether there may be more of a future in a regime that aims only to change history, not to remake it from the bottom, and whether this regime were not preferable to entering once again into the circle of revolution.[24] Such a regime of 'permanent movement' is one of reform, of a 'new liberalism.' In Venice Merleau-Ponty made the same point: was the thaw a return to the politics of Lenin and Marx? Was the 1934-53 period 'a kind of parenthesis?' Or does the thaw betoken a wholly new approach in Soviet politics? Perhaps the parliamentary road was not only an auxiliary means of expression, destined to bring to power the class considered by all good Marxists as the foundation of the new society; perhaps it was more than a means to prepare for the dictatorship of this class. But if, indeed, it is considered as a road to be followed to the end, as the means of realizing socialism, would we not be confronted with something entirely new, even with respect to Lenin's texts on the matter? And if the interpretation of the Italian Communist Togliatti were followed, that the parliamentary road was to be taken seriously, 'what difference is there between this attitude and reform?'[25] The 'thaw' seemed to mean a lessening of tension in both culture and politics, and Merleau-Ponty wished to ensure that the convergence in both areas was maintained.

What precisely was new in Merleau-Ponty's liberalism was the rejection of 'the optimistic and superficial philosophy that reduced the history of a society to the conflicts of speculative opinion, political struggle to the exchange of views about a clearly stated problem, and the coexistence of men to relations between fellow citizens in a political heaven.' Such a liberalism was practiced nowhere: 'class struggle exists, and will do so as long as there are classes.' In consequence, the workers must not only have the legal right to strike, they must also have the right to be represented by a party that refuses the rules of the democratic game because this game does not operate in its favour. More generally, 'there have been and there will be revolutionary movements, and they are justified because they exist, since their existence is the proof that the society that produces them does not permit proletarians to live.' As a practical matter, such a liberalism could never take the communists or even their enemies at face value:

Communist action and revolutionary movements are only admitted as a useful menace, as a continual call to order. One does not believe in the solution to the social problem by way of the power of the proletarian class or its representatives; one expects progress only from an action that is self-conscious and is confronted with the judgment of an opposition. As with the heroic liberalism of Weber, this one even allows what opposes it into its universe and is justified in its own eyes only on condition of understanding what opposes it. A non-communist left is for us this double resolve to pose the social problem in terms of struggle and to refuse the dictatorship of the proletariat.[26]

The objections to Merleau-Ponty's restoration of a middle way were obvious, and he anticipated his prospective critics. The most trivial objection was one that accepted the division into blocs as given and extended the logic of the situation into the future: politics is a struggle for power; therefore, either a non-communist left will be another bourgeois party, a replication of the 'socialist dream,' or it will be a transitional regime that debouches in the dictatorship of the proletariat and therefore amounts to crypto-communism. The premise of logical extension was contested by Merleau-Ponty, because it implied an inability to act in the genuine sense of introducing newness into the world. It implied that the dialectic was not only dead but could never be revived. For Merleau-Ponty, the miracle of revivification could come only through speech, through dialectic in the precise sense, and the only institution that even remotely met the requirements of dialectic was parliament. Not only was the discussion concerning the nature of communism 'open,' as Sartre said, one must take part in it. 'As for the limits of parliamentary and democratic action, they are set by the institution itself, and they must be accepted, for parliament is the sole institution known to guarantee a minimum of opposition and truth.' There was always the danger of procedural tricks and manoeuvres, but they could be denounced in parliament itself. 'The mystification of parliament consists in not posing the true problems or in posing them obliquely or too late.'[27] A genuine parliamentary debate, which recognized both the reality of class conflict and the necessity of maintaining a legitimate opposition, would revive and incarnate the dialectic in a regime of reform.

'This is not a "solution" and we well know it' because society was an ensemble of conscious lives that do not admit of solutions like crossword puzzles. 'It is rather the resolution to hold both ends of the chain, the social problem and freedom.' There could be no dialectic without freedom, but parliament did not guarantee its existence, and capitalism guaranteed even less. A non-communist left, he said, was no more tied to free enterprise than to the dictatorship of the proletariat. It would not view capitalist institutions as the sole mechanisms of exploitation, but neither would it judge them any more natural than the stone axe or the bicycle. Both elements were important: it was to be non-communist and it was to be left, and thereby non-capitalist. The revolution had evaporated as a dream, but that did not imply respect for capitalism: 'We are calling for an effort of clarification that to us appears, for reasons of principle, impossible in a communist regime but possible in the non-communist world. If we overestimate the freedom of that world, the "barometer of revolution" will say so.'[28] Such a political perspective, as Merleau-Ponty himself said, 'is not at all pessimistic, and even less is it conservative. Beyond the illusion of a realized dialectic or a revolutionary society, the idea of dialectic is always valuable, and this book, a momento to its most recent manifestations, is less the recital of a disillusion than an appeal for a new critique and a new action.'

Les Aventures was begun in July 1953, shortly after the last instalment of 'Les Communistes et la Paix' had appeared; before it was finished, Merleau-Ponty had begun to lay the groundwork for the new critique in the pages of *L'Express*. Action came later.

COEXISTENCE

Not all Merleau-Ponty's contributions to *L'Express* were political. As Professor of Philosophy at the Collège de France, he was also a prominent 'man of letters,' and well over half of his contributions during the two years he wrote with any regularity for the magazine were devoted to literary, philosophic, and aesthetic topics. It was hardly a new direction for Merleau-Ponty: before the war he had lectured at the Ecole Normale on El Greco, his first post-war article was on the novel, in 1952-3 he had given a course on the literary use of language by Valéry and Stendhal, and the last study he published was on the contemporary poet and writer Claude Simon. These other writings reflect the direction in which Merleau-Ponty's thought was moving and contain many of the themes developed in his political writings.[29]

Three major and interrelated questions dominated Merleau-Ponty's political writing after 1954: coexistence, industrial society, and French decolonization traumas.[30] The vehicle for most of Merleau-Ponty's writing in 1954 and 1955 was a weekly feature called 'Le Forum de *L'Express*.' Originally it was begun as a way for politicians, particularly supporters of Pierre Mendès-France, to reply to questions submitted by readers. In September 1954 the format was changed in the hope of appealing to a broader audience, and prominent French intellectuals took the place of politicians. Sometimes everyone responded to the same question; sometimes each person responded to an individual question.

The first important 'Forum' in which Merleau-Ponty participated addressed the question whether France was going to become a great power again. Merleau-Ponty responded not, he said, as a philosopher, but as an ordinary citizen facing political problems. If a non-communist solution to French problems were possible, it would be attained only by employing greater intellectual and political rigour than the communists, not less. One must begin by clarifying the questions at issue:

the standard Marxist notion of revolution, whereby the universal class resolved all contradictions and conflicts in creating the homogeneous society, was clearly a myth. 'Neither in the USSR nor elsewhere does the proletariat approach being in power.' Marxism as practised today, he said, created a power-organization that was not bourgeois but had nevertheless its own privileges and inertia and was certainly not about to create a homogeneous society. The sociology of the Soviet regime was practically unknown: 'One can say only that it is *another* society,' and one must seriously question whether the Soviet model has anything to teach France, particularly when the Soviet reality is covered by the ideological screens of communists and anti-communists.

When one is not a communist, Merleau-Ponty continued, naturally the question of getting along with them must be faced. Until 1953, he said, communist concessions, when they were made at all, were too little or too late; since then, however, 'the thesis of the Stalinist period according to which opposition is treason' had been abandoned, and the most pressing question was whether or not this new attitude was going to be generalized and applied to the non-communist world as well. France could play a mediating role and pave the way for a creative reply to the Soviet thaw. The key, he said, lay in domestic French politics. Coexistence and détente amounted to saying that communism and 'free enterprise' had ceased to consider themselves universal solutions. Thus it was pointless to talk of political problems in terms of revolution and class struggle, since that could only polarize unnecessarily our politics toward the West or the East. The problem with disavowing the class struggle, however, was that that always seemed to harm the workers; common sense therefore should inform us that political dynamics required a far left, and its existence owed nothing to the Soviet Union. One had the right to speak of a government beyond classes only if it demonstrated by its action that a non-revolutionary solution to economic and social problems were possible. In France, at least, there was both the theory and practice of state intervention without state control of production, a social action that appealed to no particular class for support. 'It is addressed to political consciousness, to citizens as such. In a country with a mature political culture, the enterprise is not impossible.'[31] The prospects for international peace through coexistence would be enhanced by creative French diplomacy, but this depended on sensible domestic politics that no longer even paid lip-service to either a revolutionary proletariat or the glory of free enterprise.

Over the next eight months Merleau-Ponty wrote two articles and made one radio broadcast, subsequently published in *L'Express*, which expressed his understanding of the symbiosis of communism and anti-communism. The structure of his argument was more or less the same on all three occasions. First, he noted that political action and political thought had both been frozen by the cold war;

second, he pointed to the bankruptcy of traditional Marxist and liberal ideology; and third, he suggested that the thaw was a significant opportunity to move beyond symmetrical deadlock. The stalemate of a bipolar international order was not new, he said, and would doubtless occur again in the future. Peculiar to the present, however, was that 'the antagonists have come to form a single system at war with itself. What would Senator McCarthy do if Stalinist Russia did not exist? And what an argument was lost to communist criticism when the senator was removed from the political horizon!'[32] On the anti-communist side the tattered ideology of liberalism was still expounded, though it bore no relation to events. A preponderance of intellectual effort was committed to an exposure of the difficulties of Soviet society and the threat it posed to the 'free world.' Like Sartre's vision of the ever-vigilant bourgeois, Western ideologies held up the spectre of a sleepless and relentless Communism. Their view 'is neither true nor false: it is Communism viewed through a mixture of psychology and a mechanical view of history, which is the scourge of American thought. Margaret Mead wants to replace the historical analysis of Bolshevism with some carefully chosen [psychological] tests. To do this is to decide there is nothing to understand in Bolshevism.'[33]

Yet communists were no better. Ideologically, dogmatic Marxism was as worn out as liberalism; the proletariat in the industrial countries was not revolutionary, whereas if there were a revolutionary impulse in the world at all it was to be found in the non-industrial countries, sustained by a spirit quite alien to Marx's understanding. The heirs of the October Revolution were as reluctant to talk of their own society as the liberals were of theirs and instead constantly chattered about a non-existent communism heading toward the universal and homogeneous society by way of proletarian power.[34] When systematic sociological evidence concerning the German Democratic Republic became available, Merleau-Ponty used it to reinforce his observation that the Soviet Union and communist society in general was a novel social order. The essence of revolutionary politics, he wrote, 'is in the relation of the proletariat to the party ... In philosophical terms, the party surpasses the revolt of the proletariat; it realizes the revolt by destroying it as immediate revolt; it is the negation of that negation, or in other words, it is the mediation of it ... There will be revolution if the party educates the proletariat while the proletariat animates the party.'[35] The twin principles of revolutionary politics, therefore, were that the Party was always right but that it could never be right in opposition to the proletariat. What the evidence showed in the first instance was that East Germany was far from a homogeneous society. Cleavages between workers and managers, technicians, Stakhanovites, and union officials existed; there was authoritarian rule but also appeals to elections and to consent. It was a regime, Merleau-Ponty said, torn between the two principles of revolutionary politics: it was irrefutable because the Party could always appeal to the future, but for the same reason it was undemonstrable. About all that could be said with any degree of certainty was that it was a regime oscillating between authority and relaxation and trying to confront the problems of industrialism.[36]

While it was foolish to think, having just emerged from the Korean conflict, that talking to the communists would transform the Soviet Union into a gentle liberal state, it was no less so to pretend that rearmament was the first step to arms limitation. What confronted the world, Merleau-Ponty said, was a new strategic and political situation that could not be reduced to a mixture of hard and soft lines.[37] There was a genuine détente, though it seemed scarcely to be recognized and not at all acknowledged by spokesmen for each side, habituated to hard-line thinking. Numerous people on both sides claimed it was merely a tactic. But even if it were tactical, there would be permanent consequences that could only with the utmost difficulty be countered. A policy of active coexistence, toward which the Soviet Union was moving, signified that it was giving up its claims to centralize the world revolution and was abandoning the rights of communism as a universal solution. It was aware of its own particular destination and admitted for an indeterminate time the existence and permanence of the other system. One might then expect changes on the Western front as well: if military budgets were reduced because the pretext of an anti-communist defence no longer made much sense, 'it would be difficult to defer the solution to social problems, and we can count on a renewal of the workers' movement that the cold war has frozen. The anti-communist thinks along such lines, which is why he is disturbed by peace.' But such reasoning was identical with that of the communist of yesterday since neither could contemplate a workers' movement that was not communist-inspired. If workers' movements were endemic to industrial society, however, as the East German data seemed to confirm, then the questions posed by Marx to nineteenth-century capitalism would have to be thought through again. The significance of the thaw and coexistence was to make the need for a renewal of reflection on industrial society more apparent because empirical events had given the lie to ideological pretexts.

Two sets of implications were drawn from Merleau-Ponty's reading of events. If genuine revolutionary movements were to be found in the non-industrial world, and if in industrial countries the communists had ceased to be anything more than dispensers of revolutionary rhetoric, then the avant-garde was not necessarily communist and social problems could no longer as in Marx's day be reduced to one's relation to the means of production. Second, analyses of modern industrial society were available to men of the left that took account of the changed economic conditions. More important than legal forms of property-holding was productivity. 'A new critique of capitalist societies can and must be based upon this principle ... Such ideas can animate the left, "unfrozen" by the end of the cold war, and make of it a non-communist left.' The creative application of new and empirically sound ideas would constitute the restoration of the dialectic, which had not been given the whole of its measure by nineteenth-century ideas of revolution; 'it remains to it to inspire and invent a politics of real freedom.'[38] During the balance of 1955 Merleau-Ponty was busy with the editing of *Les Philosophes célèbres*, and was not provoked again into writing on political matters until the Hungarian uprising.

Between the summer of 1955 and the fall of 1956, a great deal had happened within the French intellectual left as a result of the thaw. The French Communist Party was, under the hand of Maurice Thorez, more royalist than the king and coped poorly with the relaxation of tension. Of the numerous shifts and switches undertaken, the most important for Merleau-Ponty was by one of his communist friends, Pierre Hervé. In January 1956, a month before Khrushchev's speech to the Twentieth Party Congress, Hervé published a plea for de-Stalinization, using wholly orthodox texts from Marx, Lenin, and Stalin himself.[39] He was expelled from the Party by mid-February and exhaustively pilloried by his former comrades, Roger Garaudy and Jean Kanapa, in the pages of *L'Humanité*.[40] He was attacked by Sartre as well, who accused him of being yet another reformer scrounging after votes.[41] Hints of Khrushchev's February speech had been appearing in the Western non-communist press for some time, but *L'Humanité* persisted in passing the blame onto Beria.[42] On 4 June the American Department of State published the complete text, much to the embarrassment of communist parties in Western Europe. There was a brief moment of regret among the French Stalinists. J.T. Desanti, for example, admitted he was wrong to call Kant, Husserl, Bergson, and Merleau-Ponty all idealists.[43] But if the relaxing of Stalinist discipline was a ploy for retaining the support of the remaining Party intellectuals it did not last long.

Reformist ideas of the Hungarians had been known to the French communists at least since June 1956, and the Party doubtless found them disconcerting. In October 1956 a French communist writer, Tristan Tzara, returning from a trip to Budapest, declared through the medium of the Hungarian Embassy (not *L'Humanité*) that reform was what the Hungarian people sought. The next day *Le Monde* reported that the French Party Secretariat objected to the actions of the Hungarian officials.[44] But it was not until November and the second Soviet invasion of Hungary that the Party came under full attack from both member-intellectuals and fellow-travellers.[45] Predictably enough, the Party sent Garaudy to his typewriter and expelled the undisciplined.[46]

Merleau-Ponty published his understanding of these events in the 23 November 1956 edition of *L'Express*. The Soviet invasion of Hungary reinforced his opinion that the problem of communism was not a Marxist one. The uprising, he said, revealed a double crisis: the attempt by Imre Nagy to escape the Soviet sphere and his pre-invasion appeal to the bourgeois forum of the United Nations revealed there was no socialist solidarity between Hungary and the Soviet Union and literally no communism when the Russians invaded. Neither Nagy nor Khrushchev had made 'mistakes,' because the problem was as total as the uprising. The response of intellectuals to the invasion, he said, should not have been to counsel war, but neither should it have been simply to sign one's name to a petition expressing compassion of the moment. 'The homage we owe the Hungarians is to understand their sacrifice and explain it, for all to hear, so that it does not become vain.' To call the Budapest uprising a regrettable error, avoidable in the future, was to mock the men who died. To blame Khrushchev for de-Stalinizing too quickly or to point to unequal political and economic development in the Eastern European countries would be superficial. According to Merleau-Ponty the Hungarian insurrection meant that Stalinism had reached the very essence of the regime and that in consequence de-Stalinization was not a matter of touching up here and there or of tactical changes but a radical transformation that would involve the system in serious risks, yet one that must be taken if the system is to be honourable again. 'The only homage acceptable to the insurgents is to go back to de-Stalinization and show all its meaning without hiding anything.'[47]

There were two kinds of de-Stalinization. The first was reform, a practical consequence of *Les Aventures de la Dialectique*. The other was what the actual de-Stalinizers had done, particularly under the guidance of the French communists: denunciation of Stalin the man. It was true that Khrushchev criticized the two fundamental pillars of the Soviet system, the dictatorship of the proletariat and economic planning, but he did no more than point to facts, and the whole question was 'to know if a "planned" economy can become a planned economy, if the dictatorship of the proletariat can make itself understood by the proletariat instead of buzzing uselessly in its ears, if appearance, which has fallen away from reality, can join up with it again.' The style of Khrushchev's speech was one of a man who wanted to do something about a situation that was unsatisfactory, without acknowledging what was wrong or what he was doing. The regime had arranged its secret self-knowledge so carefully that it could succeed in not knowing about itself in good faith. 'Its greatest rule is to judge without being judged, to judge without knowing because it has stripped itself of knowledge so as not to be judged.' A genuine de-Stalinization meant calling into question not just the consequences of a regime but the spirit of the dictatorial apparatus responsible. Such a radical and frank approach was out of the question for men who had been for so long part of the apparatus they were called upon to criticize and perhaps dismantle or at least modify. Thus they hit upon the solution of presenting a criti-

cism of the regime in the form of a criticism of Stalin.[48] There would be a sufficient shock to signal the need for change, but it would be produced in such a way
that the system would remain untouched and its principles unaltered.

The line followed was delicate indeed. It was, Merleau-Ponty said, 'perhaps
the masterpiece of communism: an increase in consciousness without an awareness by the subject, an imperceptible revolution that has all the advantages of re-
dress and none of the inconveniences of confession. As with all masterpieces, this
one was difficult to achieve.' There was always the danger that some would not
understand what was being hinted, while others would try to translate hints into
clear language. The two Western European Parties characteristically voiced the
two interpretations. Togliatti brought the Russian masterpiece into the fuller
light of Marxian analysis. It was not a question, the Italian leader said, of deciding
whether Stalin was good or bad. To confine the problem to Stalin was to remain
in the realm of the cult of personality; just as Stalin was praised as a superman
who built socialism in Russia when he was alive, one would not have moved beyond him now that he was dead if he were simply denounced for superhuman
defects. The only way to go beyond Stalinism would be to question the system.
Togliatti had understood too well. The French Communist Party, Merleau-
Ponty said, could be counted upon to put things back in order.[49] It made no
sense, the French said, to follow Togliatti and view the Soviet Union as a phenomenon to be understood.[50] Merleau-Ponty wondered if the French were mocking
Togliatti or simply did not understand what they were saying. In view of the ac-
colades that Stalin and Stalinism had received in *L'Humanité* prior to the Four-
teenth Congress of the French Communist Party in the summer of 1956, it would
seem that the French leaders could not conceive of examining the USSR.[51]

Togliatti saw that genuine de-Stalinization entailed a challenge to dictatorship.
The Soviet response and the arguments of the French Party brought out the fundamental contradiction of the regime; the dictatorship was asked to challenge itself without letting itself be eliminated, and the proletariat was asked to liberate
itself without rejecting the control of the dictatorship. Khrushchev's words were
equivocal: 'Who needed to mouth the word coexistence after the Korean armistice?' There was nothing new in Soviet de-Stalinization, for there was no way to
tell if naming concessions such as the Korean armistice was anything more than
a ruse. 'The de-Stalinizers are still Stalinists. The double nature of Stalinism covers
everything, including de-Stalinization.'[52] The only sensible attitude to take,
Merleau-Ponty said, was to acknowledge that communism had its own problems:
'Communism is not a solution, since we see it going back on its principles.' The
only way to put genuine de-Stalinization into action was to form a New Left or
a Popular Front, but a Popular Front could be spoken of seriously only by taking
up again the same problem that Blum encountered – defining an action that would

be a move beyond capitalist anarchy without being the beginning of the dictatorship of the proletariat. And that is called reform. If de-Stalinization meant reform, the distinction between revolution and reform no longer made much sense because, for both East and West, more or less the same response was needed.

To evaluate the real costs of production, needs, and the potential of consumption, the market economy is a worn-out instrument, ill-adapted for unexpected practices. It is the only one we have had available up to now; if we wish a better one, it is to be invented. Analogous problems are on the horizon of dictatorship and on the horizon of capitalism. For dictatorship it is a question of moving toward a non-imperious planning; for capitalism, inversely, of subjecting the mechanisms of the market economy to management in the public interest. On both sides it is a question of creating 'artificial mechanisms' or servo-mechanisms that solicit and organize the economy without dictatorship.

Homage to the Hungarians meant, because of the Stalinist de-Stalinization of the Soviet Union, mounting a challenge to the French communists. The French Party, just as the Russian one, had squandered whatever humanist or socialist or dialectical content it ever had. Reform was the very definition of the left: 'A man of the left is one who desires the success of de-Stalinization; an unchecked and consequential de-Stalinization, extended beyond the borders of communism to the whole of the left that it has "frozen." '[53]

ALGERIA

With the decolonization of North Africa, a new kind of 'freeze' was now being imposed upon French politics. November 1956 was the month of the invasion of Suez. The motives of the three governments involved diverged greatly: Britain was no doubt concerned over the Egyptian expropriation of the canal, and Israel was undertaking one of many pre-emptive first strikes. France's participation, beyond its interest in the canal, was tied to its policy in Algeria. In October 1956 the French Air Force had intercepted an airplane belonging to the Sultan of Morocco en route to Tunisia and carrying Ahmed Ben Bella, later president of the Algerian Republic, and other Algerian rebel leaders. Guy Mollet, the socialist premier, supported the action of the military and kept Ben Bella in jail. Mollet presided over the Suez affair as well, at one point having the audacity or imagination to cite Marx in support of his action.[54] The connection between Suez and Algeria was largely symbolic. Most Algerian moslems were loyal to France, it was said, but Nasser was helping the tiny faction of rebels; a victory over Nasser, therefore, would cause the Algerian insurgency to crumble. Today, with the wisdom of hindsight and the eloquence of men such as Frantz Fanon, the events in Algeria are seen in terms of a war of national liberation. But in the 1950s it was less clear that the Algerian insurgency would end as it did.

By nearly any standard the struggle over Algeria was tragic. Legally part of metropolitan France and for up to three generations the home of a large number of European Frenchmen, who supplied 90 per cent of public and private investment and half the taxes, the country was also the home of a lumpenproletariat of between six and seven million persons out of a total population of about nine million. The French in Tunisia and Morocco had also grafted a 'French society' onto a 'native' mass, mediated by a westernized 'native' elite. The differences between Tunisia, Morocco, and Algeria were of degree, but they had the effect of making the granting of independence to Algeria much more difficult. There was no Algerian nationality nor an undisputed leader such as Bourguiba in Tunisia or the Moroccan sultan; the FLN was a lower-class movement, not a political party, and was inclined toward radicalism and violence rather than reform and negotiation. Moreover, the non-Arabs in Algeria refused to negotiate. The law of 1947, providing for a single electoral college, was ignored and two colleges were established, one for Moslems and another effectively for the European French. In addition, even the principle that one European equalled eight Moslems, which the separate electoral system ensured, was abused when French officials 'corrected' the choice of the Moslems from time to time. In 1958 when the French Algerians accepted the single electoral college it was too late: the blood of four years' fighting changed the question from one of individual equality in the liberal-democratic sense to one of national self-determination, a conflict of communities, which undercut the premise of individual rights.

The French army had always played a special role in North Africa, and following the French defeat in Indochina, which helped inspire the FLN to emulate the Viet Minh, the army became increasingly important. The Indochinese war ended in 1954, the same year as the Algerian one began, and French troops bore the brunt of the fighting in the invasion of Suez. France had been fighting more or less continually since the end of the second world war, but overseas, to preserve the image of 'a hundred million Frenchmen.' In the whole of the former French Empire, however, only Indochina and Morocco really paid their way: in those two areas, under the tutelage of giant Parisian financial houses, the spirit of capitalism had been at work. Indochina had been lost, and in 1955 so was Morocco. Nevertheless the real economic losses of these two colonies was, from the army's viewpoint, overshadowed by the Tunisian 'defeat' in 1952. The loss of Tunisia and Morocco was bound to be experienced differently by the army, which had pacified the Moroccan tribes and incorporated many of its warlike people into its own ranks, one of whom even became a general officer. The army had done little to discourage the North African proverb 'A Moroccan is a warrior, an Algerian a man, a Tunisian a woman.' How much more odious, then, was the revolt of the 'women' of Tunisia. When Morocco was also lost the army could not but believe that the system had betrayed the nation. Had Algeria been simply another Tunisia or another Morocco, army resistance could have been expected, but Algeria had an additional, almost symbolic, significance: Tunisia and Morocco had been conquered in the first place in order to secure the frontiers of Algeria. The system had abandoned the flanks, but as long as the centre held, France would not sink back into Latin mediocrity. A confederation with Tunisia and Morocco, access across the desert to black Africa, a return of grandeur, all was possible; Algeria, if saved, would also save France.

By 1958 events were becoming more critical: the politicians in Paris could not agree on the policy to be employed in Algeria; General de Gaulle was receiving many visitors at Colombey; the army had warned President Coty of 'incalculable consequences' that would follow any negotiations, which the army called capitulation, with the FLN. On 13 May 1958 the main government building in Algiers was seized, officially by patriotic Algerians but in fact by the 'red berets' of the Third Colonial Paratroop Regiment. It was mutiny. Two days later de Gaulle announced his availability to save the Republic and was subsequently accepted by the National Assembly under the threat of an air-drop by the Algeria-based paratroops.

On 5 June 1958 Merleau-Ponty published an article in *Le Monde* giving his reflections on the events of May. His tone was one of disgust. 'So,' he began, 'the *ultras* of Algiers have risen up to install a government that is going to initiate the policies demanded at least two and a half years ago by Mendès-France.'[55] The officers of Algiers broke discipline in order to get a government that would discipline them. Guy Mollet, traitor to socialism, then to the defence of the Republic and tomorrow, perhaps, to de Gaulle, had the general's esteem. Robert Lacoste, minister resident in Algiers, fled the colony when he learned about the demonstration of 13 May even though his policies ensured it would happen. Lacoste had de Gaulle's friendship, Merleau-Ponty remarked. In the Assembly the Socialists had said nothing until it was too late, and then only under their breath. 'Is politics always these stupidities, this laissez-faire, these nervous crises, these oaths no sooner taken than revoked – these oaths taken *in order to be* negotiated away? Or is it not rather the politics of decadence, and are we not condemned to parody and illusion by a deeper malady that will rot tomorrow's institutions as it has those of yesterday?' Aron had said that the change between the Fourth and Fifth Republics revealed a France steadfast and changing; for Merleau-Ponty there was no change: 'The appearance of General de Gaulle, we must not forget, is both the result and the masterpiece of Molletism.'[56] The politics of Guy Mollet were exhausted by the frenetic pursuit of dreams and the creation of intoxicating situations in order to forget the problems of political reality.

Merleau-Ponty was concerned with more than de Gaulle as the truth of Molletism. He felt the general had misinterpreted the significance of events and ignored policies needed to cope with the crisis. De Gaulle thought the regime lacked continuity: 'was continuity lacking from the Fourth Republic? Did not the governments that succeeded one another, with a single exception follow the same policy? Is it not, on the contrary, initiative, movement, and novelty that was continually lacking?'[57] De Gaulle also had doubts about party government and sought to replace it with a 'rally' (*rassemblement*) outside the structure of the parties, 'which presupposed both that opposition between parties owed nothing to circumstances, that it is, by itself the cause of the paralysis, and that it is enough to abolish it in order to be saved.' In fact, however, the opposition between parties was genuine, and the sensible policy, as de Gaulle knew but refused to say, was that of the liberal left. Thus it was vain to call the system of parties into doubt while taking up the policy of one of them. On the other hand there were many reasons to criticize the parties: 'party government could not *undertake* this policy, they could only *talk* about it' because the votes of the communist deputies were disregarded by the government when policy questions were decided, which meant that votes had to be obtained by concessions to the right. If the only possible policies were those of the centre-left, the result was that 'the right, without ideas, has become the arbiter of French politics.' What was questionable therefore, was not the passivity of the party system but the passivity of the right and the subterfuge of deducting communist votes.[58]

De Gaulle's misunderstanding could be traced to his view of France and the political order appropriate for it. The increased powers of the president of the Fifth Republic meant a decrease in the powers of the president of the Council. 'When the president of the Republic is no longer General de Gaulle, he will become once again what he has always been, a man who has followed a long career of honours, and who is more interested in customary solutions than in ones requiring imagination, new knowledge, and initiative.' It was not simply a question of de Gaulle's successors being unable to fill the general's shoes: even with de Gaulle, the question was whether the real French problem was how to find an arbiter who gives everyone a bit of what they ask for, or how to obtain a power that rules, 'that is, a power that leads and transforms the country by action rather than leaving it as it is and conceiving a grand policy behind its back, to which the country is only invited to say "yes," rather than be convinced by it.'[59] De Gaulle was a master, in Hegel's sense, which was another reason Merleau-Ponty expressed his reservations: 'General de Gaulle can change the laws, he does not change the life of France because that is not the business of a *single* man, because a single man always has too simple an idea of the system.' De Gaulle, he said, was able to work upon men with the same crude flexibility and egalitarian contempt that put him in power in 1944, but that was insufficient to keep him there, not only because the 'system' started up again but also because, while it may be sufficient to manipulate men in order to attain power, in order to keep power it is necessary to be interested in circumstances, to have inclinations and a set of ideas about problems. Thus, because he had no policy, because he arbitrated without governing, his government never had a genuine movement behind it. Needed, in Merleau-Ponty's view, were institutions to mediate properly between politicians and citizens, a genuine mediation that was not a mixture of the shadowy manipulations of an arbiter and the loud but indistinct roar of a referendum. French citizens, Merleau-Ponty said, 'owe him something other and something better than devotion: we owe him our opinions. He is too young to be our father and we have passed the age of acting like children.'[60] Merleau-Ponty's words were an exhortation as well as an analysis, for it was clear to him that many of his fellow-citizens were not acting their age.

The military had staged the 'miracle of fraternization' between Arab and European in the Algiers demonstration of 13 May but lacked 'even the outline of a policy.' When the paratroops have destroyed the system, asked Merleau-Ponty, when all the leftist intellectuals are in jail, what will they do? The absurdity of the 'miracle' was that it had been created in order to forget the problems of Algeria that the military were beginning to discover. 'Is it the slave or the queen of the state? It cannot be its slave when there is no longer a state. And what is it to do with power when it doesn't want it? ... The soldiers have no party ties to the special interests, but they must not be asked for a policy either.'[61] A month or so after the article from which we have been quoting was published in Le Monde, Merleau-Ponty was interviewed by L'Express. The structure of the interview and the tone of Merleau-Ponty's replies suggested a new element of urgency. The army was getting out of hand: Colonel Trinquier, who had commanded the troops charged with removing the occupants of the government buildings on 13 May and was the author of a book on the necessity of torture against terrorists, had on 7 June 1958 made a speech in Algiers on the need to extend to metropolitan France the means, so useful across the Mediterranean, of making the population 'commandable.' His view was the logical outcome of the now familiar notion, held by many officers, that the system had betrayed the nation. The Third World War has Begun, a book by Pierre Debray, supplied an ideology for the paranoia of the military. The war Debray wrote of was hidden. History was the record of the advance of subversion, and its phases are predictable: Tunisia and Morocco were abandoned when subversion was in its second phase; Algeria was in its fourth phase; and France? Who could deny that France had begun the first phase? 'We

are in the realm of the occult,' Merleau-Ponty commented. The magical invocation of a depth behind manifest appearance visible only to the clear-sighted was
an exact contrary to ultra-Bolshevism. Debray espoused the same faith in the
underground, internal mechanism of revolution that the Trotskyites and Sartre
had applauded. The colonels, however, did not just write fantasies; they acted.
Theirs was 'an aggressive nihilism *that excludes all policy*,' theirs was a thought
that is not even totalitarian, but a monism of terror, of anguish, defeat and shame,
uttered in despair and dressed up as a policy. 'All this is fascism in the precise
sense of the word.'[62]

On the left were the communists. They were not totalitarians as they were declared to be by Gaullist propaganda, and they were certainly nothing like the
phantoms of Debray's dreams, but they did act as accomplices for the military
extremists. 'Between the right and the communist there is no real opposition, for
they do not fight for a policy; each side has several of them. *Each side is no longer
a party; they are both "pressure groups."* Together they bring joint pressure upon
the regime and bring ministries down; neither one nor the other has taken responsibility for French political life.' The right was incapable of taking responsibility, for the reasons given earlier, and the communists, who at least retained the
heritage of a few ideas, could be asked to do anything except participate in political action.[63] All the communists could do, it seemed, was chatter alternatively
of a Popular Front and of revolution. The deduction of communist votes in the
Assembly was, in part at least, the consequence of the revolutionary rhetoric of
the Party. Since in fact communism had been won over to reform and compromise, their purely verbal Bolshevism served only to sustain the propaganda of the
right.[64] If only the communists would acknowledge what they had become, a
workers' party, and if only de Gaulle would admit that the only policies available
were liberal, Merleau-Ponty seemed to say, the atmosphere of acrimony and suspicion would evaporate, the role of an arbiter would become superfluous, and the
restoration of a genuine republic might be possible.

By mid-summer 1958 the terms of the debate seemed to have changed. In Algiers, the fascist ultras were mounting a challenge to the Republic. Clearly the regime of an arbiter was preferable to civil war, which was what Merleau-Ponty
feared if the army made any serious move to render metropolitan France 'commandable.' The choice, in any event, was an unhappy one. Merleau-Ponty doubted
that de Gaulle was willing to court the public opinion necessary to tame the ultras
because it seemed unlikely that he would pursue the necessary leftist policies.
The alternatives Merleau-Ponty saw may not have been exhaustive; de Gaulle did
seem to combine the role of arbiter between the people and a hidden France
with the role of arbiter between the image of a totalitarian left and the reality of
a fascist right. By declaring the fascists outside the nation while introducing the

spectre of communist dictatorship, de Gaulle could deal with the ultras without abandoning the bourgeoisie. Perhaps Merleau-Ponty underestimated the General's skill and his willingness to wait until the ultras had squandered their reputation as defenders of the Republic in a flurry of plastic bombs.

In addition to criticizing the ultras, the Gaullists, and the communists, Merleau-Ponty advocated some positive policies. In the area of colonial politics, even before the 13 May charade, he entertained but a modest expectation that his opinions would be effective. Asked by *L'Express* early in 1958 to give his views on Algeria, he replied: 'I have an opinion and I do not hide it. But it is perhaps no longer a solution even if it was one two and a half years ago. Nothing proves that a given problem is soluble at any time at all, and it would be excessive to reproach us for not having a solution when the problem has been allowed to grow rotten.' There were only partial truths to be seen. For example, one could be unconditionally against torture, even if Trinquier were right and torture was the appropriate reply to terror, but it would only be a moral attitude, and more was needed than morality if a policy were to be created. As for those who thought white men had no business in the non-white world, they thought so precisely because they no longer believed in the Soviet Union but had not lost faith in a universal class and, casting about to find one, discovered the native.[65] If, however, one were to look at the actual social structure of a colony such as Madagascar, the revolutionary dreams would soon be dispelled. Neither in Madagascar nor in Algeria was colonialism ordered according to the formulas of nineteenth-century economic exploitation. Economically, the Algerian Moslems under French rule were no worse off than Egyptians, who had attained independence. The problems of the non-industrial world could not be reduced to the deceptive simplicity of economics. Rather, a set of dilemmas, demographic, economic, and psychological, had conspired to create a situation where neither independence nor communism could possibly be described as solutions. Immediate independence would simply provide another source of instability and aggravate the existing tensions between East and West, because the Soviet Union and the United States would doubtless seek to influence the newly independent countries. In the short term Merleau-Ponty preferred regimes with internal autonomy or a federal system to serve as a transition toward independence, with anticipated delays and stages. France ought not abandon the colonies, according to Merleau-Ponty, because it could still do some good there. 'In essence, what really annoys me among my contemporaries who speak too easily about independence is that the duties they propose for use are always those of abstentions.'[66] As a practical matter, one may raise the question whether a policy of abstention would not have been wisest. Theoretically, one may ask whether in 1958 Merleau-Ponty was siding with the Mauriac of 1947, and whether he had, perhaps, repudiated his earlier arguments.

The second question is the easier to answer. We have seen Merleau-Ponty's practical position move from 'Marxist waiting' and advocacy of communist policies during a period of limited dialectic to a position of 'a-communism' and the advocacy of liberal policies during a period of potential civil war. It is important to keep both the change of position and the change of context in mind, and for this reason it seems inadequate to say with Simone de Beauvoir, for example, that Merleau-Ponty moved to the right. His view of the 'European project' and the relationship between Europe and the rest of the world, for example, retained the Hegelian substructure of his early writings.

In 1946, at the Rencontres Internationales de Genève, Merleau-Ponty had replied to a lengthy speech by Julien Benda which argued, among other things, that there was no 'European consciousness.' Merleau-Ponty said that no articulate representation of European consciousness existed, but that perhaps there was another kind of unity, a unity in action, 'a certain mode of relation between man and nature or between man and man.' Referring to Hegel's *Lectures on the Philosophy of History* and to the early novels of Malraux, he made precise his meaning: 'a relation between man and nature that first of all is not confusion but distinction between me and the world; correlatively, the idea of objectivity or truth.' The notions of objectivity and truth were at the origin of western science and, since this science led to a technology, the modes of European labour. Secondly, therefore, was the concept of labour itself, the Hegelian concept of productivity and the transformation of the world. Thirdly, following the Hegelian motif, was the state 'considered as the realization of freedom ... as the human milieu, properly speaking, in which human freedom can be realized.'[67] In 1958 the easy reference to Hegel was absent, but his spirit remained: 'You seem to believe in a superiority of our values, of those of western civilizations over those of the underdeveloped countries,' *L'Express* commented. 'Certainly not with respect to their moral value,' Merleau-Ponty replied,

and even less with respect to their superior beauty, but – how to put it? – with respect to their *historical* value. Landing in the dawn at Orly after a month in Madagascar, what a shock to see so many highways, so many objects, so much patience, labour and knowledge; to make out so many lights illuminating so many distinct lives who were being awakened in the morning. This great, feverish, and oppressive arrangement of so-called developed humanity is, after all, what one day will allow all the men of the earth to eat. It has already made men exist in each other's eyes rather than merely proliferate each in their own country, like trees. The encounter has been bathed in blood, fear, and hate, and it must end. I cannot seriously consider it as an evil. In any case, it is an accomplished thing; there can be no question of recreating archaism; we are all embarked and it is not nothing to have set out on that voyage.[68]

The European irruption into the rest of the world was seen by Merleau-Ponty as a fate to be welcomed. The rebellion by the rest of the world may have been inevitable, but it will have been temporary, for the technological mastery of nature and the freedom of the state, is the course mankind is launched upon, and even though the blood of both natives and Europeans flows across history a return to archaism is out of the question. A summary critique of this position was given at the 1946 conference by Marcel Raymond. 'This Western man believes that in order to be he must act, that the means of *being* is doing. It seems to me that there is something extremely serious there. In other words, in the Western spirit such as it can be seen and defined, virtues that I shall call, with all banality, contemplative, find no place or nearly no place, because of the importance given to the active virtues and even more to an erratic activism that is opposed to contemplation. The man who believes in being by doing and by fabricating no longer asks himself about the end, the raison d'être, I was going to say his soul.'[69] Merleau-Ponty neglected man's soul, in the sense that Raymond used the term, because of his faith in history. Merleau-Ponty gave no reason why history could not return us to 'archaism.' He gave no reason given why men must accept their fate. When that fate obscured the contemplative virtues and man's soul, would there not be reason to resist it? Resistance itself could also be part of our fate. There is a practical objection to his position as well. 'Developed humanity,' as Merleau-Ponty called the industrial world, had as its project more than eating, just as 'strategies of development' sought to do more than 'enable all men on earth to eat.' Put crudely, their objective is to allow all people to eat as much as they want; 'development' must also be 'liberation.' But even if there were enough food to go around, there would probably always be those who would rather go hungry and rebel than accept Western 'historical' authority. In other words, although politics may need to be liberated from the bonds imposed by the economy, even political action cannot be justified by bread alone.

POLITICAL ACTION IN INDUSTRIAL SOCIETY

No doubt the drama of decolonization and liberation from colonial masters was responsible for Merleau-Ponty's flights of fancy, for when it came to discussing the prosaic side of politics in France, he returned to *le bon sens*. He was not alone in understanding that the problems involved with decolonization in North Africa and with French domestic troubles could best be grasped in terms of an industrial and not a capitalist order. The roots of this new understanding lay in the educational experiences of a generation that grew to adulthood during the 1930s.[70] A quarter century later they had risen to positions of prominence in French society, and were responsible for formulating an appropriate response to contemporary crises. Whether the French response has in fact succeeded in coping with the problems of industrial society is a question we shall avoid. Merleau-Ponty was part of this intellectual movement, especially in his growing awareness of the obsolescence of Marx's views concerning industrial society.

The leavening of French political life by these new ideas left the Communists relatively untouched, faithful to their Stalinist principles. Likewise, the Socialists were true to their principle of *immobilisme*, and reform in the sense that Merleau-Ponty had come to understand it was advocated only by a heterogeneous collection of groups and individuals assembled under the banner of the *Union des Forces démocratiques* and subsequently the *Parti socialiste autonome*. Merleau-Ponty was a member of both organizations and in the fall of 1959, after Mendès-France announced he was becoming a socialist, worked closely with the PSA.[71] Prior to Mendès-France's announcement, a study session was held at Noisy-le-Sec at which various strategies for transforming the UFD into a reform party were debated. In addition, a more theoretical discussion, presided over by Merleau-Ponty, took place.

The Noisy-le-Sec conference was not just another stage in the regrouping of the left, Merleau-Ponty said, it also marked a stage in the evolution of ideas. 'We do not see why only two systems are conceivable: either conformist, respectable neo-capitalism, forever trying to persuade those who work that the necessities of free enterprise are the workers' as well, forever anxious to confine freedom of judgment and information, which they fear, to a carefully circumscribed terrain of "politics," or else a system of dictatorial planning where, exactly because it is dictatorial, the planning is unreal and where the real operation of production is distinct from its official operation.'[72] The question, in short, concerned democratic planning, socialism, and democracy. Discussions had been going on for over a year, Merleau-Ponty said, and there were reasons to hope for a satisfactory leftist alliance. A number of men who previously had had nothing to do with socialism had recently begun calling themselves by that name. The actual number of men was perhaps more modest than during the immediate post-war era, but they were perhaps more significant because they were accompanied by a maturation of the socialist idea and could not be explained by it. In particular, it was astonishing to Merleau-Ponty that a man such as Mendès-France, after twenty-five years of parliamentary and governmental life and extensive reflection on French politics, during which time he had always maintained a position distinct from doctrinal socialism, should declare himself a socialist. If socialism meant simply the dictatorship of the proletariat, which meant, practically, the dictatorship of the Party, or the 'Parliamentary Socialism' of the SFIO, Marxist rhetoric coupled to opportunism, there would be no reason, Merleau-Ponty said, for anyone, and certainly not a man such as Mendès-France, to lay claim to it. 'The decision that he has just taken brings to light another meaning that socialism has acquired in the context of our present times.'[73]

France was becoming an industrial society rather than an industrializing society, and its new condition was certain to require new ways of understanding: the proletariat was no longer what it once was; the middle classes, more or less integrated into the technocratic apparatus, were ceasing to be the active and vigilant supporters of traditional parliamentary democracy. To declare oneself a socialist in this new situation signified, at the very least, a willingness to take seriously the problems of industrial society, as well as a recognition that the existing institutions have done badly in meeting the new problems.

The socialism to which Mendès-France refers is a twentieth-century socialism. It is no longer a matter of a juridically and negatively defined socialism, a socialism defined, for example, in terms of the end to private appropriation. Rather, it is defined positively and concretely; its essential feature is that the entire economic and political operation be put to the service of the public interest, whatever means are employed; and these means are not necessarily nationalizations in the sense we have known them, nor are they the means used in Russia after the Revolution. I do not think that nationalizations must be excluded, but only that they must not have an a priori privilege.[74]

Specifically, he called for 'artificial mechanisms' to regulate the market, and looked to Mendès-France, as well as other members of the panel, to clarify and make more precise how such mechanisms could be made compatible with democracy.

Democratic planning and the political institutions that corresponded to it were as yet but an idea. It was an outline of a regime yet to be achieved, but, Merleau-Ponty concluded, its achievement was clearly possible. The old dilemmas 'private property *or* collective property, personal profits *or* equal salaries, class society *or* the withering away of the State, economic liberalism *or* dictational planning' had been shown by the experience of the previous thirty years to be an artificial slicing of history that allowed no understanding of any regime. These antitheses were abstract or ideological; they badly described the reality of the times and did not guarantee that it was yet possible to manage the economy by new theory and more adequate practice, to give it an orientation and a meaning. But they were enough to prescribe as an unconditional task the attempt to do so. 'It may only be an idea, but if we are to survive and revive politically, it will be along the lines of a "twentieth-century socialism." '[75] Merleau-Ponty did not live to see the theoretical elaboration of a Marxist, though not a communist, analysis of 'neo-capitalism' during the 1960s, nor did he witness the results, most spectacular in 1968, of a persistent refusal to undertake the task of orienting France in the direction of the public interest. What he had shown, nevertheless, was that the bourgeois society that Marx sought to subvert no longer existed. Events during the years after his death, which have not at all confirmed the idea of a 'twentieth-century socialism,' suggest that, like Lukács forty years before, Merleau-Ponty would have had to learn of the slowness of mediations.

FINAL POLITICAL REFLECTIONS

Merleau-Ponty's final reflections on politics were published in the preface to *Signes*. It is a serene and richly textured document, a meditation on philosophy and politics as they had come to be understood by him, a recollection of his youth, and an augury.[76]

The opening words acknowledged an immense incongruity in his book, at least at first glance, between philosophical essays and political commentary. 'In philosophy, the road is perhaps difficult but one is certain that each step along it makes other ones possible. In politics, one has the overwhelming impression of cutting a trail that is always to be reopened.'[77] The past was never clearly seen, not only because weeds grow up along the path we have cut and obscure it, but also because we cannot cut it in a straight line. As Merleau-Ponty said, 'History never *confesses*.' For that reason, many who used to be Marxists, who understood the confessional secrets of history, who had a map through the woods, have confirmed the separation of politics and philosophy. Because they had striven and failed to unite the two in their lives, because history, particularly the history that followed the Russian Revolution, failed to conform to their recipes and so failed to confirm them, they must begin all over again naked, and in the embarrassing company of those who have never done anything else, who formerly had been dismissed rather than discussed.[78] No longer having a recipe, many such men gave up cooking: if politics and philosophy have fallen apart, they say, let us interest ourselves in science or art, for the present, and preserve, if at all, an allegiance to Marxism based on faith, postponing until some vague and unspecifiable future the question of the unity of theory and action.

Postponement, at least according to Marx's teaching, was one of philosophy's vices. Modern and reluctant Marxists used it as the refuge of uncertainty. The *Aufhebung* of philosophy, which was to abolish and realize its truth in the same operation, has succeeded only in the phase of abolition, and the non-philosophical replacements of audacity and courage, according to Merleau-Ponty, were dreams and hopes. The result, and this is what concerned him, was silence, the stifling of any interrogation of the present (or of the past) on the basis of the hoped-for future dream. That is to say, the practical imagination and not philosophy alone must be understood as having some responsibility for the divorce of philosophy and politics. 'We are saying that with the events of these last few years Marxism has decidedly entered upon a new phase of its history, where it can inspire, orient analyses, and retain a serious heuristic value, but where it is certainly no longer true *in the sense that it was believed true*, and that recent experience, placing it in an order of *secondary truth*, gives Marxists a new posture and almost a new method that makes it useless to call them into court.'[79] Courts render judgments of guilt and innocence, and the question he was pondering was part of common history. There was no question of judging the guilt or innocence of history and its ideological aroma. On its own terms Marxism could be saved by the judicious addition of auxiliary hypotheses that are alleged not to touch the essential aspects of the teaching. But Marxism was as much a part of our history as Platonism, Thomism, or neo-Kantianism. In the same way and for the same reasons that it is barbarous to pronounce Plato or St Thomas or Kant 'true' or 'false' it is barbarous to pronounce such a judgment of Marx. 'We are saying that a re-examination of Marx would be a meditation on a classic and that it could not be ended by a *nihil obstat* nor by a place on the *Index*. Are you or are you not a Cartesian? The question has not much sense since those who reject this or that in Descartes only do so for reasons that owe a good deal to Descartes. We are saying that Marx is in the process of passing into this secondary truth.'[80]

A secondary truth, however, is a philosophical quest, not a recipe, and its relation to history is not at all clear: 'We have not yet learned the best use of this infringement of philosophy upon politics, above all of a philosophy that is all the less tied to political responsibilities the more it is tied to its own, all the more free to enter everywhere the less it takes anyone's place, the less it plays at passions, at politics, at life, the less it remakes them in the imagination, but discloses precisely the Being we inhabit.' The days of a first truth, of a final recipe, were over, and once again we begin, as did the Greeks, with an 'it seems to me' or a 'what is thinking?' because first truth can only be a half-truth. Thought, he said, did not bore through time; it followed in the wake of preceding thoughts, without even exercising the power, which it presumes, of tracing it anew. 'Thus I function by construction.'[81] Not that I am ever fully constructed, or in philosophical terms not that there could ever be a complete speech,[82] but that thought and speech anticipate each other and continually substitute themselves for each other. For the same reasons, there is no last analysis. In its place, to use the language of his last book, was 'the philosophy that uncovers the intersection of the visible and the invisible.'[83] Philosophy, so understood, did not play at passions, politics, or life because men of passion knew all there was to know. The philosopher did not understand men better than they understood themselves, for it was through their experience that philosophy learns of being. The difference between the passion of a philosopher and that of the man of action lay elsewhere: 'philosophy, which paints without colours, in black and white, like copperplate engravings, does not allow us to ignore the strangeness of the world that men confront as well or better than it, but as in a half-silence.' Once again it was from wonder that the philosopher sought to give a complete account, all the while knowing not just that his account was secondary but that the very strangeness that was the source of his wonder prevented his account from ever attaining completion.

Because philosophy reflected on itself it was rejoined to life and passion, so 'this sage and lofty tone' was perhaps not so false or so sterile as it appeared. It was true, Merleau-Ponty said, that 'everything that was believed to be thought out, and thought out well – freedom and power, the citizen against power, the heroism of the citizen, liberal humanism – formal democracy and real democracy, which suppressed it and realized it, the heroism and humanism of the revolutionaries – all that is in ruins.'[84] 'All that,' as the placement of dashes indicated, referred first to the young Merleau-Ponty, the liberal student of Alain and half-hearted associate of Mounier, who 'learned history,' as he put it in 1945. If liberalism was the first ruin, one is tempted to think of his early Marxism as a cathedral built upon the rubble of liberal dogma, supported in fine Gothic style with the flying buttresses of Kojève's Hegel. But the cathedral fell too: historical events and the difficult task of piercing dogmatic thought a second time produced another ruin. The final section of the preface is a reminiscence on the beauty of ruins.

Sartre's tone in the 'Avant-propos' to *Aden Arabie* 'for the first time is one of despair and revolt.' But it was a reflective revolt, the regret of not having begun by revolt, 'it is an "I ought to have," which cannot be categorical even in retrospect because, today as formerly, Sartre well knows and shows perfectly with Nizan that revolt can neither remain itself nor be accomplished in revolution.' Thus Sartre cherished the idea of a rebellious youth, and it is a chimera not only because it is too late but because his own precarious lucidity did not make such a bad figure beside the vehement errors of others; it is doubtful that Sartre would have exchanged it, were he at the age of illusions, for the illusions of anger. A page later, Sartre's lucidity was called 'damned,' and Merleau-Ponty no doubt meant that there was a lack of charity in the lecture that the mature Sartre gave to the young one and, through his younger self, to his younger contemporaries. Merleau-Ponty insisted that Nizan's life was a choice that had roots and he was not the rebel Sartre suggested because no man could be.

Merleau-Ponty's account of Nizan, which was in part a justification of the young Sartre before his elder accuser, attempted to consider as well the context of their youth. 'Nizan wished to think no more of himself, and he succeeded; he paid attention only to causal chains. But it was still him, the denier, the irreplaceable one, that ruined himself in things.'[85] With the Nazi-Soviet pact things fell apart, and Nizan realized that to be a communist is not to play a role that one has chosen but to take part in a drama where one receives another role without knowing it; it is a lifetime enterprise that continues in faith or ends in rupture, but that passes in any event beyond the conventional limits and the promises of prudence.[86] That was not what Nizan had reckoned upon, and he quit. Both Sartre and Nizan had been deceived, and so, Merleau-Ponty added, had he been. 'We were not wrong, but Nizan was right,' which was to say, in the words of a Merleau-Ponty no longer deceived, or at any rate less deceived, that 'there is an equal weakness in taking account of ourselves alone and believing only in external causes.' In one way or in the other, both are wide of the mark. Evil was not created by us or by others but born in the suffocating web we have spun between us. 'What new men will be tough enough and patient enough truly to re-do it?'[87] Certainly not, by some generational or historical necessity, the young people to whom Sartre directed his exhortation.

'The conclusion is not revolt but *virtù* without resignation.' Revolt, which was Nizan's response, was as useless as resignation, which was the youthful response of both Merleau-Ponty and Sartre. 'Nizan was right; there is your man; read him. I would like to add: read Sartre too.' But read them, Merleau-Ponty must have meant, not as one who reads a cookbook. To find the recipe for *virtù* is already to admit there was nothing more to learn. Of course Sartre, Nizan, and Merleau-Ponty had their own virtues, and young people could certainly choose worse men to emulate. But that was not Merleau-Ponty's point. The present world, which, because of its rottenness, Sartre exhorted the young to destroy, had never been made. 'It is untrue that we were at any moment masters of circumstances or that, having before us clear problems, we ruined everything by our futility. The young will learn by reading this preface that their elders have not had such an easy life.'[88] The lesson to be drawn from their lives and the history that had taken place while they lived was summarized in Merleau-Ponty's concluding sentence: 'History never confesses, not even its lost illusions, but neither does it begin them again.'

By this time in Merleau-Ponty's life the dogmas of earlier days were ruined. He surveyed them:

But we must take care. What we call disorder and ruin, others, who are younger, live as natural, and perhaps, with ingenuity, they are going to master it exactly because they no longer look for their references where we have taken them. In the fracas of demolitions, so many morose passions, so many hypocrisies or follies, and so many false dilemmas also disappear. Who would have hoped for it ten years ago? Perhaps we are at one of those moments when history moves on. We are stunned by French events or the noisy episodes of diplomacy. But beneath the noise a silence is growing, an expectation. Why could it not be a hope? [89]

He gave two reasons to justify hope. Sentences on the back cover of *Signes*, written by Merleau-Ponty himself, suggested the significance of the title: '*Signes*, that is to say, not a complete alphabet and not even a coherent sentence. But rather from these abrupt signals, like a look we receive from events, from books and from circumstances ... If the author has read well, these signs will not be such a bad augury.' Signs must point somewhere. Merleau-Ponty knew not where, but he did know that the end of one historical episode was the beginning of another, that the places from which he took his references no longer pointed anywhere but new directions and new meanings were promised by the passing of his generation.

Epilogue:
interrogation and reform

Merleau-Ponty's earliest public writings showed him to be a young philosopher acutely sensitive to what I have called, perhaps a little crudely, the transcendent dimension to human existence. In his first phenomenological studies, which included Scheler and Marcel, he learned the importance and significance of commitment as being a constituent element of knowledge. On the one hand this insight led him to abandon the dogmatic philosophical and religious traditions in which he had been reared. On the other it led him to make new commitments with a more practical significance. The first of these, the personalism of Mounier and his group centred upon the review *Esprit*, must have appeared in retrospect as a halfway house, an escape from the established structure of church and academy but still fatally compromised with Christianity.

In Kojève's interpretation of Hegel, Merleau-Ponty found a way to reinterpret his earlier beliefs, to grasp what then appeared as their limitations, and to understand where his future tasks lay. None of this happened overnight. There is no reason to doubt, for example, Merleau-Ponty's portrait of himself, given just after the war, as a sort of Machiavellian cynic. Surely the first impression of anyone who reads and accepts, even provisionally, Kojève's teaching is that finally one really understands what is going on in the world. In the vast muddle of the 1930s, Kojève's interpretation of Hegel must have been a wonderful tonic. So much now made sense. One could feel superior to confusions of others.

The war confirmed much of what Kojève said, and the Liberation seemed to Merleau-Ponty a genuine opportunity to refound French politics along more 'humanist' lines. With the expulsion of the Germans and the end of Vichy, a regime closer to the Hegelian model of mutual recognition seemed possible. But it soon became clear that France had another fate and Merleau-Ponty a different task.

His quarrels with the Communist Party revealed to him the narrow compass of their certitude. Not all fundamentalists and dogmatists were in the church. Marxists too had their scripture and formulas to be invoked as curses and anathemas against those who pointed to awkward and ambiguous factual truths that, if acknowledged, riddled certainties with doubt. Before the war the abstract ideology of liberal, Kantian moralism shored up by Christian dogmas drove him without too much difficulty to a more lively and realistic position derived from his understanding of Hegel and Marx. The problems involved in disentangling abstract ideological moralism, preached by the official representatives of Marx, from a realistic political practice was much more difficult.

First of all Merleau-Ponty was far too thoughtful to accept the stupidities of the French Communist Party and far too cultured to get along with its graceless intellectuals and 'theoreticians.' From the point of view of the Party, of course, this simply made him a petit-bourgeois individualist. But from Merleau-Ponty's perspective, it meant that the only organization in French political life that had any chance of actualizing a regime of mutual recognition was tragically squandering its opportunities. Under those circumstances, his only possible task was critical.

In *Humanisme et Terreur* he insisted, against Kantian moralists, that violence existed at the heart of liberal society even during peacetime. Political violence, he said, was our lot because we had bodies. Thoughts do not wound, but neither do they act or change anything in the world. To act, Merleau-Ponty seemed to be saying, involved doing and suffering, accepting the consequences of one's actions upon others. Moreover, he pointed out, there are circumstances – the strenuous life of war, for example – when one is constrained, willy nilly, to act. Even the lack of action is as good as action, and one is responsible too for the consequences of not acting. This is, he said, a 'hard doctrine,' but by what right may we expect life to be soft? Whatever the limitations of Merleau-Ponty's understanding of violence, by bringing it to light he reminded all his readers of a political truth they often tended to forget.

Merleau-Ponty's view of political responsibility was exemplified by Bukharin; the resulting analysis of the Moscow Trials was a model of clarity that has not been superseded. It also introduced a theme that continued to appear throughout his writings: the Soviet Union was a political regime and ought to be judged as one. It was not a liberal democracy, but it never claimed to be, so that nothing could be served by judging it by the criteria of liberalism. But neither was it a worker's paradise, the socialist, humanist society that Marx promised. Until the twin revelations of the Soviet camps and the Korean War, Merleau-Ponty maintained his neutrality. Partly this was because of a lack of reliable information on the Soviet Union in a flood of Western propaganda. But partly as well it resulted from a quite un-Marxist distinction between theory and practice. On the one hand he was thoroughly committed to the theoretical demystifying power of Hegel and Marx with regard to liberal democracy. But on the other he did not wish to charge the failures and shortcomings of Soviet life to the alleged errors of its inspiration.

His analysis of French and international politics, which showed traces of the brilliance of Marx's or Hegel's analyses, brought from him the unexceptionable recommendation that his fellow citizen 'judge of things self-evident' and not seek underground tendencies or anticipate a fatal future. France, he insisted, was not committed to one or another bloc; war was not inevitable, though the great danger lay in fatalist thinking that might make it so. As it turned out, all his insights were of no avail; their impact on real politics was nil. As a result he developed a more modest understanding of the political role of the thinker, as well as a more moderate politics, and he presented his reflections in *Les Aventures de la Dialectique.*

Whatever Marx may have meant by the unity of theory and practice, the inference that Merleau-Ponty drew from the phrase was that the barbaric side of Soviet politics was not an accidental misfortune but somehow was linked to Marx's own teaching. Merleau-Ponty did not take his reflections on this topic very far, and it is not difficult to see why. If liberalism were effectively destroyed by the critique of Marx and Hegel, and if the positive results of those who followed Marx and Hegel were also unacceptable, only two options seemed open. Either one could try to discover the common premises of Marx, Hegel, and liberal thinkers, which would entail questioning the validity of freedom as the highest political aim, for example, or one could, as Merleau-Ponty did, enter upon a new political practice. To question freedom as the highest political good is to question the goodness of modernity, and this, Merleau-Ponty several times said, he could not do. To question freedom as the highest political good is also effectively to place oneself outside the public realm, and this he would not do.

The new political practice he sought and found was a prelude to the new left of the later 1960s and even, perhaps, of the Eurocommunism of the 1970s. By calling it a *new* liberalism, its adherents, including Merleau-Ponty, wished to indicate that while it was not a tarted-up version of nineteenth-century capitalist doctrine it retained the admirable features of liberalism, the traditions of critical analysis and freedom of speech, for example, that were not to be found in the twentieth-century descendants of the opponents of capitalism, namely the communist party. The new liberalism appeared as a possibility because of the thaw. When politics refroze, Merleau-Ponty's critical remarks centred upon the common dogmatism of Western 'old' liberals and Eastern Marxists. Unlike the famous Marxist-Christian dialogue, Merleau-Ponty wished to reconsider the lived experience of class relations in industrial society, not to exchange slogans and find common or equivalent formulas.

Two aspects of Merleau-Ponty's political life seem to be consistent from be-

ginning to end. The first was that, in his own words, it was a politics nobody practised. His last efforts, directed towards defining a twentieth-century socialism, for
example, have yet to be realized anywhere. Europe, like North America and increasingly the rest of the world, seems geared to rhythms set by the large-scale private bureaucracies known as multinational enterprises. But this observation is a criticism only to the degree that the standard of politics is success. From the start,
however, Merleau-Ponty saw his task to be not winning adherents but telling the
truth as he saw it. The insights of *Humanisme et Terreur* or *Sens et Non-sens* were
thus obscured by the unreflective, opaque, ideological component of his thought.

The second consistent aspect of his thought was its common sense. In the early
work this was a less visible component, but later, in *Les Aventures de la Dialectique*, his own prior ideological commitments themselves came under scrutiny.
Henceforth, common sense appeared to be less the result of demystification than
the basis for further reflections.

In the eighteenth century the philosophers of common sense developed their
arguments as a refuge from theological and metaphysical dogmatism as well as
from the counterdogma of scepticism. Modern common sense arguments also
serve as protection against ideological dogmas. But in addition they can serve as
the foundation for a 'philosophy of appearance' such as Merleau-Ponty developed
in his final philosophical work, the unfinished and posthumous *Le Visible et
l'Invisible.*[1]

Merleau-Ponty was aware of the new direction that his reworking of the problems of perception, the body, man's being-in-the-world, was taking.[2] If, with
Remy Kwant, we describe the change as 'from phenomenology to metaphysics'
we must at the same time bear in mind two qualifications. As Merleau-Ponty wrote
in *Les Aventures*, an author does not produce ideas like a locomotive produces
smoke; there is no road from phenomenology to metaphysics except as, looking
backward, one can see a common theme in a set of questions. From the perspective of Merleau-Ponty's political writings, his later philosophical efforts seem
directed towards something like a metaphysics of common sense. Since such a notion will not be familiar to philosophers it should be explained.

The man of common sense begins with appearances, and in a sense remains
there. Appearances confirm the familiar phenomenological theme that man is
both a 'subjective' spectator and an 'objective' appearance, a characteristic common to all sentient beings. Moreover, not only do we appear, we also wish to appear, to display 'who we are'; as Kojève said, we desire recognition. And, of course
we also may wish to disappear, not finally, perhaps, but to hide. The principles
of interpretation by which what is hidden is brought to light are, in their most
fully developed form, the interrogative dialectic of questions and answers practised by Socrates.

With Socratic inquiry there is always the expectation that something will appear. The dissipation of illusion or error, then, is not followed by a direct access to truth, but by another appearance, the appearance of a meaning that is deeper or more comprehensive, and not, as with truth (whatever we mean by the term), more clear and distinct. Quite the contrary, our most profound meanings often appear to us the darkest and most obscure. It would be wrong, therefore, to say that appearances are mere appearances, that is, illusions or semblances. They are real appearances whose reality is attested by 'intersubjectivity,' the assurance I am given that others see things as I do, but also by what Aquinas called our *sensus communis*, that 'sixth sense,' as Hannah Arendt said, that fits the other five together and gives us a feeling of the realness of the world.[3] In terms of political things, this means an insistence upon the reality of the mundane and factual. This was why, for example, Merleau-Ponty accounted for his own pre-war political naïveté by saying that disregard for the facts had been a kind of duty, or why, in his many polemics, the most serious charges – indicated by terms such as magic, occult, subterranean – were that his opponents put more stock in their ideas and the logic of them than in what really appeared in the world.

The most important feature of this 'metaphysics of commonsense,' then, is that it is a philosophy of appearances, a 'philosophy of the flesh' as Merleau-Ponty said, whose first task is to uphold the realness of factual truth. It is true that factual truth is contingent in the sense that it always could have been otherwise. But this 'vice of abstract thinking,' as Hegel called it, is met by the statement that it is not otherwise: it is like this. That is, factual truth, even though contingent, is as compelling for those who witness the event as rational truth is for those who are rational. The difference, as Arendt said,[4] is that the compelling force of factual truth is more restricted in that the number of witnesses is always likely to be smaller than the number of sane people. In any event, we cannot possibly trust the testimony of others as well as we trust our own ability to reason, to know indubitably that $2 + 2 = 4$.

The question now is how a philosophy of appearance or a metaphysics of common sense would appear. To use the language that Merleau-Ponty employed, it would appear as a dialectical philosophy or a dialectical thought. The invocation of this venerable philosophical term – it means, literally, to divide or take apart in speech, dia-legesthai – does not tell us much. Let us turn, then, to *Le Visible et l'Invisible* to see directly what is involved.

The old opponents from *La Structure* and the *Phénoménologie* are there, along with the decayed dialectical philosophy brought to light by *Les Aventures*. We begin with Merleau-Ponty's critical remarks because they clear away the rubble and underbrush of error and prejudice. His criticism of Sartre's purity, for example, continued his earlier work:

It is the same thing to say that nothingness is, as to say that there is only being ... The perspective in which Being and Nothingness are absolutely opposed and the perspective in which Being itself is given by definition as identical with itself, eminently contains a contact with Nothingness that is made, broken and remade, its being recognized and its negation negated – these two perspectives are but one; as absolutely opposed, Being and Nothingness are indistinguishable ... The rigorous thought of the negative is invulnerable since it is also the thought of absolute positivity and therefore contains already everything that can be opposed to it. It cannot be shown to be faulty nor shorthanded.[5]

There could be no dialectic between being and nothingness, because each is pure and absolute. There was, so to speak, no room for the mediation of dialectic between the two mutually encompassing concepts that, taken together, imply a kind of mythical 'Hyper-being' (*Sur-être*). Consequently, there could be no internally articulated movement, but only, as a function of will, a shift in perspective, which amounts to an oscillation between the standpoints of being and nothingness and a kind of static and abstract positivity.[6]

Yet Sartre's purity was not unmotivated. Just as in *Les Aventures* where Sartre's ultra-Bolshevism expressed an incoherent and disintegrated communism, so too the definition of being as what is in every respect without restriction, and nothingness as what is not in any respect whatsoever, 'This intuition and this neg-intuition, are an abstract portrait of an experience, and it is on the terrain of experience that they must be discussed.'[7] Specifically, he said, they referred us to the experience of panoramic vision. By way of my eyes, I imaginatively command the world. But what, he asked, does this high-altitude thinking gain us? A self-cancellation. 'I have a nothingness filled up with being and a being emptied by nothingness and, if that is not the destruction of each of the terms by the other, of me by the world and of the world by me, it must be that the annihilation of being and the swallowing of nothingness by it are not exterior relations and are not two distinct operations.' On the contrary, there is but a single operation, and it resulted from an idealist prejudice whose first act is precisely the disregard of appearances.

Thus Merleau-Ponty could not accept Sartre's argument on its own terms. Once it appears as high-altitude panoramic vision, however, one's thoughts are solicited by Sartre's incompleteness to reflect upon, and so transform, the initial definitions. 'I am no longer pure negativity, to see is not simply to annihilate, and between what I see and me who sees, the relation is not immediate or frontal contradiction.' Things attracted my vision, and my vision 'caressed' things, and there existed a complicity between the two.[8] Merleau-Ponty's point was not that the examples adduced by Sartre in *L'Etre et le Néant* were wrong or misleading but that their significance was something other than what Sartre said. The terms Sartre employed did change from their initial signification, and in so doing introduced new problems that Sartre did not account for.

The changing significance of words brought about by the negative process of criticism was not mere dissembling or sophistry but the actual appearance of dialectic in the 'flesh' of the world. Dialectical thought is a process or a quest for meaning. Each of its terms is therefore already under way and proceeding towards its opposite. 'Dialectical thought becomes what it is by movement.' Like revolutions, which were true as movements and false as regimes, dialectic 'denatures itself' when captured as a determinative thesis. 'There is a trap in the dialectic: whereas it is the very movement of content such that it is realized by self-constitution or the art of retracing and following the relations between the call and the reply, the problem and the solution, and whereas the *dialectic* is in principle an epithet, it becomes, when taken as a motto, when spoken rather than practised, a power of being and an explicative principle.' But it is precisely such determinate predication that is to be avoided because it distinguishes the movement of the dialectic as a finite and abstract concept from the concrete contents that are moving. A thematized and predicated dialectic is a 'bad' dialectic, 'and this happens when the *meaning and direction* (*sens*) of dialectical movement is defined apart from the concrete constellation. The bad dialectic (*la mauvaise dialectique*) begins almost with dialectic, and the only good dialectic is the one that is criticized itself and that goes beyond itself as separated statement; the only good dialectic is hyperdialectic.'[9] A hyperdialectic, like Marcel's 'hyperphenomenology' a quarter-century earlier, took account of the ambiguous realness of appearance, the 'weight of mediations' as Merleau-Ponty had put it. Such thinking would not be in a hurry to confront meanings directly or with finality; it would accept the plurality of relationships; it would be a syllogism, a syl-logizesthai, a collecting or bringing together by words, which was not a final syn-thesis, a putting together or putting-into-place, which excluded further movement.

Against the temptation of purity, the heritage of clear and distinct ideas, and the metaphysics of knowledge, system, and synthesis, Merleau-Ponty insisted upon the unfinished business of interrogation, a task that in principle could never be finished. Philosophy, he said, interrogated perceptual faith. It was the practice of dialectic, not the speaking of it, however paradoxical such words may seem. It did not anticipate a final reply to the questions it asked, and it certainly did not receive one, 'because it is not the disclosure of a variable or an unknown invariant that will satisfy its question, and because the existing world exists in the interrogative mode. Philosophy is perceptual faith interrogating itself about itself.' Like all faiths, perceptual faith existed in conjunction with doubt, so that philosophical life would be a continuous interrogation.[10] Indeed, life itself was a con-

tinuous interrogation, and the only privilege given to philosophy over, for example, painting was that it attempted to explain itself. Yet philosophy and painting
were alike: just as there would never be a final or definitive painting, neither
would there be a final or definitive philosophy:

Philosophy does not ask questions and does not provide answers that little by
little fill in the blanks. The questions are within our life and our history; they are
born there, they die there, and, if they have found a reply, most often they are
transformed there. In any case, it is a past of experience and of knowledge that
one day ends up in this gaping wonder. Philosophy does not take its context as
given; it returns itself upon it in order to look for the origin and the sense of the
questions and that of the responses and the identity of the one who is questioning, and thereby it accedes to the interrogation that animates all questions of
knowledge but that is of another sort than they are.[11]

It is already too abstract and misleading to talk of philosophy interrogating itself
about itself; Merleau-Ponty meant by these formulas to indicate the experience
of wonder, of interrogative thinking.

To ask questions of the whole, to interrogate Being, it is necessary to ask something like What is Being? And it is clear that the form of answer, Being is X, or Y,
or Z, is incomplete to say the least. In Merleau-Ponty's words, 'Is the highest
point of reason to realize that the ground beneath our feet is shifting, pompously
to call a continuous state of stupor "interrogation," walking in circles "research,"
and what never fully is "Being"?' Pushing the questions further, one must ask
what the alternative might be, and whether any feeling of disappointment is based
upon false expectations, whether it is not the expression of 'regret at not being
everything.'[12] Beyond the logical impossibility of the part being greater than the
whole, which accounts for the incompleteness of the answer 'Being is X, or Y, or
Z,' there remained the feeling that we have some sense of the whole when we
know parts of it because answers are accompanied by a tacit recognition that they
are incomplete. ' "What is the world?" or, better, "What is Being?" – these questions become philosophical only if by a sort of double vision; they aim at the
same time at a state of things and at themselves as questions; at the same time
that they aim at the signification "being," they aim at the being of signification,
and the place of signification in Being.' Philosophical questioning, in other words,
also questioned what it meant to question and what it meant to answer questions;
it was a questioning 'at the second power,' and once begun it dragged the question-
er along after it.

Once the interrogation, the search for meaning, is begun, everything else stops.
This is why, as Heidegger said, thinking is always 'out of order.' One continues,

seduced by the movement of one's own thoughts and unable to repress it. One could make such a repression only if interrogation were simply the absence of meaning, a retreat into nothingness. 'But the one who questions is not nothing; he is – and this is entirely different – a being who interrogates himself; what he has of the negative is carried by an infrastructure of being and is therefore not a nothing that is eliminated from consideration.'[13] Human being, in short, is a questioning being. When Aristotle opened his *Metaphysics* with the statement that all men by nature desire to know, Merleau-Ponty observed, he was clearly not making an empirical statement. First of all, most men desire things other than knowledge. Secondly, it is entirely possible to gain knowledge of some things, but this achievement in no way inhibits one's quest for meaning. Aristotle's statement was simply a characteristic thinning out of Plato's more forceful proposition that the origin of philosophy is wonder. Here Merleau-Ponty simply insisted on the common experience of thinking, that men are more captivated by the interrogation than by the results.

If we confuse a search for meaning with a lack of knowledge then we raise a host of ancillary puzzles. If one were to know, all desire for knowledge would be extinguished; following Kojève to the end, one would be wise, fully, and completely satisfied. But we know from Kojève that such satisfaction (if not ironical and thus not satisfaction at all) amounts to bovine contentment stung into motion by terror. Its philosophical equivalent is found in the temptation of purity, the system, clear and distinct ideas, the complete and final speech. Whatever form it takes, 'one enters upon a cultural regime where there is neither truth nor falsity touching man and history any more, one enters a sleep or a nightmare from which there is no awakening.'[14] On the other side, the romantic or poetic sophistication of fashion and novelty, where permanence is avoided because men are conditioned by changing and antagonistic desires, contains a contradiction that is equivalent to the contradiction of complete speech. Put briefly, the pursuit of fashion, after a while, is boring in exactly the same way that a novelist who repeats the same story in a succession of books is boring. Boredom, no less than the nightmare of the system, extinguishes desire, the dialectic, and thought itself.

To avoid the boredom of repetition, desire must be deflected from things to speech, but not to completed speech, which would have nothing to say. The only kind of speech that satisfies both criteria, that it be both permanent and changing, is speech accompanied by desire to know about the whole, or, as Stanley Rosen has said, speech about completed speech.[15] This kind of speech is philosophical interrogation, a dialectical harmony of a single but invisible and never-to-be-attained goal, namely wisdom or completed speech, and a visible and apparent manifold of real speeches desiring to attain it through interrogation. The way of interrogation, this path of a philosophy of appearance, expresses the instability of human being that is experienced as novelty and forgetfulness. In this context, then, the task of philosophy is *anamnesis*, an act of recovery.[16] Again, however, the recovery can never be complete, for what is recovered is precisely the experience of interrogation.

'No question goes toward Being: by simply being a question it has already frequented Being, it is returning to it.'[17] The intelligibility of the interrogation depends upon its being part of what is interrogated, and the intelligibility of the whole of which it is a part depends, for the interrogator, upon the questions he asks. This familiar hermeneutic circle is not a vicious one, however, because the questions lead each other on to the whole: experientially, there is an 'opening to Being' that is made articulate and intelligible through dialectic. That upon which there is an opening is necessarily greater than that which experiences the opening, or in other words man as an existing interrogator experiences the truth of his being limited as human and not simply as a being limited by other existing appearances. How far Merleau-Ponty had come from the days when man was the hero for his contemporaries precisely because he knew his limitations were set only by existing appearances.

Merleau-Ponty characterized his philosophy of appearance or metaphysics of common sense as indirect. 'Direct ontology cannot be done' he said. 'My "indirect" method (being in beings) [*l'être dans l'étants*] is alone conformed to being – "negative philosophy" like "negative theology."'[18] In the end the purpose of 'negative philosophy' or of interpretative indirection and deflection is to preserve the difference between being and man, wisdom and philosophy. If the puritan attempt were a success, the puritan would be what he said: that is, there would be a unity, not a harmony, which requires at least two elements.

There is a more obvious and direct political implication to be drawn from Merleau-Ponty's incomplete remarks on the necessary indirection of ontology. It is clear from his writings after *Les Aventures* that his politics were purged of the temptation of purity. Making all possible allowances, Merleau-Ponty's immediate post-war writings, whose theoretical incompleteness I have tried to show, were certainly closer to the purity he later repudiated with such conviction. Although the textual evidence on this point is even more sparse than usual, there seems to be a coherence, a sympathetic resonance, so to speak, between the politics of reform and his 'negative philosophy' and interpretative deflection. On the philosophical side one might ask why one should be content with images, appearances, musings, with indirection, or negative philosophy, when one might speak being purely, directly, and positively. In short, why not be wise? Merleau-Ponty's short answer was that it cannot be done. His longer answer combined a critical analysis of thinkers who tried for purity and knowledge with patient description of appearances, symbolisms, and images, primarily from his experience of art, which expressed his own meditative meanings. The evidence may be found in *L'Oeil et l'Esprit* and *Le Visible et l'Invisible*; it is in essence inquiring, that is, dialectical.

An equivalent expression to this philosophical moderation may also be found in politics. Here the question would be: why accept moderate justice when pure justice may be achieved? Is not justice moderated not fully justice? And the answer is identical: pure justice, as direct ontology, cannot be attained. Just as the sense or reality of things can only be apprehended indirectly, by way of speeches about what appears, and, in general, just as philosophy is not wisdom but discourse in the light of, or about, wisdom, so too a purely just, or simply best, political order would be divine, the direct application of wisdom to human affairs. But we know that wisdom (Merleau-Ponty's direct ontology) is not possible, at least not for human beings. It may be thought a mark of human imperfection; but it is also the gap that gives us the necessary distance to see what perfection is. Here we have come some distance from the imagery of *Humanisme et Terreur*, where, to put it bluntly, a simply just order, which for Merleau-Ponty was humanism, the recognition of man by man, required the rule of wisdom. What he found in actuality was not wise or even philosophical rulers presiding over a just political order, but ideological tyrannies. Now, politics is an inherently practical enterprise, and the practical ethical implication that Merleau-Ponty drew from his later theoretical reflections was that one must learn to moderate one's indignation at suffering or beholding injustice. The spirit of revolution, whether motivated by the desire for pure justice or by more questionable passions for revenge, loses its sense when the end for which it is undertaken is impossible. If Merleau-Ponty's humanism were possible, a case could be made for terror; but because it is not, terror is unrelieved criminality. Pure justice being impossible, one learns the virtue of moderation. More tersely, justice in the absence of moderation is no longer justice.

In both politics and philosophy, therefore, what first appears as a defect – why moderate justice when one can seek pure justice? why speak indirectly of being when one can seek to speak it directly? – is in truth a necessary virtue: justice implies moderation, while ontology, in the literal sense of speech of being, implies indirection. There was, properly speaking, no new philosophy in Merleau-Ponty's later reflections because there could be no new philosophy, because philosophy (including political philosophy) is the endless task of asking the same questions under different circumstances. One can say, therefore, that an older Merleau-Ponty rejoined the youthful philosopher who found so much to admire in Scheler and Marcel. As a young man he repeated their arguments with approval but found a personal meaning only in the rejection of neo-Kantian philosophy and Thomistic Christianity; later he was able to grasp internally what previously he merely applauded intellectually and to reconstitute the living experience behind the formulas of his early teachers.

Like Scheler and Marcel, and indeed all philosophers, Merleau-Ponty was a revolutionary. He wished to 'turn men around,' as Plato said in a famous passage. But philosophers too are men of the city. They know the importance of tradition, or, what amounts to the same thing, they know that the 'conversions' of philosophy are painful, the purgative of questioning is endless, but that the city needs a kind of synthesis to survive. As Merleau-Ponty came to see, moderate speech is the public responsibility of the philosopher. The classical formulas had not lost their truth: moderate speech produced moderate deeds; the philosophical love of wisdom and the good, which are experienced by the philosopher as changeless, imply a prudent and temperate public practice, which is reform.

Notes

INTRODUCTION

1 Bernard Pingaud, 'Merleau-Ponty, Sartre et la littérature,' *L'Arc*, 46 (1971) 86

2 'Merleau-Ponty vivant,' LTM 184-5 (1961) 322-3

3 Eric Voegelin 'The origins of totalitarianism,' *Review of Politics* 15 (1953) 75

4 Theodore Gaerets, *Vers une nouvelle Philosophie transcendentale* (The Hague: Martinus Nijhoff, 1971), has provided a reliable but unfortunately incomplete account of Merleau-Ponty's intellectual development during the period. In particular, Gaerets did not appreciate sufficiently the importance of Hegel.

5 Fernandez, 'Etat de Philosophie,' *La Nouvelle Revue française* 32:226 (1932) 103-110; see also his 'A quoi sert la Philosophie?' ibid. 43-255 (1934) 901-5.

6 'Christianisme et Ressentiment,' *La Vie intellectuelle* 7 (1935) 304-5. Merleau-Ponty referred to Jean Wahl's *Vers le Concret: Etudes d'Histoire de la Philosophie contemporaine* (Paris: Vrin, 1932) a study of James, Whitehead, and Marcel from what was, in effect, the perspective of a distinctively French phenomenology, which borrowed from Hegel fully as much as from Husserl and Heidegger.

7 'Christianism et ressentiment,' 305-6

8 Léon Brunschvicg et al., 'L'Agrégation de philosophie, Séance du 7 mai, 1938,' *Bulletin de la Société française de philosophie* 38

9 Ibid. 132-3

10 Ibid. 141-2

11 Ibid. 148-50

12 (Paris: Aubier, 1935) Merleau-Ponty 'Etre et Avoir,' *La Vie Intellectuelle* 8 (1936) 98-109

13 Marcel, 'Existence et Objectivité,' in *Journal métaphysique* (Paris: Gallimard, 1927) 323. This aspect of Merleau-Ponty's intellectual debt to Marcel has not gone unnoticed. Richard M. Zaner observed that 'as regards fundamental insights, hardly anything new is added by either of his younger contemporaries [Sartre and Merleau-Ponty] as regards the problem of the body.' *The Problem of Embodiment: Some Contributions to a Phenomenology of the Body* (The Hague: Martinus Nijhoff, 1964) 44

14 'Position et Approches concrètes du Mystère ontologique,' in *Le Monde cassé* (Paris: Desclée de Brouwer, 1933) 256-61

15 *Etre et Avoir* 271-3

16 'Position ... du Mystère ontologique,' 278-83

17 'Existence et Objectivité,' 321

18 *Etre et Avoir* 145

19 Ibid. 123-4

20 Ibid. 189, 198-9

21 Merleau-Ponty, 'Etre et Avoir,' 102-3

22 Ibid. 103

23 *Etre et Avoir* 109
24 'Position ... du Mystère ontologique,' 300
25 Merleau-Ponty, 'Etre et Avoir,' 104
26 *Etre et Avoir* 248, 277
27 Merleau-Ponty, 'Etre et Avoir,' 104-5. It is often forgotten that the context of Anselm's famed 'ontological proof' is in effect a prayer.
28 *Etre et Avoir* 145
29 Merleau-Ponty, 'Etre et Avoir,' 107
30 Ibid. 108
31 Ibid.
32 Jean Lacroix (*Le Monde*, 6 May 1961, 9), for example, reported that Merleau-Ponty associated himself with Mounier and the personalist movement during the late 1930s for the somewhat naïve reason that he was searching for a philosophy and an organization that would defend and enact what he took to be the teachings of the Gospel. He left the group centred around the review *Esprit* because it did not live up to his expectations. See also SNS 305-306. For further details of Merleau-Ponty's religious opinions see M. Judith Zeiler MHSH, 'From Contingency to Hope: Merleau-Ponty's phenomenological philosophy and its impact upon his religious thought,' Duquesne University PHD thesis, 1968; Frans Vendenbussche SJ, 'The problem of God in the philosophy of Merleau-Ponty,' *International Philosophical Quarterly* 7 (1967) 44-67.
33 Kojève's lectures were given *viva voce* at the Ecole des Hautes Etudes and were collected by Raymond Queneau, along with some additional material, and published under the title *Introduction à la lecture de Hegel*, 2nd ed. (Paris, 1947). We should also note that it was at this time that Merleau-Ponty began serious study of Marx.
34 SNS 131
35 Kojève, *Introduction* 265
36 Further details may be found in my article 'Hegel and the genesis of Merleau-Ponty's atheism,' *Studies in Religion/Sciences Religieuses* 6 (1977) 665-71.
37 Kojève, *Introduction* 113-14
38 Ibid. 146
39 With a little more effort Hegel's influence can be detected in *La Structure* as well. See my 'Hegelian elements in Merleau-Ponty's *La Structure du Comportement*,' *International Philosophical Quarterly* 15 (1975) 411-23.
40 *Signes* 16-17
41 *Phénoménologie* 197. (emphasis added)
42 Ibid. 149
43 Ibid. 432 ff

44 Ibid. 438

45 Ibid. 452

46 Ibid. 455-6

47 *Phénoménologie* 520. This quotation was from Saint-Exupéry's *Pilote de Guerre.*

48 *Eloge* 11

49 SNS 50, 114-18, 169

50 SNS 225-6

51 Hegel's aphorism was quoted without reference at SNS 226. The complete version can be found in Appendix 8, 'Aphorismen aus der Jenenser und Berliner Periode,' in Karl Rosenkranz, *Georg Wilhelm Friedrich Hegels Leben* (Darmstadt: Wissenschaftiche Buchesgesellschaft, [1844] 1963) 543.

52 SNS 82

53 SNS 330-1

54 SNS 325-6

55 Friedriche Schiller, 'Was heisst und zu welchem End studiert man Universalgeschichte? Eine aksdemische Antrittsrede,' in *Werke*, ed. K.-H. Hahn (Weimar: Herman Bohlaus, 1970) Vol. 17, Part 1, 376.

56 *Eloge* 45-6

57 *Phénoménologie* 438

CHAPTER ONE: THE POST-WAR CONTEXT

1 *Humanisme et Terreur* 20

2 *Either/Or*, transl. W. Lowrie, (Garden City: Anchor, 1959) Vol. 2, 217 ff

3 For Heraclitus, consider D-K fragments B 18, B 27, B 86; for Paul, Hebrews 11:1. See also the remarks of Emil Fackenheim, *Metaphysics and Historicity, The Aquinas Lecture, 1961* (Milwaukee: Marquette University Press, 1961) 85-90.

4 SNS 330

5 *Phénoménologie* 69. See also *Signes* 20.

6 Merleau-Ponty contrasted his own 'Machiavellianism' of 1939 with the political choice of Paul Nizan in *Signes* 44.

7 SNS 245-7

8 Ibid. 250

9 Ibid. 251, 262

10 Ibid. 225

11 Ibid. 260

12 cf. *Humanisme et Terreur* xliii; SNS 266.

13 SNS 266-7

14 Ibid. 267

15 *Humanisme et Terreur* 39-40, xii

16 '*Socius* and the Neighbor,' in *History and Truth*, transl. Charles A. Kelbley, (Evanston: Northwestern University Press, 1965) 98-109

17 SNS 268

18 *Humanisme et Terreur* xxxiv. The quotations are from Montaigne's essay 'Of the useful and the honourable.'

19 *Humanisme et Terreur* xxxviii

20 SNS 134

21 Ibid. 135

22 Ibid. 188

23 Ibid. 221-2

24 Henri Lefebvre, *L'Existentialisme* (Paris: Sagittaire, 1946) 13

25 'La crise de l'Ideologie bourgeoise: à propos d'*Existentialisme ou Marxisme?* de G. Lukács,' *Cahiers de Communisme* 25 (1948) 1146

26 G. Gak, 'Un courant à la mode de la philosophie bourgeoise,' *Cahiers de Communisme* 24 (1947) 384, 398

27 Quoted in Gérard Deledalle et Denis Huisman, *Les Philosophes français d'auhourd'hui par eux-mêmes. Autobiographie de la Philosophie française contemporaine* (n.p. [Paris?]: n.d. [1959?]) 286-7. Other anecdotes and argument concerning the role of the intellectual in the Party can be found in David Caute, *Communism and the French Intellectuals* (London: Andre Deutsch, 1964).

28 *Eloge* 53, 57-8

29 SNS 271-3

30 Ibid. 280

31 Ibid. 282

32 Ibid. 275

33 Ibid. 282, 283

34 *Humanisme et Terreur* xxi ff

35 SNS 179-80

36 *Humanisme et Terreur* 8, 136, 112

37 English-speaking people often forget that the author of *Darkness at Noon* first created the French version, *Le Zero et l'Infinie* and in those days, just after the war, spent a good deal of time in Paris.

38 Koestler, *The Invisible Writing: Being the Second Volume of Arrow in the Blue, An Autobiography* (New York: Macmillan, 1954) 249-51

39 *The Invisible Writing* 363-5, 425-7

40 *Humanisme et Terreur* 178-81

41 *The Invisible Writing* 251

42 *Humanisme et Terreur* 181
43 *Humanisme et Terreur* 182
44 SNS 167

CHAPTER TWO: RECOGNITION AND VIOLENCE

1 *Phénoménologie* 382-3
2 *Humanisme et Terreur* 23-4, 204-6; SNS 111-14, 136-42, 237-41
3 *Humanisme et Terreur* 104-5, 116, 119-20, 189
4 Ibid. 104, 137-8; SNS 205
5 SNS 202-5; *Humanisme et Terreur* 138-9, 167
6 *Humanisme et Terreur* 113, 136
7 Ibid. 128, 132, 133
8 SNS 236
9 *Humanisme et Terreur* 119-27; SNS 189
10 *Humanisme et Terreur* 138
11 We are talking only of a historically immanent process and not of history as continuous creation in the sense of Saint Augustine. For Augustine, meaning was to be found only in the divine beginning and end, which were not at the disposal of men nor immanent in history.
12 SNS 294. In *Les Aventures de la Dialectique* Merleau-Ponty referred to Trotsky's metaphor of the process of natural selection and cited the French edition of his autobiography, *Ma vie*, as the source (p. 105). I have been unable to confirm the citation in either the French or English editions of Trotsky's book.
13 *Humanisme et Terreur* 166
14 *Eloge* 69
15 *Humanisme et Terreur* 129
16 Ibid. 94
17 SNS 184
18 Ibid.
19 Ibid. 213
20 *Humanisme et Terreur* 116. Consider Kant's reflections in the Third Proposition in his essay 'Idea for a universal history with a cosmopolitan purpose.' There he wrote that what was disconcerting about the doctrine of progress was 'firstly, that the earlier generations seem to perform their laborious tasks only for the sake of the later ones, so as to prepare for them a further stage from which they can raise still higher the structure intended by nature; and secondly, that only the later generations will in fact have the good fortune to inhabit the building on which a whole series of their forefathers (admitted-

ly, without any conscious intention) had worked without themselves being able to share in the happiness they were preparing. But no matter how puzzling this may be, it will appear as necessary as it is puzzling if we simply assume that one animal species was intended to have reason, and that, as a class of rational beings who are mortal as individuals but immortal as a species, it was still meant to develop its capacities completely.' Kant was, of course, silent as to why anyone should find in the immortality of the species a comfort for individual mortality. The quotation is from H. Reiss, ed., *Kant's Political Writings* (Cambridge: At the University Press, 1970) 44. The same question has been asked recently in non-Kantian terms by Raymond Beaujour, *Nemesis, ou la limite: Essai d'une Humanisme dialectique,* (Paris: Gallimard, 1965) 144-5.

21 *Humanisme et Terreur* 116-17
22 Ibid. 118-19
23 Ibid. 122; cf. Marx *Capital,* (Modern Library Edition) 824: 'Violence is the midwife of every old society pregnant with a new one.'
24 *Humanisme et Terreur* 98, 46
25 Ibid. 115, 117-18
26 Ibid. 118, 3, x
27 Ibid. xiv, 116
28 Ibid. 4, 101
29 Paul Ricœur, 'L'Homme non-violent et sa Présence a l'Histoire,' *Histoire et Verité,* 2nd ed., (Paris: Seuil, 1955) 227
30 I am not preaching non-violence. I am arguing that Merleau-Ponty's interpretation, which reduced all non-violence to hypocrisy, violated the first rule of phenomenological hermeneutics, to allow the meaning itself to appear.
31 *Discorsi,* ed. P. Gallardo (Novara: Agostini, 1966), ix:2, 181
32 'Note sur Machiavel,' *Signes* 283
33 Machiavelli, *Il Principe,* chap 18, ed. Gallardo, 109. This text, which is also frequently misunderstood and mistranslated as 'the end justifies the means,' says nothing of the kind. The translation of Merleau-Ponty, *Signes,* 274, is much more accurate; the quotation from *Humanisme et Terreur* is at 112.
34 *Signes* 267, 270-1. Cf. *Il Principe,* chap 9, 79. 'He however, who becomes prince by means of the favour of the populace must maintain its friendship; the which he will do easily, the populace demanding of him only not to be oppressed.'
35 *Signes* 272, 275
36 Ibid. 274-5
37 *Discorsi,* III:1; also his remarks on Savonarola in I:11
38 *Götzen-Dammerung,* in *Werke* VI, 3 (Berlin: de Gruyter, 1969), 74-5

39 *Signes* 279-80
40 Ibid. 281
41 Ibid. 281-2
42 Ibid. 282
43 *Humanisme et Terreur* 139-40
44 Ibid. 165
45 Ibid. 166-8

CHAPTER THREE: HISTORICAL RESPONSIBILITY AND
THE SOVIET UNION

1 *Les Aventures* 11-12
2 *Communism and the French Intellectuals: 1914-1960* (London: André
Deutsch, 1964) 127
3 See Jean-Paul Sartre, 'Preface' to Paul Nizan's *Aden-Arabie* (Paris: Maspero,
1967) 45; Ariel Ginsbourg, *Paul Nizan*, (Paris: Editions Universitaires, 1966)
82
4 *La Force de l'Age* (Paris: Gallimard, 1960) 297
5 'Merleau-Ponty vivant,' LTM 17:184-5, (1961) 315. Sartre's text said 'before
1939,' but this may be a typographical error, for lower on the same page he
wrote: 'After 1936, [there was] no doubt: it was the Party that troubled him.'
6 Arthur Koestler, *The Invisible Writing: Being the second volume of Arrow in
the Blue, An Autobiography* (New York: Macmillan, 1954) 403-4
7 *Humanisme et Terreur* 3
8 SNS 295-6
9 Ibid. 299
10 Ibid. 302
11 This was the opinion of the American ambassador as well as of Stalinist
intellectuals. See Joseph E. Davies, *Mission to Moscow: A Record of Confi-
dential Dispatches to the State Department, Official and Personal Correspon-
dence, Current Diary and Journal Entries, including Notes and Comments up
to October 1941* (New York: Simon and Schuster, 1941) 272. Lion Feucht-
wanger, *Moscow 1937: My Visit Described for My Friends*, transl. I. Josephy,
Left Book Club edn (London: Victor Gollancz, 1937), 134-5. See also
N. Besseches, *Stalin*, transl. E.W. Dickes (New York: Dutton, 1952), 277.
12 Isaac Deutscher, *Stalin: A Political Biography*, 2nd ed., (New York: Oxford
University Press, 1967) 375ff; George F. Kennan, *Russia and the West under
Lenin and Stalin* (New York: New American Library, 1962) 297; Leonard
Shapiro, *The Communist Party of the Soviet Union* (London: Eyre and
Spottiswood 1962) 428ff; Leon Trotsky, *The Revolution Betrayed* (London:

New Park, 1967) esp. chaps 5 and 12; W.G. Krivitsky, *In Stalin's Secret Service* (New York: Harper, 1939) 181ff. On the 'elimination of rivals' theme, see A. Avtovkhanov, *Stalin and the Soviet Communist Party: A Study in the Technology of Power* (New York: Praeger 1959) 223; George Katkov, *The Trial of Bukharin* (London: Batsford, 1969) 101; Robert Conquest, *The Great Terror: Stalin's Purge of the Thirties* (London: Macmillan, 1968) 277ff. Additional accounts of the trials which dwell on aspects of Stalin's 'personality' as well as on foreign and economic policy questions are: Hugo Dewar, 'The Moscow Trials,' *Survey*, 41 (April 1962) 86-95; Philip E. Mosely, 'Recent Soviet trials and policies,' *Yale Review*, NS 27 (1937-8) 745-66; Hugh Seton-Watson, *From Lenin to Khruschev: The History of World Communism* (New York: Praeger, 1961) 172-5; Robert Vincent Daniels, *The Conscience of the Revolution: Communist Opposition in Soviet Russia* (Cambridge: Harvard University Press, 1960) 370-97; Merle Fainsod, *How Russia is Ruled*, rev. ed., (Cambridge: Harvard University Press, 1964) 109-13; Boris Souvarine, *Stalin: A Critical Survey of Bolshevism*, tr. C.L.R. James, (New York: Longmans, 1939) 624-31.

13 Fitzroy MacLean, *Eastern Approaches* (London: Jonathan Cape, 1949) 90

14 Robert C. Tucker and Stephen F. Cohen, eds, *The Great Purge Trial* [an edited version of the court transcript, which preserves all Bukharin's speech] (New York: Grosset and Dunlap, 1965) 666. Some westerners took these 'absurd' explanations seriously; see Malcolm Muggeridge, *The Thirties: 1930-1940 In Great Britain*, 2nd ed., (London: Collins, 1967 [1940]) 227-9.

15 Shapiro, *The Communist Party of the Soviet Union*, 425-6.

16 See, for example, Louis Fischer, *Men and Politics: An Autobiography,* (New York: Duell, Sloan and Pearce, 1941) 518-19; David J. Dallin, *From Purge to Coexistence: Essays on Stalin's and Khruschev's Russia* (Chicago: Regnery, 1964) 113: Daniels, *The Conscience of the Revolution* 389.

17 This explanation is weakened by the fact that many prisoners regarded the confession as a formality. So far as we know, the correlation coefficient between confession and reprieve is vanishingly small. See the evidence and arguments presented in F. Beck and W. Godin (pseud.), *Russian Purge and Extraction of Confession*, transl. E. Mosbacher and D. Porter (London: Hurst and Blackett, 1951); Elizabeth Lermolo, *Face of A Victim*, transl. I.D.W. Talmadge, (New York: Harper, 1955); David J. Dallin, *From Purge to Coexistence;* Nathan Leites and Elsa Bernaut, *Ritual of Liquidation: The Case of Moscow Trials* (Glencoe: The Free Press, 1954).

18 The final plea is in Tucker and Cohen, *The Great Purge Trial*. The most thorough analysis of the psychodynamics of capitulation and confession is Leites and Bernaut, *Ritual of Liquidation*, Parts 1 and 2. See also MacLean,

Eastern Approaches 118; Beck and Godin, *Russian Purge and the Extraction of Confession* 180-1; Krivitsky, *On Stalin's Secret Service* 190, 207; Daniels, *The Conscience of the Revolution* 389-90; William F. O'Neill, 'The Yeshov Method,' *Il Politico* 34 (1969) 339; Katkov, *The Trial of Bukharin* 116.

19 Our references are to the English translation by G. Dunlop, *Memoirs of a Secret Revolutionary* (London: Boriswood, 1938). So far as I know, Koestler has never mentioned Plisnier, though Jean Kanapa accused him of plagiarism in *Le Traître et le Prolétaire, ou l'Enterprise Koestler and co. ltd. suivi d'Inédits sur le Procès de Mathias Rakosi* (Paris: Editions sociales, 1950) 27 n.1.

20 Plisnier, *Memoirs* 261, 266. The Hotel Bristol (which had once existed in Copenhagen) was alleged to have been the scene of a rendezvous between Holtzman, an alleged emissary of Trotsky, and Sedov, Trotsky's son, during the Zinoviev-Kamenev trial. In the Pyatakov trial, it was alleged that Pyatakov flew from Berlin to Oslo to meet with Trotsky. No record of the flight has ever been found, either at Templehof in Berlin or in Norway.

21 Plisnier, *Memoirs* 275-6

22 Ibid. 283-4

23 Ibid. 284

24 Ibid. 287

25 *Phénoménologie* 177

26 *The Invisible Writing* 155, 394

27 *The Invisible Writing* 405

28 *Darkness at Noon*, transl. D. Hardy (New York: Bantam, 1966), 209. First published by Macmillan in 1941. Koestler remarked that Bukharin, Zinoviev, and Pyatakov 'died for reasons which were human reasons running amuck but within the logic of their own faith.' 'Darkness at Noon again: an interview,' *Survey* 48 (July 1963) 173

29 *Darkness at Noon* 80-1

30 Ibid. 34. Cf. Plisnier, *Memoirs* 220-1.

31 *Darkness at Noon* 151, 153. Cf. Plisnier, *Memoirs* 211-12.

32 *Darkness at Noon* 206

33 For example, E. Berl, *De l'Innocence* (Paris: Julliard, 1947) esp. 46-7, 100; Harvey T. Mann, 'Totalitarian justice: the trial of Bukharin, Rykov, Yagoda, et al.,' *American Bar Association Journal* 24 (1938) 970-6, 1029-30.

34 Tucker and Cohen, *The Great Purge Trial* 328, 352-6

35 Ibid. 358-9

36 Ibid. 365-6

37 Ibid. 391-5; also 137

38 Ibid. 657

39 Ibid. 328, 337, 348, 356, 366.

40 Ibid. 328-9, 340
41 Ibid. 337-9
42 'The logic of this struggle led us step by step into the blackest quagmire. And it has once more been proved that departure from the position of Bolshevism means siding with political counter-revolutionary banditry.' Ibid. 667.
43 Ibid. 136
44 Ibid. 168
45 *Humanisme et Terreur* 56, 61
46 *The Great Purge Trial* 132 ff and 352 ff
47 *Humanisme et Terreur* 57
48 Ibid. 62-3
49 Ibid. 63
50 *The Great Purge Trial* 667. The line 'Die Weltgeschichte ist das Weltgericht' ('world-history is the world court of justice') is from Schiller's poem 'Resignation.'
51 *The Great Purge Trial* 668. From Bukharin's perspective the important question was not whether Stalin was seeking to come to terms with Hitler as one tyrant with another, but whether the threat Germany posed to the Soviet Union constituted an element in the self-recognition of his 'objective' or 'historical' guilt.
52 *Humanisme et Terreur* 67-8
53 Ibid. 68-9
54 Ibid. 69
55 Koestler has agreed that Rubashov's character did not develop its own inner possibilities but rather conformed to the disciplien of the Party. See 'Darkness at Noon again: an interview,' *Survey* 48 (July 1963) 173-4; *The Invisible Writing* 386-7, 394-5, 403-5; see also his remarks in R.H.S. Crossman, ed., *The God that Failed: Six Studies in Communism*, (London: Hamish Hamilton, 1950) 42-3.
56 *Humanisme et Terreur* 15-16
57 *Darkness at Noon* 208
58 Koestler, *The Yogi and The Commissar* (New York: Macmillan, 1945) 252-3
59 Ibid. 255. See also 'Arthur Koestler at 65: a fighter for men's minds now studies their brains,' *New York Times Magazine* 30 August 1970.
60 *The Yogi and The Commissar* 224-5; *The Invisible Writing* 427-30
61 *Humanisme et Terreur* 180
62 Ibid. 25-6
63 Ibid. xiii
64 These reflections of Kojève's were made during the 1936-7 academic year (*Introduction à la lecture de Hegel*, 2nd ed., [Paris: Gallimard, 1962] 146 ff).

In August 1936 Zinoviev and Kamenev were tried for the second time and executed after confessing to being Trotskyites; in December 1936 the new and democratic Soviet constitution was adopted; in January 1937 Pyatakov and Radek were put on trial; and in June Marshal Tukhachevsky was shot.

65 *Humanisme et Terreur* 73-5. Kojève, *Introduction* 463-5
66 Hannah Arendt, *Between Past and Future: Eight Exercises in Political Thought*, 2nd ed., (New York: Viking, 1968) 252
67 *Humanisme et Terreur* xviii
68 Ibid. 78.
69 Trotsky, *The Revolution Betrayed* (London: New Park [1937] 1967) 105. The analogy with the French Revolution as Isaac Deutscher pointed out, was not a very good one. Yet it was a powerfully emotional term during the debates of the 1920s. For details see Deutscher's biography, *The Prophet Unarmed* (New York: Vintage, 1959) 244-5, 311-16, 343-7. For a discussion of Trotsky's revision of the Thermidor concept in *The Revolution Betrayed,* see Deutscher, *The Prophet Outcast* (New York: Vintage, 1963) 313-18.
70 *Humanisme et Terreur* 79
71 Ibid. 80
72 Ibid. 81
73 Ibid. 90-1
74 Ibid. 94-6
75 L. Trotsky, 'The USSR in war,' in *The Basic Writings of Trotsky*, ed. I. Howe, (London: Secker and Warburg, 1964), 312, 313-14
76 *Humanisme et Terreur* 163-5

CHAPTER FOUR: THE ECLIPSE OF THE MIDDLE WAY

1 'Merleau-Ponty vivant,' LTM 184-5 (1961) 313
2 'Le Philosophe et le Prolétaire,' *La Nouvelle Critique* 1 (1948) 26-8
3 See, for example, Jean-Daniel Martinet, 'Les Intellectuels et le Goût du Pouvoir,' *La Révolution prolétarienne*, 303 (May 1947) 11-13.
4 *Humanisme et Terreur* 30
5 See Emmanuel Berl, *De l'Innocence* (Paris: Julliard, 1947) 12-13, for such an interpretation.
6 *Humanisme et Terreur* 31
7 Otto Kirchheimer, *Political Justice: The Use of Legal Procedure for Political Ends* (Princeton: Princeton University Press, 1961)
8 *Humanisme et Terreur* xxxiii
9 See, for example, Georges Brand, 'La nouvelle justice,' *Ecrits de Paris* 36 (Oct. 1947) 47-52; M.L. Durif, 'La justice de la IVᵉ République jugée par les

disques de Vichy,' *Ecrits de Paris* 32 (June 1947) 38-44; M. Dacier, 'Idéologies sanglantes,' *Ecrits de Paris* 34 (Aug. 1947) 1-12.

10 *De l'Innocence* 47, 94-5, 100, 115

11 Robert Campbell, 'Monsieur Merleau-Ponty et ses lecteurs,' *Paru* 5:37 (1947) 49-50

12 Aimé Patri, 'Philosophie de la police politique, à propos d' A. Koestler et de M. Merleau-Ponty,' *Masses: Socialisme et Liberté* 7-8 (Feb. 1947) 28-30; cf. Patri, 'Humanisme et Terreur,' *Paru* 42 (1948) 61-2; Patri, 'Le Yogi, le Commissaire et la Fraternité des Pessimistes,' *L'Arché* 23 (1947) 99-105; Jules Monnerot, 'Liquidation et justification,' *La Nef* 4:27 (1947) 8-19; Monnerot, 'Réponse aux *Temps Modernes*,' *La Nef* 4:37 (1947) 32-43; 5:39 (1948) 3-21; Christianus, 'Sainte Antigone,' *La Vie intellectuelle* 15:1 (1947) 1-4.

13 See H. Stuart Hughes, *The Obstructed Path: French Social Thought in the Years of Desperation, 1930-1960* (New York: Harper and Row, 1967) 199-201; Raymond Aron, *L'Opium des intellectuels* (Paris: Gallimard, 1968) 175 ff; Leszek Kolakowski, (review of *Humanism and Terror*, transl. John O'Neill [Boston: Beacon, 1969]) *New York Review of Books* 15:23 (3 Sept. 1970).

14 *Humanisme et Terreur* xviii-xx

15 Ibid. xxiii-xxiv

16 Ibid. xxv

17 Ibid. xlv

18 Ibid. xlii-xliii

19 Ibid. 105, 140-1, 145-6

20 Ibid. 191

21 Ibid. 189-90

22 'La Résistance: la France et le Monde de Demain,' *Archives du Comité d'Histoire de la Seconde Guerre mondiale*, CDD /DI 2-3.

23 *Humanisme et Terreur* 196

24 Ibid. 197-8

25 Ibid. 203-6

26 SNS 217

27 Ibid. 302, 303-4

28 Ibid. 217, 302

29 'En un Combat douteux,' LTM 27 (Dec. 1947) 961-2

30 Ibid. 962-3

31 SNS 10

32 Ibid. 303 fn. 1. 'Socialisme et Liberté' was also the name of a short-lived Resistance group to which Merleau-Ponty belonged.

33 'Note de la Rédaction,' to Lefort's 'Kravchenko et la Problème de l'URSS,' LTM 29 (1948) 1516.

34 'Et Bourreaux et victimes ... ' LTM 2:15 (1946), inserted between 384 and 385, dated 24 Dec. 1946.

35 'Le Philosophe et l'Indochine,' *Le Figaro* (4 fév. 1947) 1. Mauriac spoke of 'toute la France de l'outre-mer' and not of French possessions or the French empire. It is perhaps worth noting as well that Mauriac chose not to republish this editorial in his *Mémoires politiques* (Paris: Grasset, 1967).

36 'Indochine SOS,' republished in *Signes* as 'Sur l'Indochine.' Contributors included: Tran-duc Thao, 'Les Relations Franco-Vietnamiennes,' LTM 2:18 (1947) 1053-67; a more general interpretation by Claude Lefort, 'Les Pays coloniaux,' ibid. 1068-94; Jeanne Cuisinier, 'Service inutile,' ibid. 1095-1132; 'N ... ' 'Regards sur notre Action politique en Indochine,' ibid. 1133-49. On Lefort's article see also the response by Tran-duc Thao, 'Sur l'Interpretation trotzkyste des Evénements d'Indochine,' LTM 2:21 (1947) 1697-705. Incidentally, *Indochine SOS* was also the title of a book by Andrée Viollis published in 1935.

37 *Signes* 409, 406

38 Ibid. 406-7

39 'Le Cas de Nizan,' LTM 3:22 (1947) 181-4

40 Sartre, 'Avant-propos' to Paul Nizan, *Aden-Arabie*, (Paris: Maspero, 1960) 8

41 *Humanisme et Terreur* xli. Aragon took up the theme a few years later in his novel *Les Communistes*. Orfilat, who represented Nizan, was depicted as a snivelling coward who, when he heard of the Nazi-Soviet pact, out of fear of being sent to the front, wangled a job in the Foreign Affairs Ministry where an honest liberal put him to shame for his 'filthy treason.'

42 The transcript was quoted in *L'Ordre de Paris*, 22 Oct. 1947. Other accounts and summaries can be found in *Carrefour*, 29 Oct. 1947; *Combat*, 22 Oct. 1947; 23 Oct. 1947. See also Simone de Beauvoir, *La Force des Choses* (Paris: Gallimard, 1963) 153-4, and Michel Contat, Michel Rybalka, *Les Ecrits de Sartre* (Paris: Gallimard, 1970) 169-72.

43 'Complicité objective,' LTM 34 (1948) 1-11; Uri, 'Une stratégie économique,' ibid. 12-41. All quotations given below are from 'Complicité objective'.

44 November 1945; cf. *SNS* 303.

45 Sartre, 'Merleau-Ponty vivant,' LTM 184-5 (1961) 328; an account of the RDR 'platform' is in Sartre et al., *Entretiens sur la politique*, 11th ed. (Paris: Gallimard, 1949). A fictional account of this period is provided in Simone de Beauvoir, *Les Mandarins* (Paris: Gallimard, 1954).

46 'Complicité objective,' LTM 34 (1948) 11. The quotation is from 'La Guerre a eu lieu,' LTM, 1 (1945) 66; *SNS* 269.

47 'Le "Manifest communiste" a cent ans,' *Le Figaro Littéraire* 102 (1948) 2

48 Cf. Simone de Beauvoir, *La Force des choses* 165, 249; Sartre, 'Merleau-Ponty vivant,' 357; Sartre, 'Correspondance,' LTM 194 (1962) 183.
49 'Commentaire,' LTM 50 (1949) 1119-21; in *Signes* as 'Marxisme et superstition,' 328-9. Merleau-Ponty had met Lukács at the Rencontres internationales de Genève in 1946, which was attended also by Jaspers and was publicized as a great confrontation between existentialism and Marxism. Lukács gave an analysis of 'formal freedom' as found in the West from the perspective of 'real freedom' as described by Marx. Merleau-Ponty noted that Marx's answer to the inadequacy of formal freedom was not followed by Lenin and raised the embarrassing questions of how formal freedom, condemned by history, could have survived so long and why real freedom, promised by history, had yet to make an appearance in the home of the Revolution. Was this a detour or a derailment of the meaning of history? Lukács replied that the danger was found in fascism, into which formal freedom can very easily turn. Julien Benda et al., *L'Esprit Européen: Textes in-extenso des Conférences et des Entretiens organisés par les Rencontres Internationales de Genève, 1946* (Neuchâtel: Editions de la Baconnière, 1947) 253-5, 326
50 *Signes* 328
51 In fact, as George Steiner has pointed out, Lenin as early as 1905 wrote: 'Literature must become Party literature. Down with un-partisan *littérateurs!* Down with the supermen of literature!' *Language and Silence* (London: Faber and Faber, 1967) 335.
52 *Signes* 330. The 'autocriticism of 1949' can be found in Lukács's book *Existentialisme ou Marxisme?* (Paris: Nagel, 1948). When this book was published, early in 1949, Lukács gave a series of lectures in Paris that vigorously attacked Sartre and existentialism. For details of these charges and Sartre's no less vigorous replies, see *Combat*, 20 Jan. 1949, 3 Feb. 1949. Summaries can be found in Contat and Rybalka, *Les Ecrits de Sartre* 208-11. See also the Communist replies, one by Martin Horvath, a member of the Hungarian Politburo, 'Sur l'autocritique de Lukács,' *La Nouvelle Critique* 13 (1950) 99-107, and another by a French spokesman, Maurice Mouillard, 'J.-P. Sartre, ou la trafiquant des lettres,' ibid. 15 (1950) 32-43.
53 *La Force des Choses* 219-20
54 'Les jours de notre vie,' LTM 51 (1950) 1153-68. Although signed by both Sartre and Merleau-Ponty, the editorial was the work of Merleau-Ponty alone. See 'Merleau-Ponty vivant,' 330. It is reprinted in *Signes* 330-43. The title is a parody of a book by Rousset on the Nazi camps, *Les Jours de notre Mort* (Paris: Pavois, 1947) parts of which had appeared in LTM 1 (1945) 1015-44; 1231-61
55 *Signes* 332

56 Ibid. 334

57 Ibid. 336

58 See Hannah Arendt, *The Origins of Totalitarianism*, new ed. (New York: Harcourt Brace and World, 1966) 444, fn. 135 and references cited.

59 *SNS* 173 ff

60 *Signes* 337

61 The objection could have been stated more strongly: since the universal recognition of man by man was an unattainable goal, and since human beings were real and were conceived as obstacles, all that could in fact take place was their destruction.

62 *Signes* 336-8

63 Dwight Macdonald, *Politics Past: essays in political criticism*, (New York: Viking, 1970) 29-30. The article from which we have quoted was published in 1946.

64 *Signes* 341-2

65 Ibid. 343

66 *La Force des choses* 221

67 Pierre Daix, 'Sartre et Merleau-Ponty refusent de choisir, mais les deportés prennent le Parti de la Paix,' *Les Lettres françaises* 295 (19 Jan. 1950) 1. The original article by Daix, which celebrated the re-educational successes that the camps had attained and labelled Rousset a 'filthy liar,' was published in *Les Lettres françaises* 286 (17 Nov. 1949).

68 'Lettre ouverte aux *Temps modernes*,' *La Révolution prolétarienne* 339 (May 1950) 3

69 In fact, in the July 1948 issue of *Les Temps modernes* Merleau-Ponty wrote: 'We think that forced labour or concentration camp labour in the USSR is not simply one of the means of repression through which no revolution fails to pass, that it has become a permanent element of Soviet production (and that correlatively the police have become a permanent power), and that in consequence the system has no chance of realizing socialism.' 'Complicité objective,' LTM 34 (1948) 10. Later in the same issue he said that the extent of concentration camp labour and the independence of the police made it ever more difficult to speak of a transition regime. 'Communisme-anticommunisme,' LTM 34 (1948) 188, reprinted in *Signes* 327. In July 1949, Roger Stephane reviewed M. Buber-Neumann's book *Deportée en Siberie*, LTM 45 (1949) 180-2.

70 'L'Adversaire est complice,' LTM 57 (1950) 1-11

71 'Merleau-Ponty vivant,' 338. Simone de Beauvoir wrote: 'Merleau-Ponty, who in practice ran the review, has been converted to apolitism by the Korean war: "The guns are speaking and we have no longer anything to say" was the substance of what he told us.' *La Force des Choses* 249

72 'Note de la Rédaction' to E.-N. Dzelepy, 'Le Drame de la politique ameri-
caine,' LTM 60 (1950) 601

73 'Merleau-Ponty vivant,' 338-9

74 See the comments of Pierre Labar, 'A travers les revues,' L'Observateur 32
(16 Nov. 1950) 18-19.

75 'Merleau-Ponty vivant,' 337

76 LTM 81 (1952) 1-50; 84-5 (1952) 695-760; 101 (1954) 1731-1819. The
articles were later collected in Situations VI (Paris: Gallimard, 1964) 80-384,
and constitute an important, though regrettably neglected, stage between
L'Etre et le Néant and the Critique de la Raison dialectique.

77 See Caute, Communism and the French Intellectuals 195, for details.

78 Henri Martin was a young ex-Resistance fighter who joined the navy for the
last round of fighting against Japan. Rather than stopping Japanese imperialism, he found himself present at the shelling of Haiphong and the attempt to
re-establish French imperialism. Disillusioned with the government attitude
toward the Viet Minh, he began his own 'subversion' by talking to friends in
the Navy about the Indochinese war. In October 1950 he was sentenced to
five years in the brig for handing out leaflets to sailors in Toulon. In his
defence he said he was a Republican sailor, not a mercenary, and that he had
been defending the interests of France then just as he had done against Vichy.
He was retried in July 1951, again found guilty, and later pardoned by the
president of the Republic. Sartre's book was devoted to a political defence
of Henri Martin. See L'Affaire Henri Martin (Paris: Gallimard, 1953).

79 'Merleau-Ponty vivant,' 348

80 La Force des Choses 280

81 'Merleau-Ponty vivant,' 320

82 Naville, 'Etats-Unis et Contradictions capitalistes,' LTM 86 (1952) 899-914

CHAPTER FIVE: A REAPPRAISAL OF DIALECTIC

1 There is no point in giving a complete list of reviews and review articles. The
right-wing, or at least anti-communist, criticisms were found in journals such
as Preuves and the Revue des deux Mondes; those of the communists can be
found primarily in La Nouvelle Critique.

2 This meeting illustrated some subsidiary themes in the repertoire of Communist Party struggles on the intellectual front: when it was learned that
Merleau-Ponty was to be in Kenya, the meeting was billed in L'Humanité as a
revival of the grand tradition of public debate. One of the sponsors, Georges
Cogniot, went so far as to declare that Merleau-Ponty had been specifically
invited; in fact, M. Cogniot had called upon Mme Merleau-Ponty and knew
beforehand that Merleau-Ponty could not be there. See 'Procédé élégant,'

L'Express 165 (29 Nov. 1955) 4. In any event, as *France-Observateur* pointed out, there was no intention of debating anything: the purpose was to vilify Merleau-Ponty's book and link it to the 'New Left' conference supported by *France-Observateur* a few weeks earlier. See 'Les Aventures de la polémique,' *France-Observateur* vi:291 (8 Dec. 1955) 2-3. The results of the 'debate' were published in Roger Garaudy et al., *Mésaventures de l'Anti-marxisme* (Paris: Editions sociales, 1956). See also Garaudy, 'La Lutte ideologique chez les intellectuels,' *Cahiers du Communisme* 31:7-8 (1955) 891-905; Henri Lefebvre, 'M. Merleau-Ponty et la philosophie de l'ambiguité, 1,' *La Pensée* 68 (1956) 44-58.

3 'Merleau-Ponty et le pseudo-sartrisme,' originally appeared in LTM 114-15 (June-July 1955) 2072-122 and was re-issued in *Privilèges* (Paris: Gallimard, 1955) 201-72. Jean Kanapa, 'Situation de l'intellectuel,' *La Nouvelle Critique* 68 (1955) 22-3. At the time of publication, Sartre was engaged in the production of his play *Nekrassov*.

4 J. Muglioni, 'L'Histoire et la verité,' *Revue socialiste* 90 (Oct. 1955) 312-21; Jean-Jacques Sorel, 'Merleau-Ponty contre Sartre, ou les mésaventures des mandarins,' *France Observateur* 6:263 (26 May 1955) 16-18

5 *Les Aventures* 7; cf. George Lichtheim, *Marxism in Modern France* (New York: Columbia University Press, 1966) 80, fn. 5

6 Henry van Lier, 'A propos des *Aventures de la Dialectique*,' *La Revue nouvelle* 22 (1955) 230, fn. 11. See also the appreciation of Mikel Dufrenne, *Jalons* (La Haye: Martinus Nijhoff, 1966) 169-73.

7 *Les Aventures* 253

8 Ibid. 310

9 Ibid. 307-8

10 Ibid. 308-9

11 Ibid. 310-11 (emphasis added)

12 Of purely biographical interest is the fact that Merleau-Ponty lost his mother in the fall of 1952; her death also motivated a more personal stock-taking.

13 *Les Aventures* 11

14 Ibid. 8. Strictly speaking, Merleau-Ponty began with a brief critical appraisal of Alain's distinction between the politics of reason and the politics of compromise. He dismissed that distinction with a citation from Aron's *Introduction à la Philosophie de l'Histoire*, 2nd ed., (Paris: Gallimard, 1948) no pages given, but probably 413-15. He also dismissed in the Preface the 'sham of systematizing,' on familiar grounds.

15 *Les Aventures* 17-18

16 Ibid. 19-21

17 Ibid. 23-25. This citation from Weber is from *Gesammelte Aufsätze zur Religionssoziologie*, vol. 1 (Tübingen: J.C.B. Mohr, 1947) 37.

18 *Les Aventures* 33-4. Thus, for example, Kojève wrote: 'The "truth" of the Master is the Slave; and his Labour. In fact others recognize the Master as Master only because he has a Slave.' *Introduction à la Lecture de Hegel* 26. This understanding of truth, most forcefully argued by Heidegger, is widely accepted, though not philologically unshakable: see P. Friedlander, *Plato*, vol. I, transl. H. Meyerhof (New York: Bollingen, 1958), chap. 11.

19 *Les Aventures* 37, 42

20 Originally published by Malik Verlag, Berlin, 1923. Reissued as vol. 2 of Lukács, *Werke* (Neuvied: Hermann Luchterhand, 1968).

21 *Les Aventures* 43-4. Incidentally, Weber described himself as a follower of the German historical school. See his *Gesammelte politische Schriften*, ed. J. Winckelman, (Tubingen: J.C.B. Mohr, 1971) 16-17; *Gesammelte Aufsätze zur Wissenschaftslehre*, ed. J. Winckelman, (Tübingen: J.C.B. Mohr, 1968) 208.

22 *Les Aventures* 45-6

23 Ibid. 49

24 This is the burden of a long paragraph that began by introducing Marx's understanding of alienation and ended by concluding with a restatement of 'a historical selection that eliminates antinomical realities from the course of history.' We dealt with the concept of historical Darwinism above in chapter 2.

25 *Les Aventures* 51

26 Ibid. 54

27 Ibid. 53

28 Ibid. 55

29 Ibid. 56

30 Ibid. 61

31 Ibid. 61-2

32 Ibid. 64-9

33 Ibid. 69-70

34 *Phénoménologie de la Perception* 506-11

35 *Les Aventures* 71-2

36 Ibid. 73-5

37 Ibid. 77-8; *Geschichte und Klassenbewusstsein* 348

38 *Les Aventures* 82

39 Ibid. 79

40 The term appears, so far as I know, only once in *Les Aventures* (at 88) but was developed extensively and thematically in Merleau-Ponty's lectures at the Collège de France during 1954-5. See *Résumés* 59-65

41 *Résumés* 64-5

42 Ibid. 65

43 *Les Aventures* 90

44 Ibid. 82-4

45 Ibid. 86, 87 fn. 2

46 Ibid. 88, 90

47 Ibid. 88

48 Ibid. 91

49 Ibid. 97-8

50 For details see Isaac Deutscher, *Trotsky*, vol. 2 *The Prophet Unarmed, 1921-1929* (New York: Vintage 1959).

51 *Les Aventures* 108-10

52 Ibid. 112

53 Ibid. 113

54 Ibid. 117-18. The quotation is from Guérin, *La Lutte des Classes sous la Ire République* (Paris: Gallimard, 1946) vol. 1, 9.

55 *Les Aventures* 119-20

56 Ibid. 121 (emphasis added)

57 Ibid. 122-3

58 Ibid. 127

59 Ibid. 131

60 *Résumés* 78, 84

61 *Les Aventures* 133

62 One review, of Sartre's *L'Imagination*, in the *Journal de Psychologie normale et pathologique* 33 (1936) 756-61, was generally favourable but criticized Sartre only for being too severe with Bergson; the other review, of his play *Les Mouches*, in *Confluences* 25 (1943) 514-16, was entirely favourable and took issue with some reviewers who based their judgments on formal aesthetic criteria and so overlooked the political significance of the play, performed during the occupation.

63 Compare Sartre's *L'Etre et le Néant* (Paris: Gallimard 1943) 508-10, 531-5, with Merleau-Ponty, *Phénoménologie de la Perception* 497-8, 504-5. See also *Les Aventures* 264-9.

64 *SNS* 73 ff, 120, 125, 133, 140. In addition, the 'Notes de Travail' of *Le Visible et l'Invisible* contained numerous references to Sartre, always with the implication that Sartre's dilemmas were to be avoided. See also Sartre's remarks in 'Merleau-Ponty vivant,' 354.

65 *Les Aventures* 143, 146; Cf., Sartre, 'Les Communistes et la Paix,' in *Situations VI* (Paris: Gallimard, 1964) 342-3.

66 *Les Aventures* 148-54. See *Situations VI* 207-9. The notion of an oath reappeared in Sartre's *Critique de la Raison dialectique*, vol. I (Paris: Gallimard, 1960) 440 ff. Merleau-Ponty commented that Sartre's analysis was incomplete in that he did not reflect on the relationship between death or terror

and betrayal of the oath but moved on to a discussion of Malthusianism. The *Critique* certainly dealt with terror as the prophylaxis of betrayal, but it was still 'exchanged outside of life.'

67 *Les Aventures* 156
68 Ibid. 178-9
69 Ibid. 185, 190, 192, 197-8, 206
70 G. Myrdal, *The Political Element in the Development of Economic Theory* (New York: Simon and Schuster, 1969) 54, 115; Karl Marx, *Capital*, vol. 1, chap. 1, section 4
71 *Les Aventures* 208-9
72 Ibid. 203-4, 209
73 Ibid. 213-14
74 Ibid. 215-17
75 Ibid 181 fn
76 Ibid. 220-1.
77 Ibid. 223, 230
78 Ibid. 236-7, 239-41, 160
79 Ibid. 240, 135-6
80 Ibid. 166, 178, 222-3
81 Ibid. 160
82 'Dialectique en action: à propos des *Aventures de la Dialectique* de M. Merleau-Ponty,' in *Recherches de Philosophie*, vol. 2, *Aspects de la Dialectique* (Paris: Desclée de Brouwer, 1956) 332.
83 Ibid. 273-4
84 Ibid. 276
85 Ibid. 276-7
86 Ibid. 277
87 Ibid. 277-9
88 Ibid. 294. As shown in detail in the next chapter, Merleau-Ponty concluded from these reflections that a sensible political attitude demanded that he moderate his expectations and the revolutionary severity of his judgments. Sartre, whose theoretical conclusions were in some ways comparable, found an opposite practical lesson: if the revolution decayed it was only through want of terror. For details of Sartre's argument in his *Critique de la Raison dialectique* and a criticism of them based on assumptions similar to those that governed Merleau-Ponty's autocriticism and our own earlier remarks, see Raymond Aron, *History and the Dialectic of Violence*, transl. B. Cooper, (Oxford: Blackwell, 1975).

CHAPTER SIX: *Virtù* WITHOUT RESIGNATION

1 See Lefort's 'Avertissement' to *La Prose du monde* (Paris: Gallimard, 1960) esp. ix-x, xiii.

2 See *Résumés* for details. Consider Merleau-Ponty's remarks on Sartre in *SNS* 125-6, 133; *Les Aventures* 185-8, 192, 259; *Signes* 33, 196.

3 *Les Aventures* 238-9, 270-1

4 See *Eloge* 49-50; *Les Aventures* 240.

5 *Les Aventures* 236

6 Ibid. 245-6

7 *SNS* 275

8 *Les Aventures* 246, 248

9 Ibid. 253-60

10 *Eloge* 79 ff

11 'Dialogue entre Est et Ouest, Rencontre à Venise,' *Comprendre: Revue de Politique et de la Culture* 16 (Sept. 1956) 211-12

12 Ibid. 212-13

13 Ibid. 215-16

14 Ibid. 217

15 Ibid. 218

16 'Le Philosophe, est-il fonctionnaire?' *L'Express* 72 (9 Oct. 1954) 3; 'Sur la déstalinisation,' [1956] *Signes* 366; 'Sur le 13 Mai 1958,' *Signes* 422

17 Interview, in Madeleine Chapsal, *Les Ecrivains en Personne* (Paris: Julliard, 1960) 145, 156

18 *Signes* 10

19 'Truth and politics,' *Between Past and Future*, New ed., (New York: Compass, 1968) 250

20 *Les Aventures* 241

21 Ibid. 248-9

22 Ibid. 249-50

23 Ibid. 301-2

24 Ibid. 278-9

25 'Dialogue entre Est et Ouest,' 211

26 *Les Aventures* 303-4

27 Ibid. 304

28 Ibid. 305-6

29 As the following analyses have clearly shown: S.K. Levine, 'Merleau-Ponty's philosophy of art,' *Man and World* 11 (1969) 438-52; Thomas Langan, *Merleau-Ponty's Critique of Reason* (New Haven: Yale University Press, 1966) 42 ff; Eugene Kaelin, *An Existential Aesthetic: The Theories of Sartre*

and Merleau-Ponty (Madison: University of Wisconsin Press, 1962); Robert Klein, 'Peinture modern et phénoménologie,' *Critique* 161 (1963) 336-53.

30 In addition, he wrote a few topical pieces: 'Comment repondre à Oppenheimer?' *L'Express* 91 (19 Feb. 1955) 3; 'M. Poujade a-t-il une petite Cervelle?' ibid. 95 (19 Mar. 1955) 3; 'Le Marxisme est-il mort à Yalta?' ibid. 98 (9 April 1955) 3-4, in *Signes* 343-8.

31 'France, va-t-elle se renouveler?' *L'Express*, 74 (23 Oct. 1954), pp. 3-4. On the lack of a sociology of the Soviet Union see also *Les Aventures*, pp. 222 *et seq.*

32 'Où va l'Anticommunisme?' *L'Express* 109 (25 June 1955) 12

33 'D'Abord comprendre les Communistes,' *L'Express* 85 (8 Jan. 1955) 8

34 'Où va l'Anticommunisme?' 12

35 'L'Avenir de la révolution,' in *Signes* 350

36 *Signes* 359-65

37 'D'Abord comprendre les Communistes,' 9

38 'Où va l'Anticommunisme?' 12. In this article Merleau-Ponty mentioned the work of a fellow contributor to *L'Express*, Alfred Sauvy, author of *La Prévision economique*, (Paris: PUF 1954).

39 *La Révolution et les Fétiches* (Paris: La Table ronde, 1956)

40 See, in particular, *L'Humanité* 25 Jan. 1956, 10 Feb. 1956.

41 Sartre, 'Le Réformisme et les fétiches,' LTM 122 (1956) 1153-64. Also in *Situations VII* 104-8

42 See the series of articles in *L'Humanité* appearing over the week of 23-30 March 1956.

43 J.T. Desanti, 'Les intellectuels et le communisme,' *La Nouvelle Critique* 76 (1956) 97

44 *Le Figaro* 19 Oct. 1956; *Le Monde* 21 Oct. 1956

45 See *Le Monde* 1 Nov. 1956; Sartre, 'Après Budapest,' *L'Express* 281 (9 Nov. 1956) 13-16; Sartre, 'Le Fantôme de Staline,' LTM 129-31 (1956-7) 577-696, also in *Situations VII* 144-307.

46 *Le Monde* 16 Nov. 1956; *L'Humanité* 22 Nov. 1956; *Le Monde* 24 Nov. 1956

47 'Sur la Déstalinisation,' *Signes* 366-7

48 *Signes* 372-3

49 Ibid. 374-6

50 See *L'Humanité*, 3 July 1956.

51 A year later, for example, Pierre Daix admitted only that 'a certain untidiness' followed Khrushchev's speech but no apologies were needed. *Réflexions*, (Paris: Editeurs de France Réunis, 1957) 180

52 *Signes* 378-80

53 Ibid. 384-5. The term 'artificial mechanism' was borrowed from Mendès-France.

54 See *Le Monde* 2 July 1957.
55 *Signes* 418. Merleau-Ponty was referring to the single electoral college.
56 Ibid. 419
57 Ibid. 427-8
58 Ibid. 428-30, 442
59 Ibid. 428
60 Ibid. 421, 434
61 Ibid. 419-20
62 Ibid. 424-5
63 Ibid. 433
64 Ibid. 422
65 Ibid. 408-9
66 Ibid. 416-17. This is why in 1960 Merleau-Ponty refused to sign the 'Manifesto of the 121,' which justified the refusal to take up arms against the Algerian people. Among the signatories were Sartre, Simone de Beauvoir, and Simone Signoret. See *Le Monde* 5 Sept. 1960. Shortly thereafter Merleau-Ponty signed a petition calling for a negotiated peace in Algeria and affirmed support for the '121.' See also the editorial in *L'Express* 487 (13 Oct. 1960) 7; M.-A. Burnier, *Les Existentialistes et la Politique* (Paris: Gallimard, 1966) 137-8; *France Observateur* 534 (20 Sept. 1960) 2.
67 'Intervention' by Merleau-Ponty in Julien Benda, et al., *L'Esprit européen: Textes in-extenso des Conférences et des Entretiens organisés par les Rencontres Internationales de Genève, 1946*, (Neuchâtel: Editions de la Baconnière, 1947) 74-5
68 *Signes* 418
69 In Benda et al., *L'Esprit européen* 133
70 This is the thesis of Stanley Hoffman, 'The effects of World War II on French society and politics,' *French Historical Studies* 2 (1961) 29-63; see also his essay in Hoffman et al., *In Search of France*, (Cambridge: Harvard University Press, 1963); Pierre Andreu, 'Les Idées politiques de la jeunesse intellectuelle de 1927 à la Guerre,' *Revue des Travaux de l'Académie des Sciences morales et politiques et Comptes rendus de ses Séances*, 4th series, 110:2 (1957) 17-35.
71 For details, see 'Lettre ouverte aux Démocrates,' *France Observateur*, 442 (23 Oct. 1958) 2; 'Un grand Débat au sien d l'UFD,' ibid. 442 (6 Nov. 1958) 2; 'L'Avenir de l'UFD,' ibid. 455 (22 Jan. 1959) 2; 'Accord en vue à l'UFD,' ibid. 459 (19 Feb. 1959) 2; 'Accord complet à l'UFD,' ibid. 463 (19 March 1959) 2; 'Les Projets de Mendès-France et de Mitterand,' ibid. 474 (4 June 1959); 'Que va faire Mendès-France?' ibid. 489 (7 Sept. 1959) 6.
72 'L'avenir du socialisme,' *Les Cahiers de la République* 22 (Nov.-Dec. 1959) 42

73 Ibid. 30-1
74 Ibid. 31-2
75 Ibid. 42
76 The preface was divided into four sections of unequal length. The first three were written in February 1960 and the last in September 1960. The final section was a discussion of Sartre's 'Avant-propos' to the new edition of Nizan's *Aden Arabie*, issued during the summer of 1960.
77 *Signes* 7
78 Ibid. 12-13
79 Ibid. 14-15
80 Ibid. 17
81 Ibid. 20-1
82 'Now, the very idea of a *complete* statement inconsistent: it is not because it is complete in itself that we understand it; it is because we have understood that we say it is complete or sufficient.' Ibid. 25
83 Ibid. 25, 28, 30
84 Ibid. 32
85 Ibid. 40
86 Ibid. 42. According to Merleau-Ponty, what made Nizan resign was not the pact itself, 'which beat the Western friends of Hitler at their own game,' but that the French Communist Party did not at least retain the dignity of independence that a mock indignation would have expressed.
87 Ibid. 44, 47
88 Ibid. 46-7
89 Ibid. 32

EPILOGUE: INTERROGATION AND REFORM

1 For details on the relationship between this last work and his other writings, see Remy Kwant, *From Phenomenology to Metaphysics: An Inquiry into the Last Period of Merleau-Ponty's Philosophical Life*, (Pittsburgh: Duquesne University Press, 1966); A. Lingis, Translator's Preface to *The Visible and the Invisible*, (Evanston: Northwestern University Press, 1968); Claude Lefort's masterly 'Postface' to *Le Visible* is the most eloquent meditation on Merleau-Ponty's interrogative discourse.
2 *Le Visible* 222, 237, 253
3 *The Human Condition* (Chicago: University of Chicago Press, 1958) 208-9
4 See her 'Truth and Politics,' in *Between Past and Future*, new ed., (New York: Viking, 1968) 227 ff.
5 *Le Visible* 94-5

6 Ibid. 105, 126
7 Ibid. 105
8 Ibid. 106-7
9 Ibid. 128-9
10 Ibid. 139-40
11 Ibid. 142; *L'Oeil et l'Esprit* 91-2
12 *L'Oeil et l'Esprit* 92
13 *Le Visible* 160
14 *L'Oeil et l'Esprit* 12
15 Stanley Rosen, *Nihilism: A Philosophical Essay* (New Haven: Yale University Press, 1969) 209
16 *Résumés de Cours* 153
17 *Le Visible* 161
18 Ibid. 233. See also *Résumés de Cours* 125.

Bibliography

Numerous primary and secondary bibliographies of Merleau-Ponty are now available. None is complete, and all are in need of some minor revisions, but the following, if taken together, constitute an extensive collection:

MÉTRAUX, ALEXANDRE. 'Bibliographie de Maurice Merleau-Ponty.' In X. Tilliette, ed., *Merleau-Ponty, ou la mesure de l'homme*, 173-83. Paris: Seghers, 1970

O'NEILL, JOHN. *Perception, Expression, and History: The Social Phenomenology of Maurice Merleau-Ponty*, 90-101. Evanston: Northwestern University Press, 1970

RABIL, ALBERT. *Merleau-Ponty: Existentialist of the Social World*, 301-25. New York: Columbia University Press, 1967

LANIGAN, RICHARD L. 'Maurice Merleau-Ponty Bibliography.' *Man and World*, 3 (1970) 289-319

GOOD, PAUL and CAMTO, FREDERICO. 'Bibliographie des Werkes von Maurice Merleau-Ponty.' *Philosophisches Jahrbuch*, 77 (1960) 439-43

LAPOINTE, FRANCOIS H. 'Works on Maurice Merleau-Ponty.' *Journal of the British Society for Phenomenology*, 2 (1971) 99-112

The only items missing from these bibliographies, so far as I know, are *Titres et travaux* (Paris: Centre de Documentation Universitaire, 1951) and the anonymous pamphlet, *La Résistance, la France et le monde de demain* (Archives of the Comité d'Histoire de la Seconde Guerre mondiale, 32 rue de Leningrad, Paris 8e, number CCD/D.I).

The following secondary materials on Merleau-Ponty either have influenced my interpretation of Merleau-Ponty but have not been referred to in footnotes or else are of relatively recent appearance. The first section is on philosophy, the second is on politics.

Philosophy

ACTON, H.B. 'Philosophical survey: philosophy in France.' *Philosophy*, 24 (1949) 77-81

BACHELARD, S. et al. *Hommage à Jean Hyppolite.* Paris: PUF, 1971

BANNAN, JOHN F. 'Merleau-Ponty mismanaged.' *Journal of Existentialism*, 7 (1967) 459-76

BATAILLON, M. 'Eloge prononcée devant l'Assemblée du Collège de France, 25 juin 1961.' *Annuaire du Collège de France*, 37-40. Paris: Imprimerie Nationale, 1961

BELAVAL, YVON. 'Les recherches philosophiques d'Alexandre Koyré.' *Critique*, 207-8 (1964) 675-704

BERTRAM, MARYANNE J. 'Subjectivity in the monism of Merleau-Ponty.' PHD thesis, Marquette University, 1971.

BRUNNER, AUGUSTE, SJ. *La personne incarnée: étude sur la phénoménologie et la philosophie existentialiste.* Paris: Beauchesne, 1947

CAILLOIS, ROLAND-P. 'De la perception à l'histoire: La philosophie de M. Merleau-Ponty.' *Deucalion*, 2 (1947) 57-85

– 'Le Monde vécu et l'histoire.' In *L'Homme, le monde, l'histoire*, 7-110. Paris: Cahiers du collège philosophique, 1948

– 'L'Ambiguïté de l'histoire et la certitude de la philosophie.' *Critique*, 77 (1953) 867-74

COOPER, BARRY. 'Hegelian elements in Merleau-Ponty's *La Structure du Comportement.*' *International Philosophical Quarterly*, 15 (1975) 411-423

DEVAUX, ANDRÉ A. 'Idealisme critique et positivisme phénoménologique (l'esquisse d'un dialogue entre M. Joseph Moreau et Maurice Merleau-Ponty).' *Giornale di Metafisica*, 17 (1962) 72-91

DONDEYNE, ALBERT. *Contemporary European Thought and Christian Faith* (Duquesne Studies, Philosophical Series, no. 8). Pittsburgh: Duquesne University Press, 1963

– 'L'historicité dans la philosophie contemporaine.' *Revue philosophique de Louvain*, 54 (1957) 5-25, 456-77

DUHRSSEN, A. 'Some French Hegelians.' *Review of Metaphysics*, 7 (1953-4) 323-37

EECKE, WILFRIED VER. 'Interpretation and perception: from phenomenology through psychoanalysis to hermeneutics.' *International Philosophical Quarterly*, 11 (1971) 372-384

FESSARD, GASTON, SJ. 'Deux interprètes de la *Phénoménologie* de Hegel: Jean Hyppolite et Alexandre Kojève.' *Etudes*, 255 (1947) 368-73

– 'Existentialisme et Marxisme au Collège philosophique.' *Critique*, 252 (1947) 399-401

- *De l'actualité historique.* Paris: Desclée de Brouwer, 1960
GERGER, RUDOLPH J. 'Merleau-Ponty: the dialectic of consciousness and world.' *Man and World*, 2 (1969) 83-107
HYPPOLITE, JEAN. *Sens et existence dans la philosophie de Maurice Merleau-Ponty* (The Zarhoff Lecture for 1963.) Oxford: Clarendon Press, 1963
- 'Existence et dialectique dans la philosophie de Merleau-Ponty.' *Les Temps Modernes*, 184-5 (1961) 228-44
JOLIF, J.-Y. 'Maurice Merleau-Ponty ou la vertu du dialogue.' *Economie et humanisme*, 134 (1961) 10-20
KAELIN, E.F. 'Merleau-Ponty, fundamental ontologist.' *Man and World*, 3 (1970) 102-15
KLINE, GEORGE. 'Some recent interpretations of Hegel's philosophy.' *The Monist*, 48 (1964) 34-75
KOYRÉ, ALEXANDRE. *Etudes d'histoire de la pensée philosophique.* Paris: Colin, 1961
KWANT, REMY C. *From Phenomenology to Metaphysics: An Inquiry into the Last Period of Merleau-Ponty's Philosophical Life* (Duquesne Studies, Philosophical Series, no. 20). Pittsburgh: Duquesne University Press, 1966
- *The Phenomenological Philosophy of Merleau-Ponty* (Duquesne Studies, Philosophical Series, no. 15). Pittsburgh: Duquesne University Press, 1963
LACROIX, JEAN. *Marxisme, existentialisme, présence de l'éternité dans le temps.* Paris: PUF, 1949
LEFORT, CLAUDE. 'L'Idée d'être brut et d'esprit sauvage.' *Les Temps Modernes*, 184-5 (1961) 255-86
- 'Maurice Merleau-Ponty.' In R. Klibansky, ed., *Contemporary Philosophy: A Survey*, vol. 3, *Metaphysics, Phenomenology, Language and Structure*, 206-14 Firenze: La Nouva Italia Editrice, 1969
LORENZ, H.S. 'Hierarchic man: philosophy and the individual in the work of Maurice Merleau-Ponty.' PH D thesis, Tulane University, 1971
LUIJPEN, WILLIAM. *Phenomenology and Atheism* (Duquesne Studies, Philosophical Series, no. 17). Pittsburgh: Duquesne University Press, 1964
MAYER, WILLI. *Das Problem der Leiblichkeit bei Jean-Paul Sartre und Maurice Merleau-Ponty.* Tubingen: Max Niemeyer, 1964.
MOREAU, JOSEPH. *L'Horizon des esprits.* Paris: PUF, 1960
MURPHY, RICHARD T., SJ. 'A metaphysical critique of method: Husserl and Merleau-Ponty.' In F.J. Adelmann, SJ, ed., *The Quest for the Absolute*, 175-207. The Hague: Martinus Nijhoff, 1966
ROOSJEN, SJOERD. *De Idee der Zelfvervreemding bij Maurice Merleau-Ponty.* Delft: Drukkerijen Hoogland en Waltman, 1963
SAPONTZIS, STEVE F. 'Merleau-Ponty and philosophical methodology.' PH D thesis, Yale University, 1971

SAID, EDWARD M. 'Labyrinth of incarnations: the essays of Merleau-Ponty.'
Kenyon Review, 29 (1967) 54-68

WAELHENS, A. DE. 'Phénoménologie husserlienne et hegelienne.' *Revue philosophique de Louvain*, 52 (1954) 234-49

WAHL, JEAN. 'A propos de l'introduction à la phénoménologie de Hegel par A. Kojève.' *Deucalion* 5. Neuchatel: Baconniere, 1955

- 'Commentaire d'un passage de la "Phénoménologie de l'esprit" de Hegel.' *Revue de Métaphysique et de Morale*, 34 (1927) 441-71

ZANER, RICHARD M. 'Existentialism as a logos of man: the case of Merleau-Ponty.' *Memorias del xii Congreso Internacional de Filosofia* (Sesiones plenarias: communicaciones sobre el tempa: I 'The problem of man'). Vol. 3, 409-21. Mexico: Universidad Nacional Autonoma de Mexico, 1963

Politics

A[DRIAN], A.-H. 'Hegel était-il marxiste?' *La revue internationale*, 12 (1947) 72-4

ARON, RAYMOND. 'Le fanatisme, la prudence et la foi.' *Preuves*, 63 (1956) 8-22

- 'Aventures et mésaventures de la dialectique.' *Preuves*, 59 (1956) 3-20
- 'La Responsabilité sociale de la philosophie.' *Preuves*, 88 (1958) 18-25
- 'Les Intellectuels français et l'utopie.' *Preuves*, 50 (1955) 3-14
- *La Tragédie Algérienne*. Paris: Plon, 1957
- 'La notion du sens de l'histoire.' *Revue des travaux de l'Académie des Sciences morales et politiques et comptes rendus de ses séances*, 4e série, 110:1 (1957) 53-74
- *Polémiques*. Paris: Gallimard, 1955
- *D'une Sainte Famille à l'autre: Essais sur les marxismes imaginaires*. Paris: Gallimard, 1969
- *History and the Dialectic of Violence*. Transl. Barry Cooper. New York: Harper and Row, 1975
- *L'Opium des intellectuels*, 2nd ed. Paris: Gallimard, 1968
- 'Remarques sur les rapports entre existentialisme et marxisme.' In *L'Homme, le monde, l'histoire*. Paris: Cahiers du Collège philosophique, 1948

AUBENQUE, PIERRE. 'Dialectique en action: à propos des aventures de la dialectique de M. Merleau-Ponty.' In *Recherches de philosophie*, Vol. 2, *Aspects de la dialectique*. Paris: Desclée de Brouwer, 1956

BATTAGLIA, FELICE. 'Existentialisme et Marxisme.' *Synthèses* 49 (1950) 36-48

BEAUFRET, JEAN. 'Vers une critique marxiste de l'existentialisme.' *La Revue socialiste*, 2 (1946) 149-54

BERL, EMMANUEL. *De l'Innocence*. Paris: Julliard, 1947

BERNSTEIN, SAMUEL. *The Beginnings of Marxian Socialism in France*. New York: Russell and Russell, 1965

BIEN, JOSEPH. 'Man and the economic: Merleau-Ponty's interpretation of historical materialism.' *Swedish Journal of Philosophy*, 3 (1972) 121-7

BILGER, PIERRE. *Les Nouvelles gauches de janvier 1956 à mai 1958: étude de stratégie politique.* Paris: Mémoire, Fondation Nationale des Sciences Politiques, 1960

BILLOUX, FRANCOIS. 'Sur les problèmes de nouvelles gauches.' *Cahiers du communisme*, 31:3 (1955) 563-78

BON, F. et M.-A. BURNIER. *Les Nouveaux intellectuels.* Paris: Ed. Cujas, 1966

BORG, JOHN LUCIAN. 'Le Marxisme dans la philosophie socio-politique de Merleau-Ponty.' *Revue Philosophique de Louvain*, 73 (1975) 481-510

BORNE, ETIENNE. ' "Les Aventures de la dialectique" de Maurice Merleau-Ponty.' *La Vie Intellectuelle*, 26 (July 1955) 6-19

BOURGIN, HUBERT. *De Jaurès à Léon Blum: L'Ecole Normale et la politique.* Paris: Fayard, 1938

BRIONNE, MARTIN. 'Ni Zéro ni infini.' *Esprit*, 122 (1946) 697-702

BRISSAND, ANDRÉ. 'Existentialisme, Marxisme, Christianisme.' *Synthèses*, 4:3 (1949) 354-66

BROMBERT, VICTOR. 'Raymond Aron and the French intellectuals.' *Yale French Studies*, 16 (1955-6) 13-23

CAILLOIS, ROLAND-P. 'Destin de l'humanisme marxiste.' *Critique*, 22 (1948) 243-51

CAMPBELL, ROBERT. 'Monsieur Merleau-Ponty et ses lecteurs.' *Paru*, 37 (1947) 49-51

CANTRIL, HADLEY and D. RODNICK. *On Understanding the French Left.* Princeton: Institute for International Social Research, 1956

CAPALBO, CREUSA. 'L'Historicité chez Merleau-Ponty.' *Revue Philosophique de Louvain*, 73 (1975) 511-35

CARAT, JACQUES. 'La Deuxième "enfance d'un chef." ' *Preuves*, 18-19 (1952) 94-7

CARRUBA, GERALD J. 'The phenomenological foundation of Marxism in the early works of Maurice Merleau-Ponty.' *Dianoia*, 10 (1974) 37-55

CASANOVA, LAURENT. *Le Parti communiste, les intellectuelles, et la nation.* Paris: Ed. Sociales, 1949

CAUTE, DAVID. *Communism and the French Intellectuals: 1914-1960.* London: André Deutsch, 1964

CHALLAYE, FÉLICIEN. 'Immoralité et existentialisme.' *Synthèses*, 128 (1957) 286-96

CHANLIEU, PIERRE. 'Sartre, le stalinisme et les ouvriers.' *Socialisme ou barbarie*, 12 (1953) 63-88

CHÂTELET, F. *Logos et praxis: recherches sur la signification théorique du marxisme.* Paris: SEDS, 1962

CHIAROMONTE, NICOLA. 'Paris letter,' *Partisan Review*, 15 (1948) 1007-14

CHRISTIANUS. 'Sainte Antigone.' *La Vie Intellectuelle*, 15:1 (1947) 1-4

CIVICUS. *M. Mendès-France et les communistes.* Paris: Amiot, 1957

LA COMMISSION DE CRITIQUE DU CERCLE DES PHILOSOPHES COMMUNISTES. 'Le retour à Hegel: dernier mot du révisionnisme universitaire.' *La Nouvelle Critique*, 20 (1950) 43-54

CORNELL, KENNETH. '*Les Temps Modernes:* peep-sights across the Atlantic.' *Yale French Studies*, 16 (1956) 24-8

CRASTRE, VICTOR. 'Un tour d'horizon sur le monde.' *Critique*, 36 (1949) 470-4

DAIX, PIERRE. 'Réponse à David Rousset.' *Les Lettres Françaises*, 286 (17 Nov. 1949) 1, 4

- 'Sartre et Merleau-Ponty.' *Les Lettres Françaises*, 295 (19 Jan. 1950) 1

DAVENHAUER, BERNARD P. 'Renovating the problem of politics.' *Review of Metaphysics*, 29 (1976) 626-41

DEBRAY, RÉGIS. 'Avec *Signes* Merleau-Ponty veut faire parler l'histoire.' *Arts*, 3, no. 802 (Jan. 1961) n.p.

DELASNERIE, CH. 'Des actuelles tentatives de synthèse entre l'existentialisme et le marxisme.' *La Revue internationale*, 13 (1947) 184-6

DEPREUX, EDOUARD. *Le Renouvellement du socialisme.* Paris: Calmann-Lévy, 1960

DESANTI, JEAN-T. 'Les Intellectuels et le communisme.' *La Nouvelle Critique*, 76 (1956) 92-102; 77 (1956) 90-101

- 'Le Philosophe et le prolétaire.' *La Nouvelle Critique*, 1 (1948) 26-36

- 'Hegel est-il le père de l'existentialisme?' *La Nouvelle Critique*, 56 (1954) 91-109

DUCLOS, JACQUES. 'Le parti et les intellectuels.' *La Nouvelle Critique*, 57 (1954) 2-7

DUFRENNE, MIKEL. *Jalons.* The Hague: Martinus Nijhoff, 1966

DUVIGNAND, JEAN. 'France: the neo-Marxists.' In L. Labaedz, ed., *Revisionism: Essays on the History of Marxist Ideas,*' 313-23. London: Geo. Allen and Unwin, 1962

ETCHEVERRY, AUGUSTE. *Le Conflit actuel des humanismes.* Paris: PUF, 1955

FETSCHER, I. 'Der Marxismus im Spiegel der französischen Philosophie.' *Marxismusstudien*, 1 (1954) 173-213

FOUGEYROLLAS, PIERRE. 'Les intellectuels entre la morale et la politique.' *Cahiers de la République*, 28 (1960) 7-11

- *La Conscience politique dans la France contemporaine.* Paris: Denoël, 1963

- 'Sartre et le marxisme.' *Cahiers de la République*, 27 (1960) 89-95

- *Le marxisme en question.* Paris: Seuil, 1959
- *Contradiction et totalité: surgissement et déplorements de la dialectique.* Paris: Minuit, 1964
GARAUDY, R. 'La lutte idéologique chez les intellectuels' *Cahiers du communisme,* 31:7-8 (1955) 891-905
- *Perspectives de l'homme: existentialisme, pensée catholique, marxisme.* Paris: PUF, 1960
- *L'humanisme marxiste.* Paris: Ed. Sociales, 1957
GARAUDY, ROGER, et al. *Mésaventures de l'anti-marxisme.* Paris: Editions Sociales, 1956
- *Literature of the Graveyard.* Transl. J.M. Bernstein. New York: International, 1948
GODFREY, E. DREXEL. *The Fate of the French Non-Communist Left.* New York: Random House, 1955
GOLFIN, C. 'Chroniques de philosophie politique.' *Revue Thomiste,* 56 (1956) 353-75
GORDON, DAVID C. *The Passing of French Algeria.* London: Oxford University Press, 1966
GRAHAM, D.B. *The French Socialists and Tripartisme 1944-1947.* Toronto: University of Toronto Press, 1965
GROSSER, ALFRED. *La Quatrième République et sa politique extérieure.* Paris: Colin, 1961
HAKIM, ELEANOR. 'Jean-Paul Sartre: the dialectics of myth.' *Salmagundi,* 1 (1966) 59-94
HERVÉ, PIERRE. *La Révolution et les fétiches.* Paris: La Table ronde, 1956
- *La Libération trahie.* Paris: B. Grasset, 1945
HOFFMAN, STANLEY, et al. *In Search of France.* Cambridge, Mass.: Harvard University Press, 1963
HONDT, JACQUES D'. 'Violence et histoire.' *Etudes philosophiques,* NS 23:1 (1968) 39-46
HUGHES, H. STUART. *The Obstructed Path: French Social Thought in the Years of Desperation 1930-1960.* New York: Harper and Row, 1966
IGLESIAS, JUAN ANDRÉS. 'Le marxisme communiste de Merleau-Ponty.' *Akten der xiv Internationalen Kongresses für Philosophie,* Wien, 2-9 Sept. 1968, Vol. 2, 62-8
INVITO, GIOVANNI. *Merleau-Ponty politico: L'eresia programmatica.* Rome, Lacaita, 1971
JUNG, HWA YOL. 'The radical humanization of politics: Maurice Merleau-Ponty's philosophy of politics.' *Archiv für Rechts-und Social-philosophie,* 53:2 (1967) 233-56

- 'The political relevance of existential phenomenology.' *Review of Politics*, 33 (1971) 538-63

KANAPA, JEAN. *Le Traître et le prolétaire: ou, l'Entreprise Koestler and Co. Ltd.* Paris: Ed. Sociales, 1950

KUHN, HELMUT. 'Existentialisimus und Marxismus: Zu Merleau-Ponty's Philosophie der Zweidentigkeit.' *Philosophisches Jahrbuch*, 62 (1953) 327-46

KLEIN, A.N. 'On revolutionary violence.' *Studies on the Left*, 6:3 (1966) 62-82

KRUKS, SONIA. 'Merleau-Ponty, Hegel, and the dialectic.' *British Journal of Phenomenology*, 7 (1976) 96-110

LAGUEUX, MAURICE. 'Y-a-t-il une philosophie de l'histoire chez Merleau-Ponty?' *Dialogue*, 5 (1966) 404-17

LEBOND, J.-M. 'Le Sens de l'histoire et l'action politique.' *Etudes*, 287 (1955) 209-19

LEFORT, CLAUDE. 'Le Marxisme et Sartre.' *LTM*, 8:89 (1953) 1541-70
- 'De la réponse à la question.' *LTM*, 9:104 (1954) 157-184
- 'La Politique et la pensée de la politique.' *Les Lettres Nouvelles*, 32 (1962) 19-70

LEFRANCE, GEORGES. *Le mouvement socialiste sous la Troisième République.* Paris: Payot, 1963
- 'Histoire d'un groupe du parti SFIO: Révolution constructive.' In *Mélanges d'histoire économique et sociales en hommage au Professeur Babel*, Vol. 2, 401-25. Genève: Tribune, 1963

LUETHY H. and DAVID RODNICK. *French Motivation in the Suez Crisis.* Princeton: Princeton University Press, 1956

LICHTHEIM, GEORGE. *Marxism in Modern France.* New York: Columbia University Press, 1966

LIER, HENRI VON. 'A Propos des *Aventures de la dialectique*, philosophie et politique.' *La Revue Nouvelle*, 22 (1955) 222-32

LIGOU, D. *Histoire du socialisme en France (1871-1961)*, Paris: PUF, 1962

LORWIN, VAL. R. *The French Labor Movement.* Cambridge: Harvard University Press, 1969

LUKACS, GEORG. *Existentialisme ou Marxisme?* 2e ed. Transl. E. Kelemen. Paris: Nagel, 1960

MANN, HARVEY T. 'Totalitarian justice: trial of Bukharin, Rykov, Yagoda, et al.' *American Bar Association Journal*, 24 (1938) 970-6, 1029-30

MARTINET, GILLES. 'Possibilités et limites d'une "Nouvelle gauche." ' *LTM* 112-13 (1955) 1922-34

MARTINET, J.-D. 'Lettre ouverte aux *Temps Modernes.' La Révolution Prolétarienne*, 339 (mai 1950) 3
- 'Les Intellectuels et le goût du pouvoir.' *La Révolution Prolétarienne*, 303 (1947) 43-5

MEISEL, JAMES A. *The Fall of the Republic: Military Revolt in France.* Ann Arbor: University of Michigan Press, 1962

MENDÈS-FRANCE, PIERRE. 'Pourquoi le socialisme.' *Cahiers de la République,* 22 (1959) 7-16

MEYER, RUDOLF W. 'Merleau-Ponty und das Schicksal des französischen Existentialismus.' *Philosophische Rundschau,* 5:3-4 (1955) 129-65

MICAUD, CHARLES A. *Communism and the French Left.* New York: Praeger, 1963

– 'The "New Left" in France.' *World Politics,* 10 (1957-8) 537-59

– 'French intellectuals and communism.' *Social Research,* 21 (1954) 286-96

MICHEL, HENRI. *Les Courants de la pensée de la Résistance.* Paris: PUF, 1962

MILLER, JAMES. 'Merleau-Ponty's Marxism: between phenomenology and the Hegelian absolute.' *History and Theory,* 15 (1976) 109-32

MIRKINE-GULTZÉVITCH, BORIS. 'La Pensée politique et constitutionelle de la Résistance.' In Henri Michel et Boris Mirkine-Gultzévitch, eds, *Les Idées politiques et sociales de la Résistance.* Paris: PUF, 1954

MONNEROT, JULES. 'Réponse aux *Temps Modernes.' La Nef,* 37 (1947) 32-44

– 'Du Mythe à l'obscurantisme, réponse aux *Temps Modernes* II.' *La Nef,* 39 (1948) 3-21

– 'Liquidation and justification.' *La Nef,* 4:27 (1947) 8-19

MORIN, EDGAR. *Autocritique.* Paris: Julliard, 1959

MOUGIN, H. *La Sainte famille existentialiste.* Paris: Ed. Sociales, 1947

MOUILLARD, MAURICE. 'J.-P. Sartre, ou le trafiquant des lettres.' *La Nouvelle Critique,* 15 (1950) 32-43

MOUNIER, E. *Mounier et sa génération.* Paris: Seuil, 1956

MUGLIONI, J. 'L'histoire et la vérité.' *Revue socialiste,* 90 (Oct. 1950) 317-21

MUNZER, THOMAS. 'A-propos de Lukács.' *Arguments,* 3 (1957) 17-22

NAVILLE, PIERRE. *L'Intellectuelle communiste: A-Propos J.-P. Sartre.* Paris: Rivière, 1957

– 'Marxistes, marxiens et marxologues.' *Critique,* 126 (1957) 968-81

– 'Marx ou Husserl?' *La revue internationale,* 3 (1946) 227-43; 5 (1946) 445-59

ODAJNYK, WALTER. *Marxism and Existentialism.* Garden City: Doubleday, 1965

OLAFSON, F.A. 'Existentialism, Marxism and historical justification.' *Ethics,* 65 (1955) 126-34

PARIENTE, JEAN-CLAUDE. 'Lecture de Merleau-Ponty.' *Critique,* 186 (1962) 957-74; 187 (1962) 1067-78

PATRI, AIMÉ. 'De l'opium des intellectuels à la cure de désintoxication.' *Preuves,* 53 (1955) 81-5

– 'Madame de Beauvoir et le pseudo-marxisme.' *Preuves,* 56 (1955) 94-5

– 'Sartre et Merleau-Ponty.' *Preuves,* 135 (1962) 84-6

– 'La Philosophie de la police politique.' *Masses,* 7-8 (1947) 28-30

- 'Vue d'ensemble sur l'existentialisme.' *Paru*, 26 (1947) 60-6
- 'Humanisme et Terreur.' *Paru*, 42 (1948) 61-2
- 'Le Yogi, le commissaire et la fraternité des pessimistes.' *l'Arche*, 23 (1947) 99-105
- 'Le Yogi et le commissaire.' *Paru*, 26 (1947) 67-9

PAX, CLYDE. 'Merleau-Ponty and the truth of history.' *Man and World*, 6 (1973) 270-9

PEJOVIC, D. 'Maurice Merleau-Ponty.' *Praxis* (Zagreb), 1 (1965) 339-50

PIERCE, ROY. *Contemporary French Political Thought*. New York: Oxford University Press, 1966

PIERRARD, ANDRÉ. 'A propos de la gauche des *Temps Modernes*.' *Cahiers du communisme*, 31:9 (1955) 1048-63

POSTNER, MARK. *Marxism in Postwar France*. Princeton: Princeton University Press, 1975

RICOEUR, PAUL. 'Le Yogi, le commissaire, le prolétaire et le prophète.' *Christianisme sociale*, 57 (1949) 150-7

RIEBER, ALFRED J. *Stalin and the French Communist Party*. New York: Columbia University Press, 1962

RÉGNIER, M. 'Existentialisme et personalisme.' *Etudes*, 250 (1946) 134-6

RITSCH, FREDERICK F. *The French Left and the European Idea*. New York: Pageant Press, 1967

ROUSSET, DAVID. 'L'URSS concentrationnaire.' *La révolution prolétarienne*, 333 (Nov. 1949) 27-30

SCHMIDT, STEPHEN, 'Adventures of the dialectic.' *Philosophy of Social Science*, 5 (1975) 463-78

SCHUMANN, M. *Le Vrai Malaise des intellectuels de gauche*. Paris: Plon, 1957

SÉRANT, PAUL. 'Maurice Merleau-Ponty, Raymond Aron et la pensée de gauche.' *Revue des Deux Mondes*, (1 July 1955) 117-27

SHERIDAN, J.F. 'On ontology and politics: a polemic.' *Dialogue*, 7 (1968), 449-60

SIMÉON, J.-P. 'Vérité et idéologie.' *L'Arc*, 46 (1971) 48-55

SOMMERVILLE, JOHN. 'Violence, politics and morality.' *Philosophy and Phenomenological Research*, 32 (1971) 241-9

SOREL, JEAN-JACQUES. 'Merleau-Ponty contre Sartre, ou les mésaventures des mandarins.' *France-Observateur*, 6, no. 263 (26 mai 1955) 16-18

SPIEGELBERG, H. 'French existentialism: its social philosophies.' *Kenyon Review*, 6:3 (1954) 446-62

SPIRE, ALFRED. *Inventaire des socialismes français contemporains*, 2nd ed. Paris: Medicis, 1946

SUTTERT, G. 'Maurice Merleau-Ponty.' *Cahiers de la République*, 33 (1961) 81-2
TRAN-DUC-THAO. *Phénoménologie et matérialisme dialectique.* Paris: Gordon and Breach, 1971
- 'Marxisme et phénoménologie.' *Revue internationale*, 1:2 (1946) 168-74
ULLMO, JEAN. 'Une Etape de la pensée politique (*A propos des Aventures de la dialectique*).' *Critique*, 98 (1955) 625-43
Y.G. 'Le Zéro et l'infini.' *Paru*, 17 (1946) 47-50

Index

27,613

DATE			